QUEEN MARY AND THE CRUISER

David A. Thomas has also written

Naval History
WITH ENSIGNS FLYING
SUBMARINE VICTORY
BATTLE OF THE JAVA SEA
CRETE 1941: THE BATTLE AT SEA
JAPAN'S WAR AT SEA: PEARL HARBOUR TO THE CORAL SEA
ROYAL ADMIRALS
A COMPANION TO THE ROYAL NAVY
THE ILLUSTRATED ARMADA HANDBOOK
THE ATLANTIC STAR 1939–45
CHRISTOPHER COLUMBUS: MASTER OF THE ATLANTIC
QUEEN MARY AND THE CRUISER: THE CURACOA
DISASTER
(with Patrick Holmes)

Social History
THE CANNING STORY 1785–1985
CHURCHILL: THE MEMBER FOR WOODFORD
Bibliography
COMPTON MACKENZIE: A BIBLIOGRAPHY
(With Joyce Thomas)

Juvenile
HOW SHIPS ARE MADE
WHAT DO YOU KNOW?
BIBLE SUPER PUZZLE BOOK NO. 1
BIBLE SUPER PUZZLE BOOK NO. 2

QUEEN MARY

AND THE

CRUISER

The *Curacoa* Disaster

DAVID A. THOMAS
AND PATRICK HOLMES

NAVAL INSTITUTE PRESS
ANNAPOLIS, MARYLAND

First published in the United Kingdom in 1997 by Leo Cooper,
an imprint of Pen & Sword Books Ltd.
Published and distributed in the United States of America
and Canada by the Naval Institute Press, 118 Maryland Avenue,
Annapolis, MD 21402–5035

Library of Congress Catalog Card No. 96–71990
ISBN 1–55750–698–1

This edition is authorized for sale only in the United States,
its territories and possessions, and Canada

Typeset by Phoenix Typesetting, Ilkley, West Yorkshire.

Printed in the United Kingdom on acid-free paper
by Redwood Books, Trowbridge, Wilts

CONTENTS

ACKNOWLEDGEMENTS

A book such as this can only be compiled with the generous help of a great number of people to whom we wish to extend our grateful thanks. In particular we acknowledge our gratitude to the following, many of them survivors of the disaster, most of them men of HMS *Curacoa*, nearly all of whom have corresponded with or met Patrick Holmes:

A.E. (Ted) Beavis, R. Beilby, Harry Bell, Mrs F.B. (Jean) Black, Norman Blundell, Howard Bodger, Anthony Boosey, Jeremy Boutwood, John Wilfred Boutwood, Eric Bower, Philip Brocklesby.

Ken Cartright, Geoffrey Carter, Mr Charlton, C.H.C. Clarke, Harry Clarke, Len Clarke, Kenneth Clarkson, Margie Clover, K. Coggin, Anthony Corlett, Olive Croft, Harley Crossley, Fred Dennis, J.G. Dixon, Sid Dobbs.

E.L. Eadie, Clive Edgar, Harry Ellis.

Stan Farrow, E. (Ted) Freeborn.

W. Garfitt, R.W. (Bob) Garner, N. Good, C. Gray (HMS *Skate*), W.M. (Mac) Gray.

Dennis Hearn, J.W. Honey, Ken Huntley, Vic Jones, Ted King, Iain McKilligan, Tom McMeekin, Bill Mant, R. (Bob) Markham, Don Marshall, Allin Martin, George L. Moore, Joe Murray, John Nicholas.

E.W. (Bob) Richards, R. Roach, C.A.M. Robertson.

C. John Rooke.

John Sewell.

C. Taylor, John Tether, Gofton Thorley, Jess Turner, Allen Whalen (HMS *Cowdray*), Edgar (Tug) Wilson, Fred Woodger.

Of these, we wish to emphasize our gratitude to the late John Tether, organizing secretary of the association known as the Men of *Curacoa*, and his worthy successor, Allin Martin. Both of them helped point the way and introduced us to many Curacoans. Deserving of special mention are the late Dr John Rooke, the late Lieutenant-Commander Anthony Corlett and Lieutenant-Commander Robert Garner. They all provided help beyond what could reasonably be expected.

The late Captain Bill Heighway of Sydney, New South Wales, kindly allowed publication of his correspondence with Patrick Holmes; as did Lieutenant-Commander Jeremy Boutwood, son of Captain John W. Boutwood. We are grateful. Owing to the declining health of Captain Boutwood he was unable to give a formal interview nor to engage in correspondence but was content to allow his son to do so. It is a pity he has not lived to see the publication of this book.

We are pleased to record our appreciation too for the valuable help given by Marcus Holmes whose constant encouragement to his father in Australia was sustaining, as was that of Elizabeth Richardson in England. Our gratitude is also extended to three secretaries, Nan Skead in Western Australia and June Corbett and Joan Weir in England. We are also appreciative of the courtesy of William M. Winberg, Historian and Archivist aboard *Queen Mary* at Long Beach, California.

We should also like to express our appreciation to Valerie Thomas LRPS for her photographic work, and to Dr Peter Boutwood.

Libraries and Museums

The staff of the following have shown their customary professional assistance for which we are grateful: the Naval Historical Branch of the Ministry of Defence; the Reading Room of the National Maritime Museum, the Imperial War Museum, David Male of the RNC Greenwich Library and the reference sections of the Redbridge Central Library, the Bristol Central Library and the Public Record Office at Kew. The archivists of the Liverpool University Library were specially helpful with the Cunard Archives in their charge. The Corporation of Trinity House assisted with information.

Publishers and Authors

We are grateful to the following for allowing us to quote from their published works:

Chatto & Windus and Ralph Barker (*Against the Sea*)

William Kimber and G.G. Connell (*Valiant Quarter*)

Hodder & Stoughton and Gordon Holman (*The King's Cruisers*)

Patrick Stephens and Neil McCart (*Passenger Ships of the Cunard Line*)

David & Charles, William H. Miller and David F. Hutchings (*Transatlantic Liners at War*)

Weidenfeld & Nicolson and John Mills (*Up in The Clouds, Gentlemen, Please*)

Hodder & Stoughton and Peter Padfield (*An Agony of Collisions*)

Macdonald & Janes and A. Temple Patterson (*Tyrwhitt of The Harwich Force*)

Magazines & Newspapers

The editors of the following publications have kindly allowed us to quote from them:

Ships Monthly	*The Etruscan*
Time Magazine	*Daily Sketch*

Transactions of the Royal Institute of Naval Architects

Daily Mirror *Truth Magazine*

Sea Breezes *The Naval Review*

Lloyd's List of Law Reports *The Times*

Journal of Commerce (Liverpool) *Yours* (Choice Publications)

INTRODUCTION

The afternoon of 2 October, 1942, was uncommonly clear and bright with good visibility. A moderate-to-rough sea was running with a heavy westerly swell and the air was fresh. One survivor described it as 'a brisk, healthy day with cumulo-nimbus clouds'. It was probably better than could be expected at that time of year in the waters immediately NW of County Donegal's Bloody Foreland.

The old First World War cruiser HMS *Curacoa*, having already experienced three years of the Second World War, was steaming into the Western Approaches at 25 knots to rendezvous with the majestic Cunarder, the 81,237 gross tons *Queen Mary*, heading for the United Kingdom with more than 10,000 American troops aboard.

Aboard the cruiser there was all the alertness of the forenoon watch, experienced lookouts and watchkeeping officers long used to their duties and to handling their ship in far worse sea conditions than those running on this special afternoon. The *Curacoa* thumped into the waves, shipping it green over the fo'c'stle, the sea cascading away into the waist scuppers. Most of the twenty-seven officers and 412 men aboard her were down below or between decks going about their normal cruising watch duties.

There was nothing in the world to suggest any danger from the enemy – from lurking U-boats or raiding long-range Condor aircraft, despite this being the height of the Battle of the Atlantic – let alone that they were to become the unwitting principals in a maritime disaster of awful proportions, and that for the majority of them it was to be their last day alive.

For those who survived the tragedy, like Patrick Holmes in the Air Defence Position, high in the ship's fore structure, it left them branded with the dreadful memory which has never left them. As one of them was to relate nearly fifty years later, 'Since 2 October, 1942, every day has been a bonus.' John Tether, writing to fellow survivors in 1988 commented, 'Like me, I suppose many of you will have regarded yourselves as living on borrowed time since 1942.'

338 men were to perish that afternoon, engulfed in the agony of a collision, obliterated in a brief moment of time, most of them within five or six minutes: those who survived – there were 101 of them – were rescued within two or three hours: perhaps a few others lingered longer, never to be rescued, their fate only to be guessed at. A dozen or so bodies reached land, the

isolated Scottish Isle of Skye, nearly 200 miles ENE from the scene of the disaster, swept there no doubt by the North Atlantic Drift. It was a long way to come home.

Those on watch on the cruiser's bridge sighted their charge, her splendour barely dimmed by her wartime grey paint, approaching from the west on one of her many crossings of the North Atlantic, packed with American troops on passage to the United Kingdom. She was speeding at 28½ knots (about 33½ mph) steaming independently, without escort of any kind, her speed being her main protection against U-boats. As a precaution she was zigzagging to make it unlikely for a U-boat to be able to take up a position to torpedo her.

This was the fifth time, either outward or inward bound that the ships had met. *Curacoa* had also escorted the *Queen Elizabeth*, Cunard's larger two-funnelled consort, under similar circumstances on two occasions.

As *Queen Mary* approached the waters off the NW coast of Ireland the threat of air attack increased, and the threat remained as she entered the North Channel between Ulster and Scotland. To counter this threat from patrolling Focke–Wulf Condors and Heinkel 177s she was provided with AA escorts – destroyers and light cruisers well equipped with high-angle guns. Such protection was provided by HMS *Curacoa*, a 4,290-ton light cruiser launched as long ago as 1917, and converted into an AA cruiser in 1939–40. She carried eight 4-inch guns in four mountings, sundry 2 pounder Pom Poms and .5" AA Oerlikon guns.

She was commanded by Captain John W. Boutwood and it was he who commanded the escort group which comprised an additional six destroyers which had joined from Londonderry.

It was the practice of Captain Boutwood to turn his cruiser about as soon as the Cunarder hove in sight. He would then head for the Clyde at 25 knots, as fast as the cruiser could go. In her heyday she could maintain 27 knots and in short spells at speed trials she even exceeded her design speed with 29 knots. Realizing that the high seas running would make it almost impossible for the destroyers to maintain anything above 20 knots, he signalled them to turn about and head for the Clyde straightaway. They soon disappeared over the eastern horizon, a seemingly unimportant action which was to have sad consequences later.

When *Queen Mary* was sighted to the NW about two hours behind her estimated time of arrival Boutwood altered course to position *Curacoa* more or less directly ahead of the troopship on a straight line course at maximum speed of 25 knots. *Queen Mary* would follow her escort, still zigzagging along the same mean course but at a higher speed. The great liner thus slowly closed the distance so she lay astern of the cruiser.

The liner made a magnificent sight. One survivor put it simply: 'She looked beautiful.' Smoke streamed from her three giant funnels; her great length, her high bridge with its wings well out over the sea giving good sight lines fore and aft, the curved front of her superstructure stepped down steeply for'ard and gently aft, made a stunning picture. The great bow wave was thrust apart by the tall raked stem. As the clouds parted her grey hull glistened in the sunlight and when they closed again she looked sombre and menacing in shadow. Every four or eight minutes she altered course by twenty-five or fifty degrees so that her angle of heading was constantly, or almost constantly, changing.

By contrast, her relatively tiny escort with her low profile, two squat funnels and four pairs of 4-inch guns pointing skywards, wallowed in the sea, displaying her curious Mountbatten pink camouflage, designed by Lord Louis for his famous 5th Destroyer Flotilla and supposedly more effective under dawn and dusk conditions. For many of the GIs aboard the *Queen Mary* she was the first British warship they had ever seen. She looked small, but business-like and impressive.

Shortly after two-o'clock that afternoon (1400 hours), the massive bulk of *Queen Mary* scythed the small cruiser into two with the finality of a guillotine.

How was it that, on such a bright if boisterous day, with good visibility and both ships with ample sea room for manoeuvring, one ship could plough into the other causing the death of 338 men? It is to answer this question that we have set out to examine the facts of the disaster itself, of the hearing before the Court of Enquiry aboard HMS *Argus*, the protracted Law Courts hearing, the subsequent Appeal and the Judgement of the House of Lords nearly five years after the sinking, and to discover if we can where the blame lay.

Ostensibly the *Curacoa* Incident, as it came to be called, was a matter between the Admiralty and the Cunard White Star Company as protagonists, or it was a matter between two ships – *Queen Mary* and *Curacoa*. But at the end of the day it was between none of these contestants: it was between the two men who had charge of the ships – troopship and escort – Captain Illingworth of *Queen Mary* and Captain Boutwood of *Curacoa*.

The news of the tragedy was kept secret; in the terminology of the day, it was hushed up. The loss of the cruiser was not announced until the end of the European war, about two and a half years after the loss. Such censoring of wartime information was perfectly acceptable for security reasons, to deny it to the enemy, although curiously, many statements exist to suggest that Lord Haw Haw* broadcast the news from the German radio station at Hamburg.

When the news was released in May, 1945, it was accompanied by inaccurate reports which have persisted over the years. Indeed, almost every report of the *Curacoa* Incident is plagued with distortions and errors of omission as well as commission.

---

* William Joyce (1906–46) was executed after a treason trial. Lord Haw Haw's broadcasts from Germany and his distinctive 'Jairmany Calling' became a feature of the war.

Captain Boutwood was one of *Curacoa's* survivors. Only one other officer escaped with his life. He was Temporary Sub-Lieutenant Patrick Holmes RNVR. He witnessed the terrifying collision from a peculiar advantage point, virtually a ringside seat, high up in what was known as the ADP or the Air Defence Position, where he had charge of twelve lookouts. All his adult life since the collision Patrick Holmes has been dismayed at these published inaccuracies and the abounding errors.

One of the most persistent ones, even if insignificant, is the spelling of the ship's name – correctly *Curacoa* and incorrectly *Curacao*. Thus, incidentally, the pronunciation is CURASOWER. One national newspaper transformed a bright October afternoon into a stormy night with poor visibility, and this same newspaper's naval correspondent got the date as well as the time of day wrong – 22 November. Another correspondent had it that *Queen Mary* had 15,000 American troops aboard, and that the cruiser was carried 'a considerable distance with one half each side of the liner: there were only twenty-six survivors.' All these so-called facts are wrong as will be related in due course.

One report introduced the U-boat fable which has lasted to this day. 'The *Queen Mary* was travelling all out for the Clyde,' the report states, 'with an escort of *two* cruisers when the lookout man raised the alarm that a suspected U-boat had been sighted on the port bow ahead. Immediately, that great liner wheeled round to starboard to take avoiding action and at the same moment HMS *Curacoa* was racing towards the submarine . . .' Not so. Nor did the troopship then proceed at top speed. She reduced it to 10 and then 13 knots.

Another report tells us that the collision occurred in dense fog, that the cruiser was carried along for three miles on the liner's bows. Some book accounts of the tragedy locate the sinking in wrong positions; most do not agree where the cruiser was struck – anywhere from midships to eleven feet from the stern. Another book wrongly interprets the judgements of the Court of Appeal and the House of Lords when it states *Queen Mary* was found to be blameless.

Here, in this book, Patrick Holmes has co-authored the whole story, detailing the life and death of the cruiser in which he served, correcting the errors, extensively researching sources, examining contemporary documents, corresponding with and interviewing dozens of survivors, including their commanding officer, Captain John Wilfred Boutwood. Theirs is a compelling story. We hope that its telling will also serve as a memorial for all the lost men of *Curacoa*. We conclude with a moral for this work, taken from a letter of Jeremy Boutwood's: 'The only touchstone to documentary literature for us is the search for Truth.'

DAVID A. THOMAS   PATRICK HOLMES
Sheering   Cottesloe
Essex   Western Australia

SHOWING THE FLAG: PRELUDE TO WAR

'After nine months of keeping the peace in Turkish waters the ship came home. I had saved enough to buy a bike.'

Able Seaman Jack Philip-Nichols describing Curacoa's commission to Eastern Europe, 1923.

The *Curacoa* story began as long ago as 1 January, 1807, when Captain Charles Brisbane* led a small squadron of three frigates in his flagship *Arethusa* and captured the island of Curacoa† from the Dutch.

The island enjoys a Caribbean climate, lying, as it does, off the coast of Venezuela. It was discovered by the Spaniards in 1527 during their 15th–16th century early colonization period, but the Dutch seized it in 1634. And the Dutch, regarded by many as harsh colonizers, held the island until modern times except for the short period when Captain Brisbane came on the scene and Curacoa came under British rule between 1807 and the end of the Napoleonic Wars.

The first HMS *Curacoa*, named after the island, was launched at Ichenor in September, 1809. She was a vessel of 953 tons mounting 36 guns and classed as a 5th rate. She was commissioned at Plymouth and it was under the command of Captain J. Tower that she sailed on her first important convoy duty to the East Indies in June, 1810.

After a chequered career as a 42-gun ship, then as a 24-gun corvette, she was commissioned for the East Indies again. Later she served on the American Station for six years. She was paid off for the last time in 1847 and two years later she was taken to pieces. The gallant little ship had given service for nearly forty years.

---

* Later a distinguished admiral (c1769–1829). Entered RN 1779. Served under Hood, Rodney and Nelson. Knighted for his Curacoa incident. KCB 1815. Vice Admiral 1820. Governor of St Vincent 1808–29.

† The island's name is most commonly spelled Curacao throughout the world, but the British prefer the alternative Curacoa. It is this spelling which is always adopted for HM ships.

The second *Curacoa* was launched on 13 April, 1854, at Pembroke, the yard that built the fourth ship of the name fifty or more years later. She was a steam screw frigate of 31 guns and a tonnage of 1,571. She was fitted with a 350 hp engine. In 1855 she saw active service in the Crimea and some years later she was present in the New Zealand War where she landed 232 officers and men in 1863 to help defeat the Maoris. She made her last appearance in the Navy List in April 1869. She had served the Queen's Navy for fifteen years.

The third *Curacoa* was built at Glasgow in 1878 and was a 2,300 hp screw corvette of 2,383 tons with 14 guns. In July, 1893, she was involved in fighting between rival chiefs in Samoa. In 1896–97 she was a tender to HMS *Northampton*, a sea-going training ship for boys, on the Home Station. She was finally disposed of in 1904 after twenty-six years of service.

During this great period of history known as Pax Britannica, the three *Curacoas* had served the nation throughout the world for seventy-nine years under the command of eighteen captains.

It was to be the fourth Royal Naval vessel to carry the name *Curacoa* which gave rise to controversy when disaster overwhelmed her in a tragic incident in the greatest battle at sea, the Battle of the Atlantic, 1939–45.

She was laid down in Pembroke Dockyard in Wales on 13 July, 1916, and was launched less than ten months later, on 5 May,1917, and was finally fitted out and completed on 18 February, 1918.

Her first commanding officer was Captain Barry Domvile.* He was later to describe her as 'a fine little ship,' and she became his first flagship fourteen years later. He took her from her fitting-out basin to Harwich on 20 February where she joined the renowned Harwich Force of light cruisers and destroyers.

Commanding the Harwich Force was the daring and charismatic Rear-Admiral Reginald Tyrwhitt† and the very next day after the newcomer's arrival Tyrwhitt hoisted his flag in the brand new ship. A few days later, to crown a happy week, *Curacoa* was inspected by HM King George V.

However, her wartime service was short-lived for on 11 November the war ended and amid scenes of tremendous celebration Tyrwhitt signalled his Force from *Curacoa*:

---

* Later Admiral Sir Barry Domvile (1878–1971), Director of Plans Division, Admiralty; commanded *Royal Sovereign* 1925–26; Director of Naval Intelligence Division 1927–30; commanded 3rd Cruiser Squadron (Mediterranean) 1931–32; retired list 1936.
† Later Admiral of the Fleet Sir Reginald Tyrwhitt (1870–1939). Created baronet 1919. Commodore commanding Harwich Force 1914–18. C-in-C China Station 1927–19. C-in-C the Nore 1930–33. Retired list 1939.

SUMMARY OF CURACOAS

Ship	Type	Launched	Length × Breadth	Tonnage	Guns	Disposal
I	5th rate	1809	145' × 38½'	953	36 & 24	Scrapped 1849
II	Wooden Steam Frigate	1854	192' × 43'	1,570	1 × 10" 30 × 32 pdrs	Sold 1869
III	Steam Corvette	1878	225' × 44½'	2,383	2 × 7" 12 × 64 pdrs	Sold 1904
IV	Light Cruiser	1917	451½' × 43½'	4,390	5 × 6" Later: 8 × 4" 4 × 2 pdrs	Sunk 1942

'On this day of rejoicing I wish to thank the captains, officers and ships' companies of the Harwich Force for the unbounded gallantry, zeal and endurance they have invariably displayed during the war.

'The Harwich Force has made its name and will not be forgotten during the future annals of history. I particularly wish to call attention to the uniformly good conduct and cheerfulness of the Harwich Force. . . . It is well to remember that though peace is assured a period of hard and possibly unpleasant work is at hand. I know that I can trust the Harwich Force to carry out any work ordered in the same cheerful spirit that they have shown throughout the war.'*

A few days later *Curacoa* took Tyrwhitt to Rosyth where he took part in the arrangements for all German U-boats to be surrendered to him at Harwich: other surface forces were to be surrendered at Scapa Flow and the Firth of Forth. There was disappointment that German destroyers had not been among the vessels surrendering to the Harwich Force, because they had been the Force's main antagonists throughout the war.

Domvile was dismayed at missing the surrender ceremony; he had fallen victim to the influenza epidemic that was sweeping the Force, as well as Europe.

The surrender was an elaborate naval evolution and *Curacoa* played a leading part. On 20 November twenty U-boats were escorted by the Force in a five-mile-long procession with the German crews fallen in on the forecasing, RN prize crews manning the boats, now flying the White Ensign. Further surrender by batches resulted in about 170 U-boats being handed over.

With the war at an end, the dispersal of the Harwich Force began. Early in 1919 *Curacoa* conveyed Queen Maud of Norway and Crown Prince Olaf back to Christiania (now Oslo) after they had taken the opportunity of visiting friends and relations in England. Tyrwhitt escorted them aboard his flagship, gave up his cabin to the Queen then travelled to Sandringham to spend a few days with the royal family. In Norway, King Haakon was welcomed aboard to greet his returning family.

Curacoa proceeded to show the flag to the Scandinavian and other Baltic countries, a cruise which became a regular annual event for the cruiser throughout the twenties. On 1 May, 1919, *Curacoa* became flagship of the 1st Light Cruiser Squadron of the Grand Fleet under Rear-Admiral Walter

---

* *Tyrwhitt of the Harwich Force* by A. Temple Patterson, Macdonald & Janes, 1973.

Cowan.* Just over a fortnight later she hit a mine aft, which damaged the steering. With bulkheads shored up she was towed by two tugs to Chatham where she was paid off and remained out of commission till 26 August, 1921.

She was recommissioned as flagship of the 2nd Light Cruiser Squadron in the Atlantic Fleet wearing the flag of Rear-Admiral Wilmot Nicholson. He immediately took her on her first cruise with the squadron to the Baltic where extensive goodwill visits were made. Later that year *Curacoa* exercised at Scapa Flow, Invergordon and Rosyth. While at Rosyth in November, 1921, she was joined by two Boys First Class, Jack Philip-Nichols and his friend, Grimes, both of them fresh from the training establishment HMS *Ganges* at Shotley near Harwich. Philip-Nichols recorded his first sight of the light cruiser:

> 'HMS *Curacoa* came in, a flourish of bugles as the boats were lowered, the booms were run out, the Royal Marines paraded and the cable secured to a buoy. Grimes and I were ordered down into the duty motor boat to join our first sea-going ship . . . the motor boat thrust out into the Forth with us two boys in the fore end under a canvas dodger and our bags and hammocks in the after cabin.'†

Philip-Nichols's impressions of the cruiser were complimentary: he referred to the sacred quarterdeck which was so clean he feared to stand on it. The boys were given in charge to Petty Officer Haseldene, the Boys' Instructor, responsible for all thirty-two boys aboard. Those were hard times and taught the boys to look after themselves. Mealtimes in the congestion of the mess decks were described by Philip-Nichols:

> 'The cooks of the mess brought the dinner down from the galley. . . . The Senior Boy slashed the meat into roughly thirty-two parts, shovelled out the grey potatoes and spooned out a few peas to every person present. There were about twenty plates and five china basins, and seven portions were left in the cooking dishes where the owners jealously guarded them, as they ate, mostly with the help of Pusser's Dirks [the sailor's knife] only half-a-dozen knives and about eight forks being available. The mess tables could not hold thirty-two boys so a few sat on the bottom steps of

---

* Later Admiral Sir Walter Cowan KCB, MVO, DSO* (1871–1956). He distinguished himself by earning a DSO in both World Wars. Created Baronet 1921. C-in-C North America and West Indies Station 1926–28. Retired List 1931. Served with the Commandos in WWII.
† *Ships Monthly*, December, 1979, and January, 1980, 'Keeping the Peace.'

the ladder and dug into the communal dish like hungry Arabs. . . .
Tea was worse – a fraction of a slice of bread and a dab of canteen
margarine. Those with really rich parents, at teatime bought two
pennyworth of cheese at the canteen. . . . Grimes and I had some
money and we went halves on a tin of sardines.'

After describing the scrubbing, sanding, holystoning, swabbing and
mopping of the quarterdeck in the charge of a greatly respected Petty
Officer, Tim Coleman, with a row of campaign medal ribbons, a jolly, good-
natured man who nevertheless would readily bully his quarterdeckmen with
punches, Philip-Nichols thought the quarterdeck looked beautiful, made
more so by the gleaming brasswork and spotless paintwork. He described
his action station in the Transmitting Station:

'I followed down two decks through the Stokers' Mess, past the
Petty Officers' Mess, past the Stoker Petty Officers' Mess and
down a little square hatchway: then across a space and through a
watertight door . . . it was the Transmitting Station – a halfway
house between the Gun Director up the mast . . . and the five 6-
inch guns.'

In the late summer of 1922 *Curacoa* sailed from Portland for San Sebastian
in northern Spain where King Alfonso XIII and his English Queen Ena were
celebrating the anniversary of his accession to the throne. The British
squadron of ships lay at anchor in the picturesque bay under the ancient
guns of the castle of Monte Urgull.

From this beautiful setting *Curacoa* departed with all despatch to the
eastern Mediterranean where the politico-military situation between Turkey
and Greece was deteriorating rapidly. *Curacoa* reached Smyrna [now Izmir]
on 23 September. Philip-Nichols recalled the activity of those days vividly
and gave a graphic account:

'There was much coming and going as War Staff officers
compared notes and studied rumours. Out came the tampions
from the guns and we were on a war footing, real ammunition
being brought up. Some officers had not forgotten that in this area
mines and submarines had accounted for several battleships in
1915. It was an easy job to mine the Dardanelles, or even float
mines down with the south-going stream out of the Sea of
Marmora.

'The Greek ships kept at a distance. After all, the Turks still had
the *Yavuz* (ex-*Goeben*) in a more or less effective condition. With
11-inch guns she was a ship to be watched. We wished to be considered neutral and to bring the Graeco-Turkish war to an end.'

Curacoa moved up to Constantinople [now Istanbul] to find the moorings crowded with French, Dutch, American and Spanish ships, together, of course, with a preponderance of British warships; periodically battleships of the Mediterranean Fleet would make an ostensible courtesy call and pay respects to Mustapha Kemal.

Philip-Nichols recalled that there were no hostile acts by either the Greeks or the Turks. He recalled seeing:

> 'Landing parties of sailors march round Constantinople and packing thousands of Greek refugees into old inter-island steamers, taking them to refugee camps which the British government had set up for them.'

On 7 February, 1923, Philip-Nichols celebrated his 18th birthday and became rated an Able Seaman. On the next day an impressive force of British warships assembled and it was decided to reply to an ultimatum from the Turks who forbade the British Fleet entry to Smyrna. Any attempt to do so would be met with gunfire.

While four Royal Navy battleships lay outside the port *Curacoa* was ordered to enter Smyrna and 'bell the cat'. She wore the flag of her admiral, Rear-Admiral Nicholson, and had a spotting plane allocated to her to direct the cruiser's gunfire and that of the four battleships with their 13.5-inch guns. Philip-Nichols continued his narrative:

> 'HMS *Curacoa* gets under way, streaming her paravanes. We are loaded with HE shell and cordite. I am down in the Transmitting Station, the ship is trembling with high speed, and a voice from the spotting top comes over my headphones: "Both paravanes are running perfectly, the Bird Man [the plane] is approaching and has made a signal to the ship [in morse, of course]; our guns are following the director."
>
> 'Our AA guns (the two 3-inch) are also loaded, but the Turks are believed not to have any planes near Smyrna. The time drags on. We are just entering. The fort has hoisted a signal. I think it has been interpreted as 'The port is closed'. We are increasing speed, the Bird Man says that the battleships are beyond the headland, with maximum elevation on their 13.5s.
>
> 'Ah, a little excitement: the signal is going down. Ah yes, there is a puff of smoke from a small gun in the fort: a blank, I think. We are maintaining our speed. We are turning to starboard in a big circle. The Director is turning round and all guns are following the pointers. Stand by now; it is now or not at all. . . . It was over . . . we had called their bluff. For my part I was disappointed and glad, both at the same time. After nine months of keeping the

peace in Turkish waters the ship came home. I had saved enough money to buy a bike.'

In June of that year, 1923, Rear-Admiral Thomas Gilbert took over command of the 2nd Light Cruiser Squadron, hoisted his flag in *Curacoa* and headed off with the squadron on a seven-week cruise in the Baltic, *Curacoa's* third. Throughout the remaining years of the 1920s the routine followed a pattern, all part of the Royal Navy annual programme of maintaining and improving relations with other nations and at the same time hopefully impressing the hosts by demonstrating the Navy's awesome strength and power.

In May, 1925, Captain C.B. Prickett recommissioned *Curacoa* and Rear-Admiral W.A.H. Kelly hoisted his flag in her as Rear-Admiral 2nd Cruiser Squadron in the Atlantic Fleet. This acknowledged, incidentally, that the Admiralty now regarded *light* cruiser squadrons as cruiser squadrons: the Cs were no longer *light*.

Two years later Captain F.T.B. Tower assumed command under the flag of Rear-Admiral R.A.F. Larken and when they took *Curacoa* on her Scandinavian cruise the King of Sweden and the King of Norway were entertained aboard at Stockholm and Oslo. And in the following spring, in 1928, the ship dressed overall when moored in the Tagus at Lisbon and a twenty-one gun salute was fired in honour of the President of Portugal when he visited the ship.

A year later *Curacoa* was recommissioned as flagship of the 3rd Cruiser Squadron in the Mediterranean Fleet and spent the next 2¾ years based at Malta. It was one of the choicest commissions she ever experienced. The list of ports she visited reads like a holiday brochure. Most of July and August, 1930, was spent off Greece and in the Aegean Sea with Fleet manoeuvres and 6-inch gun competitions, and 'Hands to bathe' at 1600 hours each day became the custom when at anchor.

Jim Dales, who joined *Curacoa* in 1930, has recalled those days more than sixty years ago when *Calliope*, *Calypso*, *Caradoc*, *Cardiff*, *Comus*, *Cambrian*, *Caledon* and *Coventry*, as well as *Curacoa*, all formed part of the Mediterranean Fleet. He remembers spending much of the time in white duck uniform showing the flag and recalls one cruise when a visit was made to Constanza on the Black Sea coast of Romania where Queen Helena and Crown Prince Michael came aboard to the thunderous cracks of a 21-gun salute, the ship dressed overall, with sun-bleached awnings spread over the quarterdeck.

Jim Dales also recollects visiting Haifa, Jerusalem, Bethlehem and Nazareth. And when *Curacoa* called at Alexandria he remembers the crew touring the Pyramids, the Sphinx and Cairo, and even sailing up the Nile.

'Looking back as I have done,' he writes wistfully, 'I would say that my happiest days were those times spent on the Cocoa Boat.'

The year 1931 was highlighted by *Curacoa's* first captain, Barry Domvile, rejoining the ship as Rear-Admiral of the 3rd Cruiser Squadron in February. His flag captain was Captain C.M. Graham. And there now came a change in the centre of gravity of the squadron's cruises: the Baltic gave way to Eastern European countries – Romania, Greece, Turkey, Bulgaria and islands such as Rhodes. In addition, during the 1930s *Curacoa* served a commission on the China Station which gave her crew new experiences at the traditional naval stopping-off ports to the east – Alexandria, the Suez Canal, Aden, Colombo, Singapore, Hong Kong, Nanking, Hankow and Shanghai: all became familiar to the Curacoans.

In March, 1933, a new commanding officer joined the cruiser in the Mediterranean; it was Captain Henry Rawlings* who was to distinguish himself in the Navy and in particular during the Second World War.

Two other young men joined the cruiser during this month. They were Boy First Class R.W.J. Helyer and Able Seaman J.W. Honey. They both served aboard her for eight months. Honey recalls that there were engine room troubles which delayed the cruiser's departure for the Mediterranean. Full power trials, basin and sea trials all proved below standard and it was not until 9 May that *Curacoa* sailed, five weeks late.

The magazine *Truth* carried a critical article about *Curacoa*, and its issue of 11 May, 1932, commented, a little tongue in cheek:

> 'A good many people will recall the joke about the original British airship which was called the *Mayfly* in intelligent anticipation that she never would. Portsmouth Dockyard has applied a similar tag to the cruiser *Curacoa* which has been dubbed HMS *Maygo.* . . . The disquieting aspect of this experience is that the *Curacoa* is one of six cruisers of her type which have passed the efficient age limit, but are yet retained on the Active Service List. Three years ago the *Curacoa* had £120,000† spent upon her in a big refit, but the simple fact is that she and her sisters are approaching the worn-out stage and will be well beyond it in 1936 when they must still be retained if we are to show the total of fifty cruisers allowed under the London Treaty.'

Bob Helyer was a Boy First Class when he joined *Curacoa*, straight from

---

* Later Admiral Sir Henry Rawlings (1889–1962). Served throughout WW I. Commanded *Valiant* 1939. Rear-Admiral 1st Battle Squadron 1940. 7th Cruiser Squadron 1941. CB 1942. Vice Admiral 1943. GBE and Admiral 1946.
† About £2.5 million at today's values.

HMS *Ganges*, and, like Honey who was soon to become a Leading Seaman, experienced this business of having to return to Pompey time and time again to the cheers and jeers of the sailors on Fort Block House. Even the RN Band on Southsea Fort played 'Here we are Again'.

Maygo was just one of three sobriquets by which *Curacoa* became known. In 1942 she spent so much time in dry dock in Rosyth near the shore establishments known as HMS *Cochrane I* and *Cochrane II* that she gained the nickname *Cochrane III*. But Curacoans shrugged off these christenings and were happy to settle for the one they always used – that of *Cocoa Boat*.

This incident was not to be the end of *Curacoa's* engine troubles. After entertaining King Boris III of Bulgaria and King Carol of Romania aboard, *Curacoa* returned to Malta and was just about to leave for her second cruise when, in the words of Bob Helyer:

> 'The Captain had flag in hand ready to slip the buoy, when the Engineer Commander arrived on the bridge to inform him he could not go – condenser trouble once more. The Admiral – not in a very good frame of mind – transferred his gear and staff to (I think) HMS *Cardiff* – while *Curacoa* remained at her buoy. When the fleet returned, *Curacoa* was ordered home.'

Shortly after Rear-Admiral R.A. Tottenham arrived on board *Curacoa* in June, 1932, he introduced a new exercise. Honey recalls it in detail:

> 'General drill was being carried out including exercising fire stations, tow aft, collision stations, and eventually action stations. During this, the Admiral's staff handed out envelopes to some of the ship's company containing notes saying they were wounded or a breakdown had developed or that there was a fire; in fact anything that could really happen in action. It so happened, closed up at his station in the wheelhouse below the bridge was a Cockney, Tommy Tucker, at the engine room telegraph. He had an envelope which enclosed the information that he was shell shocked. This was right up his street – remember that they are at action stations, doing about 25 knots, guns firing, battle flag flying, torpedoes about to be fired – the whole bang shoot! So what did Tommy do? He rang down FULL ASTERN, then FULL AHEAD on one engine, causing complete chaos – especially with the gunnery department. . . . Somebody eventually realized what was wrong and the sick berth staff arrived and stretchered him off to the sick bay. In the Admiral's report read out to the ship's company there was a remark that some incidents were a little too realistic.'

At the end of the year 1932 Captain the Honourable E.R. Drummond took over command of the ship and he brought her home to Portsmouth where she joined the Reserve. Her days as a flagship were over. She had had a good run.

However, her days of service were far from over. During the whole of January and February, 1933, she refitted in preparation for a Far East commission. Her passage to the east was marked by her meeting many splendid British passenger liners. On one day alone, 21 March, 1933, she spoke the 16,700-ton P & O liner *Rajputana* out from Bombay; the *Ballarat* from Australia belonging to the P & O Branch line: then there was the Aberdeen & Commonwealth Line vessel *Jervis Bay* (14,164 tons), also from Australia, and later to sacrifice herself in an heroic bid to defend Convoy HX 84 on the afternoon of 5 November, 1940,* against the German pocket battleship *Admiral Scheer.*†

On arrival at Hong Kong the new Commanding Officer, Captain 'Bob' Burnett, assumed command.‡ He was a man destined to distinguish himself in command of the cruiser squadron which helped sink the 31,800-ton German battlecruiser *Scharnhorst* on Boxing Day, 1943. Captain R.L. Burnett, thick-set, fair haired, with a ruddy complexion, was a born sailor and a born leader.

The Far East commission proved to be very short-lived. After a matter of a few weeks *Curacoa* was ordered home. She left Shanghai on 10 June and retraced her wake to arrive at Portsmouth on 27 July where she was de-ammunitioned and placed in the Reserve Fleet. Her days of glory, it seemed, were rapidly coming to an end.

But a further injection of life was given her with the appointment of Captain A.M. Peters and another refit. She was re-commissioned before the end of the year to take up training duties as the Gunnery and Torpedo School Ship at Portsmouth. She relieved HMS *Champion* and settled down to an undemanding phase of her life. Little did anyone know that 1935 was the beginning of the countdown to war.

During her six-and-a-half years as a training ship *Curacoa* became as familiar a sight in Portsmouth as the Naval Barracks. In the waters around the Isle of Wight, in Spithead and the Solent, and in the English Channel she was often seen and heard on her gunnery and torpedo exercises with or without other ships.

It all became a busy routine for her, and for several days a month for years

---

* This action earned her Commanding Officer, Captain E.S.F. Fegen, a posthumous VC.
† 12,100 tons, six 11-inch guns. Launched 1933. Suffered the curious fate of being bombed by Allied aircraft, capsizing in dock then being buried when the dock was filled in.
‡ Later Admiral Sir Robert Burnett (1887–1959).

on end she occupied herself and others in AA firings at smoke bursts, coastal bombardments, torpedo-firing exercises, streaming paravanes on voyages to Plymouth and Falmouth, simulated attacks by aircraft of several types, submarine attacks with destroyers 'depth charging' them, mining trials with experts and trainees from the torpedo shore establishment HMS *Vernon*.

Army officers from Camberley and the Imperial Staff College, and RAF officers from Basingstoke came aboard to witness combined service attacks: inter-service activity went a long way towards understanding each other's difficulties and was a fine platform for viewing new developments and gunnery techniques.

Every spring there was an RNVR cruise; every conceivable activity was embarked upon to give these part-time sailors training and sea-time, including much boat-work and, for the officers, ship handling.

Occasionally these Portsmouth-based years were enlivened with experiences a little out of the ordinary. One such occasion was in February, 1934, when Field Marshal Lord Allenby and Admiral of the Fleet Sir Roger Keyes were embarked at Dover for a Remembrance Day visit to Zeebrugge. Royal Navy, Royal Marine and RAF funeral parties were landed to take part in a moving ceremony; a one-minute silence was observed and the ceremony was marked by the firing of 59 one-minute guns.

In lighter vein, in September of that year a week's filming by Gaumont British was carried out aboard *Curacoa*, ashore in Cornwall, at Portland and in Weymouth Bay. John Mills, as a young man, had a leading part in the film *Brown on Resolution*. Many years later he wrote in his autobiography:

> 'In those early days of filming I always insisted that whenever possible I should be allowed to do my own stunts. . . . The scene was to be shot at night. It entailed Able Seaman Brown's escaping from the German cruiser. The camera would pick me up creeping through a cabin door, rifle in hand, boots tied round my neck; then, when no crew were in sight, I was to cross the deck, climb the rail, drop overboard into the sea and start the swim to Resolution Island. . . . The weather was appalling, bitterly cold, with a damp sea mist. . . . I walked to the ship's rail and looked down. . . . [It] seemed like a hundred feet below.'*

As John Mills waited in one of the cabins, out of the wind and cold, the door opened and a Petty Officer offered him the traditional PO's hospitality: 'Scuse me, sir,' he said, 'but I hear you are going in the drink tonight. And as it's a bit on the nippy side, we thought you might like to have a small tot to keep out the cold.' Mills continued the story:

---

*   *Up In The Clouds, Gentlemen Please*, by John Mills, Weidenfeld & Nicolson, 1980.

'The small tot turned out to be half a tumbler of that marvellous, oily, amber-coloured liquid called Navy Rum. In a few minutes I was a new man. That tot really hit the jackpot. The effect on an empty stomach was electric – courage spurted from every pore. Then they came to tell me there was a camera problem. "Time for the other half, sir?" Twenty minutes later when they were ready to shoot, Able Seaman Albert Brown was happily "smashed" and willing, if asked, to jump off the Eiffel Tower with no safety net.'

But the drop looked horrific. Mills took a deep breath, mentally crossed himself and jumped. He hit the water, which felt like concrete, and by the time he had struggled to the surface he was sober and nothing in the world would have persuaded him to give a repeat performance. Before he left *Curacoa* the Petty Officers insisted that the best place to restore circulation before leaving the ship was in their mess.

On 22 July, 1936, the cruiser made her first contact with *Queen Mary* who was outward-bound to America. Polite signals were exchanged. This was two months after her maiden voyage, and on her following voyage she captured the Blue Riband of the Atlantic.* It was to be nearly six years before their paths were to cross again for the last time.

1937 was a special year for the twenty-year-old cruiser, the highlight of which was the Coronation Review of the Fleet at Spithead. For the purposes of this event *Curacoa* joined the 9th Cruiser Squadron. For a whole week from the 13th to 20th there was hectic activity involving the battleships *Queen Elizabeth* (32,700 tons) and *Barham* (31,100 tons), the battlecruisers *Repulse* (32,000 tons), and *Hood* (48,000 tons), the carrier *Glorious* (22,500 tons), the cruiser *Galatea* (5,220 tons),† the 1st Destroyer Flotilla and the 1st Cruiser Squadron before mooring in their review positions at Spithead. On the 14th *Curacoa*, followed by *Cardiff* (4,190 tons) and *Carlisle* (4,290 tons) took station astern of *Dunedin* (4,850 tons) wearing the flag of the C-in-C Reserve Fleet, and steamed for Weymouth Bay for manoeuvres and rehearsal of illuminations with searchlight and firework displays. The Admiral took the opportunity of inspecting *Curacoa*, still a smart and attractive ship despite her age.

On the return to Spithead on 19 May the scene had grown in majesty and splendour out of all recognition. In addition to the Home, Mediterranean and Reserve Fleets, there were warships from the Royal Canadian and

---

* *Queen Mary's* fastest crossing was between 10 and 14 August, 1938, when she covered the 2,938 miles from the Ambrose Light to Bishop Rock at an average speed of 31.69 knots (36.49 mph.)

† All of these ships with the exception of *Queen Elizabeth* were sunk in the Second World War with enormous loss of life.

Indian navies, from the United States Navy, from Germany, France, the Argentine, Russia, Greece, Holland and Japan. Furthermore, there were representative ships from Sweden, Denmark, Finland, Portugal, Romania, Poland, Turkey, Estonia and Cuba. Liners of the British Merchant Navy also took part. It was perhaps the greatest assemblage of the world's warships that had ever been seen: certainly it was the last great gathering of the Royal Navy before the Second World War.

Next day, between 1530 and 1730 hours, 21-gun salutes resounded as the Trinity House vessel *Patricia* led HM Yacht *Victoria and Albert* down the lines of moored ships. Aboard the yacht the new King, George VI, took the salute. Bringing up the rear was the Admiralty yacht *Enchantress*. It must have been a most impressive sight for the King, and a moving experience, if only because he was a true naval officer who had seen action at the Battle of Jutland in the battleship *Collingwood*.

In celebration of the day the mainbrace was spliced and at 1800 hours tens of thousands of electric lamps illuminated the fleet in a brilliant display of light that shimmered across the waters.

It was a scene that gave rise to that famous gaffe by a radio commentator who kept repeating, 'The fleet's all lit up'. It was to be a life-long embarrassment to both the BBC and to Lieutenant-Commander Thomas Woodroofe who was acting as the commentator for the BBC's first live outside broadcast: kinder critics say he was emotionally overcome by the magnificence of the scene before him. Others, less charitably, suggest he might have been entertained in a wardroom or two, or, worse still, like John Mills, in a Petty Officers' Mess.

After these celebrations in 1937 the spectre of war loomed, making its presence felt throughout Europe; the 1930s were approaching a climactic end. Spain was gripped in internecine strife: Abyssinia (Ethiopia) lay under the heel of the blackshirt dictator, Mussolini: Czechoslovakia had been ravaged, and the year of Munich in 1938 rumbled forward with almost mesmeric certainty towards confrontation and war. For *Curacoa* the year was a normal one of activity for a training ship, paravanes were streamed and recovered and submarine exercises carried out. The annual refit necessitated no less than seven weeks in dry dock. And already new plans were afoot for *Curacoa*. All ships of the Royal Navy were being considered for extended life; especially was this so for escort vessels, for in the event of war they would be needed in vast numbers.

Others, like *Curacoa*, were being considered for re-equipping as AA ships, and it was in June, 1939, with Europe on the threshold of war, that she gathered her skirts about her, headed for Chatham and embarked on a refit to make her better suited for the type of warfare expected in the near future. *Curacoa* was, in fact, the last of the six 'C' Class cruisers to be taken in hand for conversion into AA ships before the start of the Second World War. Work began on her in Chatham Dockyard in June, 1939, three months before the outbreak of war, and finished in January, 1940. It was a radical transformation. Her original armament was completely stripped out. All her five 6-inch low-angle guns and two 3-inch AA guns of First World War vintage were replaced with four twin HA/LA (High Angle/Low Angle) AA guns, two for'ard and two aft, positions known as A and B, and X and Y.

A multiple Pom Pom (four x 2 pounder quick-firing guns), sometimes called the 'Chicago Piano', was fitted for'ard of the bridge and the AA armament was completed by eight .5-inch guns in two mountings of four each, placed on either side of the for'ard funnel.

Later still, during a refit at Rosyth in May/June, 1941, two single Pom Poms were added to either side of X gun deck aft, and a year later, during the big Rosyth refit of April/May, 1942, the eight .5-inch guns were removed and four Oerlikons substituted abreast the funnel and on either side of the signal deck in the bridge structure.

A lot more structural changes were made. All the torpedo tubes were removed. The bridge was enlarged. An ADP (Air Defence Position) was fitted on to the top of the tripod which formed the lower foremast. From a master sight on either side of this enlarged crow's-nest the close-range weapons could be brought to bear against attacking aircraft.

Finally, two HA Director Control Towers (HADCTs) and two Transmitting Stations (the for'ard and aft TSs) were incorporated deep in the ship to relay orders to the 4-inch guns. The for'ard director was up the foremast and was reached by way of a ladder from the bridge via the ADP. The after director was situated between the mainmast and X gun.

By the end of 1939 the war which had been threatening for years was now a reality in Europe, though it was the period of the phoney war when the only evidence of shooting appeared to be at sea in the Atlantic. The Battle of the River Plate in December occurred in the same month that Captain E.A. Aylmer DSC was appointed to command *Curacoa*. On 1 January, 1940, he re-commissioned her for service as an AA cruiser and she left Chatham for Portland before joining the 1st Anti-Aircraft Squadron (AAS1) on the Humber, comprising *Calcutta*, *Curlew* and *Cairo*. This squadron was to provide protection for East Coast convoys between Southend on the Thames estuary and Methil on the Firth of Forth. In naval circles these unglamorous duties were regarded as a bed of nails.

It was while *Curacoa* lay here that a substantial draft of RNVR gunnery ratings joined the ship, including Sub-Lieutenant R.R.K. Clover. They all came from the Humber Division RNVR. Robin Clover was a wartime member of the wardroom longer than anyone else; he enjoyed an infectious sense of humour and, with the great good fortune that few experience in life, he left the ship a few weeks before she went down.

During a period of intensely cold and strong weather in March and April, 1940, *Curacoa* worked out of Immingham near Grimsby on a roster with her sister ships. For four or five days she would steam about 150 miles each day, returning to anchor at night, then spend a couple of days and nights in port.

At last it seemed that His Majesty's AA cruiser *Curacoa* was in all respects ready for war. It was not long in developing.

BOMBED IN NORWAY

Wearied to exhaustion by air attacks, Ordinary Seaman Anderson complained: 'Roll on death and let's have a long sleep.' Later, after an air attack, mess mates found him: 'At the mess table there was Anderson. When we went up to him we realized he was dead. He had been killed by blast. His earlier wish had been granted.'

Report of Norwegian campaign, 1940, by Able Seaman (later Lieutenant-Commander RN Ret'd) Bob Garner.

In 1940 Norway and Denmark were neutral countries with insignificant armed forces. In the port of Narvik in the north of Norway vital Swedish iron ore supplies were shipped south to Germany. The regular Royal Navy blockade threatened this traffic and the danger to German interests was demonstrated by the *Altmark* affair in mid-February. In a moment of swashbuckling action, HM destroyer *Cossack* (1,870 tons), with Captain P.L. Vian★ in command, sent an armed boarding party aboard the *Altmark* prison ship for crews whose ships had been sunk by the *Graf Spee* and liberated 299 British seamen. The prison ship was violating Norwegian territorial waters. Vian's instructions from the Admiralty were clear: 'You should board *Altmark*, liberate prisoners and take possession of ship. Suggest to Norwegian captain [of attendant torpedoboat] that honour is served by submitting to superior force.'

British minelaying off the Norwegian coast, partly to stop the iron ore traffic, was regarded by Germany as further provocation.

On 9 April Germany ended the phoney war by launching an all-out attack called Operation *Weserübung*, the assault on Norway and Denmark. Jutland and Copenhagen were occupied immediately and a German seaborne invasion began to land troops at Kristiansand, Trondheim, Bergen, Narvik, Oslo and Stavanger. An airborne attack seized Oslo, the Norwegian capital. Norwegian shore batteries sank the German cruiser *Blücher* and the *Luftwaffe* flew in more supporting troops.

★ Admiral of the Fleet Sir Philip Vian DSO★★ (1894–1968).

30,000 British and French troops were thrown into the battle for Norway. They were put ashore at Namsos and Andalsnes in central Norway, while a smaller force was landed at Narvik. The forces in central Norway were subjected to a heavy pounding by bombers and the Germans gradually gained the upper hand.

The situation seemed tailor-made for the converted AA cruisers; where permanent AA sites were not available ashore, as in these Norwegian ports, the AA cruisers were able to provide splendid mobile AA batteries. Air support from the RAF and Fleet Air Arm was sparse and, although some was provided from the aircraft carrier *Glorious*,* she and some destroyers were intercepted and sunk by the *Scharnhorst*† and *Gneisenau*.‡

The 'C' Class cruisers were promptly despatched to Norway to give supporting AA protection to the Allied forces ashore and to units of the Royal Navy at sea. An operation conceived to capture Trondheim, the key to central Norway, was mounted by landings at Namsos, to the north of the target, the Mölde and Andalsnes, forming the southern prong of the movement, with the intention of effecting a pincer movement. The enemy opposition on all fronts was stubborn and well-conducted, resulting in frequent sharp engagements in all sectors.

But the terrain did not lend itself to naval operations. True, at Narvik, two naval battles had been fought with conspicuous success for the Royal Navy. In the first Captain B.A.W. Warburton-Lee in the destroyer *Hardy* (1,505 tons) led his flotilla into the fjords and sank two German destroyers and sundry support craft for the loss of two of his own ships, including his own destroyer. Warburton-Lee suffered mortal wounds and was subsequently awarded a posthumous VC.

Conspicuous success marked the Second Battle of Narvik which took place a few days later. Warburton-Lee had flushed out anything up to ten German destroyers and the Admiralty decided to send in a more powerful force to intercept and sink them. The 30,600-ton battleship *Warspite*, with her eight 15-inch guns and a powerful force of destroyers, intercepted and mercilessly pounded to destruction eight German destroyers and the U-boat *U-64* at no loss to themselves. It was an exemplary exhibition of the handling of destroyers in relatively confined waters.

Despite these successes, the town of Narvik, too far north to seem to be

---

* HMS *Glorious* (22,500 tons) was a former light battlecruiser converted to a carrier in the late '20s. She carried sixteen 4.7-inch guns and up to 48 aircraft. She sank with heavy loss of life on 8 June, 1940. The two 1,350-ton destroyers *Ardent* and *Acasta* were sacrificed in her defence.
† *Scharnhorst*, 31,800-ton battlecruiser, was launched 1936. Successfully carried out the Channel Dash. Was sunk in Battle of the North Cape, 1943, with enormous loss of life.
‡ *Gneisenau*, 31,800-ton battlecruiser, launched 1936. Bombed at Kiel 1942, virtually total loss. Scuttled 1945.

of strategic value to anyone, fell to the Germans; the Navy had not been able to capitalize on its two splendid successes. It was not at ease in these waters with their fjords and narrows, the overbearing snow-capped mountains, the near impossible routes round the islands and promontories, and the lack of searoom, the prerequisite of naval officers throughout the ages.

In addition to this almost claustrophobic feeling, the naval ships were subjected to remorseless air attacks. Junkers 87 dive bombers, Dornier 17s, Heinkel 111s and the remarkably versatile Junkers 88s dropped thousands of bombs and completely obliterated many of the small Norwegian town-ships which the Allies hoped to make their bases. The first troop convoy for this operation left the Clyde on 11 April, 1940, and it was not long before *Curacoa* herself was severely damaged. She left Rosyth for Mölde on the 17th of the month in company with the cruisers *Galatea*, *Arethusa* and *Carlisle*, carrying the 148th Infantry Brigade as part of Operation Sickle. *Curacoa* had one hundred Artists' Rifles aboard. In fact, it was to Andalsnes that *Curacoa* went.

Andalsnes was described by Christopher Buckley as

> 'a mere village of some 1500 inhabitants and the port was of the most rudimentary nature. It comprised a concrete jetty about 150 yards long, one side of which could be used for berthing ships, and a simple wooden quay. Under peacetime conditions it had a capacity of perhaps 700 tons daily. . . . Under the conditions of total German air superiority which prevailed throughout the campaign, unloading could not be carried out in safety for more than four or five out of the 24 hours. . . . It would be a good day on which 100 tons were unloaded.'*

Logistics alone were to make this a forlorn campaign.

Able Seaman Bob Garner, aboard *Curacoa*, remembers the cruiser's arrival off the Norwegian coast after a fairly stormy passage:

> 'We entered Romsdal Fjord and picked our way past Mölde towards the town of Andalsnes. As we cleared the mountains on the port beam we could see the town ablaze. We went alongside and landed the troops, who were glad to get ashore after a miser-able trip – not that they had much to look forward to, and many were killed or captured. With *Arethusa*, *Galatea* and our sister ship, *Carlisle*, we were ordered back to Scotland on the 19th. Half-way across, *Carlisle* returned to Norway. As soon as we had refuelled at Scapa Flow we headed back to relieve *Carlisle* who had

---

* *Norway, The Commandos, Dieppe* by Christopher Buckley, HMSO, 1977 edition, p 44.

run out of ammunition. On 22 April we steamed into the fjord, went past Andalsnes and anchored close to the mountains.

Having taken over as AA guardship, we were warned that we might have to pick up the King of Norway and his government who were somewhere in Andalsnes awaiting transport to Great Britain.

We settled down to the normal routine; decks were scrubbed and brightwork was cleaned. Commander's 'Requestmen'* was rudely interrupted by the appearance of a Heinkel which, coming over the mountains, did not see us at first, but as she went over us we opened fire with everything we had. This was at 0930, and twenty minutes later another plane appeared low over the top of the 2,000-ft mountain, and we fired a number of rounds as it dipped out of sight. After that, German aircraft appeared at fairly frequent intervals. There were many near misses but no major damage, merely damage from bomb splinters.'

Garner remembers that the ship's company behaved magnificently while under fire. Morale, he noted, was very high. During the later attacks Garner recalls that the cruiser had slipped her moorings and got under way, trying to gain some sea-room to enable her to take avoiding action. At midday, during a lull in proceedings, sandwiches and hot soup were brought round to all the guns' crews. Garner moved from the Pom Pom he was manning and was put in charge of the multiple .5 machine guns on the port side of the funnel. Attacks continued throughout the day, being brought to a halt by dusk. Guns' crews were allowed to go to their messes for supper and turning in. Before going below Garner spent some moments gazing at the scenery, absorbing the beauty and serenity of the completely calm waters of the fjord and the towering mountains reflected in them.

Careful Herman!
It's the CURACOA.

* This is a regular muster of ratings wishing to discuss requests – such as application for compassionate leave or for promotion – with their First Lieutenant, Commander or Captain.

He can remember the next morning – the 23rd. It was beautiful. The air was crisp as the sun rose over the mountains. It was a peaceful scene which belied what was to follow. After breakfast, ship was cleaned and guns' crews closed up. Very soon a Heinkel was spotted flying low up the fjord. At the same time a Walrus flying boat from an RN ship appeared over the mountains. Garner writes:

'It was amusing to see the Heinkel turn round to attack the Walrus whose maximum speed was 100 knots, for, as the Heinkel banked, so did the Walrus, and because of its smaller turning circle, continually thwarted the Heinkel pilot in his attempts to get the guns to bear. He gave it up and decided to attack us instead. He came in very low which gave a chance for our guns – the point fives – to open fire. He dropped his bombs close astern, which shook the ship up, and then disappeared over the mountain belching out smoke.

We had the usual high-level attacks throughout the day with only minor damage, due largely to our being under way and making last-moment alterations of course. During the afternoon we were attacked by a Ju 87 dive bomber which was a frightening experience, but having survived the first attack, we realised that dive bombers were easy targets as they came straight down our line of fire.

Later that day there was an alarm when a plane with twin tail-fins flying quite low and out of the sun was sighted. The 4-inch guns opened up, and after about twelve rounds the aircraft was smoking and seen to hit the sea. There were cheers from the guns' crews, but consternation on the bridge as they realised we had shot down a Hudson. There had been no indication that there were any British planes in the area and we had seen no RAF aircraft in Norway: and the Hudson was a new plane which no one had seen before. A boat was put out to rescue the pilot but he refused to come on board, so the boat took him ashore.'

By the end of the day thousands of rounds had been expended and *Curacoa* was beginning to run short of ammunition. Another ship returning home had been ordered to unload her surplus ammunition at a nearby jetty and arrangements were made for *Curacoa* to help herself from this hoard.

Garner recalls a strange atmosphere on the mess decks that evening. Everyone was relating his experiences during the air attacks and he noticed how this had a bonding effect: any friction between the reservists and the permanent ratings disappeared and all seemed to feel they had been truly christened by common battle experience.

The following morning, as soon as it was light, at about 0530, *Curacoa* weighed anchor and prepared to go alongside the jetty to pick up the ammunition. But in going alongside a wire hawser got caught around the screw.

'The captain sent for Dicko who was the diver and explained to him that he wanted him to go down and clear the wire, but if we were attacked we would have to get under way. Dicko agreed to do it and went over the side. It was a nail-biting hour, but he did the job. However, in the haste to get him aboard his leg was injured and he was put in the sick bay, which, as it turned out, saved his life – but only just.'

The third day, again, was one of almost continuous bombing attacks, and Garner can remember gossiping around the gun during the day and saying, 'When you're bombed ashore you can always convince yourself that they're aiming at someone else. Here it's not like that!'

Captain Aylmer decided to take advantage of a lull in the action to anchor closer inshore, in the shadow of the mountain, 'our stern tucked as close as possible to the sheer cliff which was assumed to afford us some measure of security – which was not borne out by events.'

On Bob Garner's gun the trainer was Peter Fenton whose form of relaxation was playing the piccolo: it made an odd sight, a piccolo concert with an audience of guns' crews sitting around below a mountainous cliff.

The ship's Gunner, Mr Charlton, has left an account of a ship's party being sent ashore to locate the ammunition:

'The captain ordered a fusing party to be landed to locate a known stock of 500 boxes of ammunition and fifty boxes of fuses. They were eventually discovered strewn about a beach.'

Charlton's team of eight men, supplemented by more men from the base, worked like Trojans to fuse the cartridges. An air raid developed, bombs were seen to fall and a soldier came running to them shouting, 'She's hit! She's sinking!'

Failing to find the cruiser, the fuse party commandeered a Norwegian trawler, loaded her with the ammunition and set out to search for the cruiser. Charlton continues his report:

'A thousand rounds of Pom Pom were [also] embarked on commandeered lorries. . . . We shoved off flying the Norwegian flag with a total complement of two officers, eight ratings, two Royal Marines, two Norwegian naval ratings, a skipper, two deck hands and an engineer.'

Enough adventures were experienced in the next few hours to last everyone all their lives. They were nearly shot at by an RN trawler during an air raid ('This is my 19th air raid since daylight,' the skipper shouted) and were closely scrutinized by one of three loitering Heinkels:

'The plane descended in ever decreasing circles until it came to within 800 ft. The four beautiful black bombs stood out plainly. Orders were passed to blow up lifebelts, keep out of sight and jump overboard when ordered. Our poor skipper was frantic, he wanting to go full speed ahead and hard-a-port, and myself wishing to go on just as normal to avoid arousing further suspicion. . . . To our surprise – and relief – Jerry gave us the benefit of the doubt.'

Mr Charlton took the trawler close inshore and secured alongside a derelict pier. Startled inhabitants fled, returning chastened when they discovered the party was mainly British. Communication with base was established and orders received to return to Andalsnes. En route the trawler was attacked by an aircraft, the bomb salvo exploding about 100 feet ahead:

'The trawler seemed to jump clean out of the water. Bombing was going on all around; the base was afire and under attack; a cricketer-named trawler was fighting off five Heinkels and the pier alongside which the trawler was proposing to secure was blown up in good enough time for the trawler to head across the fjord to anchor in relative safety.'

At dusk the ammunition was laboriously heaved ashore; naval units entered the fjord and the *Curacoa* party embarked in a cruiser, rejoining their own ship eight days later, to learn of the cruiser's exploits, the damage sustained and the deaths of their comrades, while they themselves had been having equally hair-raising experiences.

*   *   *

Guns' crews and those on duty up top were advantaged in many ways, but especially when the ship was in action. They could, more often than not, follow the action, see much of the battle, watch the movements of the enemy and know what the bangs and explosions were all about. Those down below were less privileged. Author G.G. Connell expressed this when writing about *Curacoa's* sister ships off Norway:

'Those below decks, in boiler and engine rooms, in gun control transmitting stations, in the ship's lower steering conning position and in the magazines, suffered to a point of numbed apathy and mental torpor. News of what was happening was sparse, the hard-pressed upper deck parties could only shout occasional often garbled descriptions of events or warnings through ammunition chutes. . . . Deep down in brightly-lit magazines, cold, clammy, stark and claustrophobic . . . little news percolated.'*

Sub-Lieutenant (E) Tony Corlett[†] paints a similar picture of endurance in the engine room when under attack, a situation he experienced many times during the Norwegian campaign:

'In action, the closest the engine room crew came to knowing what was going on above them was by the noise of gunfire. We could hear and feel the thuds of the 4-inch shells being hurled at the enemy aircraft. We felt strangely secure until it gave way to the rapid Pom Pom fire followed by the rattle of the multiple machine guns. By then anything could happen. On the after bulkhead the clanking and hissing of the steering engine indicated the endless twisting and turning of the ship to avoid bombs. No machinery failure now – every man was tensed up making sure his charges were doing their bit. Then, just as quickly, the quiet descended, accompanied by the steady rumble from the shafts and gearing. The whiff of battle came down the ventilators, mixing with the smell of hot oil and steam. Nobody spoke. Over in the boiler room grim faces watched the water gauges, peered through the sight glasses into the furnaces. Deft hands adjusted the air flow to the oil burners, while the big feed pumps strove to satisfy the thirst of the boilers. A cacophony of sound to some, a symphony of precision to others.'

After Bob Garner and the rest of the guns' crews had listened to Peter Fenton's piccolo playing they went below off watch. Garner continued his account:

'The warmth of the mess deck was very welcome after the cold evening on deck. There was argument because someone had swiped all the butter, but there were mugs of hot tea, a stew and plenty of bread. An OD (Ordinary Seaman) – Anderson – was grumbling about no sleep and remarked, "Roll on death, and let's have a long sleep." At this moment the Action Station alarm rattlers went. We all cursed, grabbed our duffle coats and scrambled up the ladder. In the passageway leading to the upper deck

* *Valiant Quartet* by G.G. Connell, William Kimber, 1979, pp. 82–3.
† Later Lieutenant-Commander (E) A.E. Corlett DSC.

24

there was a solid mass of people trying to get out to the upper deck, whilst trying to go the other way were others heading for the for'ard magazine. I had almost got to the door when there was a tremendous bang and then a rush of hot air, followed by débris falling from the deckhead, then silence with just someone moaning.

As we emerged from the passageway on to the upper deck we were amazed to see it was covered in twisted metal, and the port side of the bridge was only held up by two struts. There were fires burning in the wreckage. It took a little time to adjust to the situation and think what to do. I made my way to my gun on the port side. It had been pushed back from its mounting. I went round to the starboard gun and the layer and trainer were slumped over it. As I was examining them to see what was wrong the Doc arrived, took a look and said, "Leave them, they're dead."'

Captain Aylmer evidently had fears of the cruiser settling in the deep waters of the fjord because he gave orders for the boats to be turned out in their davits and to prepare to beach the ship. The engines had stopped and all electric power had been cut off. But even before the boats had been turned out the order was cancelled, probably as damage control parties began a better assessment of the real damage to the ship. Garner takes up the story again;

'The gunner was calling for men to fight a fire on the mess deck, which was in danger of reaching the magazine. After this was put out, I returned to the upper deck and saw a body hanging in the rigging round the mast. This had to be got down. There were a number of bodies in the wreckage. There were injured men there, too, who had to be extracted and taken down to the wardroom and Royal Marines' mess deck, which had been turned into emergency sickbays. All the dead we could get at were placed on the upper deck and covered with canvas.'

An actual eyewitness of the bombing attack was Gofton Thorley. He was a Humber RNVR man who had been called up in August, 1938, and after four months' intensive gunnery training was drafted to *Curacoa* as an OD along with fifty-three other ratings and two officers, all of them reservists of the Humber Division. He relates the story of the evening attack on 24 April, 1940:

'At 1700 we anchored again under the shelter of the mountain and everybody was overjoyed to see some twelve Skuas of the Fleet Air Arm pass overhead. That night we were allowed to go below for our supper, and I was relieving on A gun [the foremost 4-inch] about 1930 when a Heinkel appeared flying in from ahead at about 12,000 ft. A gun and the Pom Poms were the only guns able to bear on her and we fired two rounds when I heard the bombs whistling down towards us. From my experience of the past few days I knew that the Germans had made no mistake. I had a peculiar detached feeling, and fatalistically thought, "So this is it!" Then the bombs, three 250-pounders, tore into the ship. There was a terrific crash as the ship lifted out of the water. I looked up from my post, realizing that I had been neither killed nor injured. All the CPOs who were in or near their mess when we were hit were killed outright, leaving only two aboard – and they were seriously injured. Altogether some forty ratings were killed and a similar number injured.'

At some stage Bob Garner remembered Dicko in the sickbay, which had been destroyed:

'I made my way into the wreckage, found him in his nightshirt and helped him out. The engine room had got one engine working and the torpedo party had rigged emergency lighting. All the bridge steering gear had been destroyed, so the next job was to arrange emergency steering aft. The ship was then controlled from the after gun platform.

It was now completely dark, so I collected some of the seamen together to go below and see how our mess deck had fared. It was only partly lit by the emergency lighting. At the mess table was Ordinary Seaman Anderson. When we went up to him we realized he was dead. Between us we got his body out onto the upper deck. He had been killed by the blast. His earlier wish had been granted . . .

We didn't feel like sleeping on the mess deck that night so we huddled round the funnel.'

By early light on the 25th the cruiser was seaworthy and made her way slowly down the fjord to the open sea. The two remaining serviceable guns were manned and as many of the crew as possible mustered on the upper deck in case the ship should founder.

The Bo'sun called for volunteers to search the wreckage for bodies. A young shipwright, two RNVRs and Garner stepped forward. One of their early tasks was to shore up the side of the bridge and then remove some of the débris with tackles. Bodies were identified and labelled: parts of bodies and remains were more difficult to identify. All were placed into canvas bags and labelled appropriately.

Later that day Garner went to the wardroom flat to see the injured. They all put on brave faces, including two seamen who had had leg amputations. One of them, an RNVR called Prest, had lost both his legs. The ship seemed strangely deserted: the Captain and Navigator had both been injured and were confined to their cabins, and the only officers to be seen on the upper deck were the Gunnery Officer and two RNVRs.

Stoker 2nd Class Bob Richards leaves us with a view of the action from between decks. His action station was in the wardroom and office flat as ammunition supply for Y magazine. His job was to collect a 4-inch shell from a hoist in the office flat, carry it to the wardroom and push it up a metal chute to the upper deck. He recalled that there was a fusing party ashore which was to have come aboard that evening but had failed to do so.

Bob Richards should have had the first watch (2000 to 2400 hours) in B boiler room. He was on his way there when action stations sounded. He was unclipping the hatch to Y magazine when the bombs hit for'ard at the base of the bridge. The ship was plunged into darkness. Orders were passed for the ammunition parties to go for'ard and help the fire-fighting parties. He found there was a huge heap of débris just inside the break of the fo'c'sle and alongside it a Royal Marine. Bob Richards tells a grisly tale:

'I went back with someone to fetch some sort of stretcher and managed with the help of a two-and-a-half ringer [Lieutenant-Commander] to remove a length of canvas from the potato locker. On our return we found the Royal Marine. Only then we discovered his body had been decapitated. I dashed up the companion way to be sick in the heads, but found they had vanished over the side. At the top I found a young seaman hanging on a metal spar by the straps of his life jacket. He did not appear to be injured, but he was dead, and I helped to lift him down to the deck.'

Bob Richards then climbed up towards the bows and was spotted by an officer who was playing a hose into a compartment. He was told to take over, and with another hose under his other arm managed to put out the fire which had been threatening the Pom Pom ready-use locker. That finished, he was ordered up to the Pom Pom where he was given a hurried gunnery lesson. When he was relieved he was told to go aft and collect a tot of rum – his very first taste of it, as he was too young to draw the daily ration. Warmed by the experience, he found a space in the hammock netting in the mess and fell asleep.

A memo attached to *Curacoa's* log book (preserved in the Public Record Office) for 23 August, 1940, four months after the bombing, appears to have the stamp of authority:

'The bombs appeared to explode on the port side of the ship just for'ard of the ship's company's galley. The force of the explosion occurred upwards, causing extensive damage in the sick bay flat and the superstructure as far as the lower bridge, and opening up the whole of the port side of the Pom Pom deck.

The Pom Pom and point fives were put out of action, and all communications from the director and compass platform were destroyed or badly damaged. All 4-inch guns could be fired in local control.

The ship had been steered from the lower conning tower, but as all communication between the compass platform and the LCT was destroyed by the explosion, a change-over to the engine room steering position was made, and the ship was conned from the emergency conning position abaft B gun.

The casualties amounted to 45 ratings killed and 36 injured. Most of the casualties occurred in the upper mess decks and in the superstructure, where personnel who had been relieved for supper were proceeding to their action stations.'

*   *   *

Arriving back at Scapa Flow on 26 April, *Curacoa* transferred the wounded to a hospital ship, took on board sailmakers to help prepare the corpses for sea burial and two padres for the service.

On 28 April, accompanied by the 1,340-ton destroyer *Hotspur*, *Curacoa* set off for Chatham via the Atlantic and English Channel – two lame ducks, one with next to no ammunition and the other with defective Asdics. Fog delayed their arrival but spirits were raised when soldiers and sailors ashore at Sheerness cheered in rousing fashion as the ships passed by.

Bob Garner's father was president of the Warrant Officers' mess at Chatham. He came aboard and as he shook hands with his son the strain showed; people ashore only had numbers of casualties revealed to them – no names. Mr Garner had kept all this from his wife until he knew their son was safe and well.

The following day the whole ship's company went on a fortnight's survivor's leave and a care and maintenance party from Chatham barracks took over.

NORWEGIAN AFTERMATH: THE NORTH-ABOUT CONVOYS

3

'Air attacks on convoys at this time were extremely frequent, always occurring about dusk and usually when a convoy was in the vicinity of Kinnaird Head.'

Captain C.C. Hughes Hallett in The Naval Review, May, 1948.

Curacoa's fierce ordeals in the Norwegian fjords had lasted just one week. The other five 'C' Class cruisers which had been converted to AA cruisers before 1940 all had longer stints in these inhospitable waters. Throughout April and May they gave support to the British and French troops who were being pounded almost at will by squadrons of *Luftwaffe* aircraft which enjoyed total command of the air.

Gradually the precarious Allied footholds in central Norway were loosened and an attempt to recapture Trondheim failed. Andalsnes was evacuated on 1 May and Namsos the following day. Further north, the Allies were unable to dislodge the Germans holding Narvik. The campaign then deteriorated to one of evacuation as more convulsive battles erupted in France and the Low Countries. By early June Norway was virtually abandoned and on the 14th of the month Paris fell to the Germans.

At the expense of chronology, it is appropriate here to glance briefly at the effectiveness of the six 'C' Class AA cruisers converted or re-built before 1940.

Their gallant performance in Norway can be gauged by the damage sustained by *Curacoa* and the loss of HMS *Curlew*, bombed to destruction on 26 May. She had relieved *Coventry* as AA guardship, patrolling close by Skaanland airstrip when she was struck aft by one or more bombs and severely damaged. *Curlew's* survivors packed into *Cairo*, then she was struck by a bomb and also needed much damage control attention before she was able to limp back to Scapa Flow. There she deposited *Curlew's* survivors before proceeding to Tyneside for repairs and a much-needed three weeks' leave.

It seems, on the face of it, ironical that three light cruisers recently converted specifically for AA duties were bombed and sunk or severely damaged by the very weaponry they were designed to combat.

Connell suggests that much of the trouble at this stage of the war was the unsophisticated, even primitive, weapons used by the Navy:*

'With few exceptions all the long-range AA guns were of 4-inch calibre manufactured for the 1914–18 war. Guns and mountings used hand-operated elevation and training mechanical shaft and cog drives, devoid of any form of power assistance. Gunlayers and trainers followed pointers on step-by-step dial repeaters that required endless pointer checks in harbour and at sea. Elevation and training mechanical systems on gun mountings and director top controls allowed a tolerance of error of plus or minus two degrees; it was rare for any mounting to better plus or minus three to four degrees. Fixed charge and shell, 4-inch ammunition in the fleet was fitted with powder-activated time fuses of uncertain accuracy . . . few ships as yet possessed mechanical fuse setters. Fuse settings were transmitted to guns over gun telephone head sets, and repeated on dials.'

Connell goes on to point out that elevation, training and fuse-setting data came from primitive mechanical computers called High Angle Fire Control Systems (HACS). The information digested by this unit was acquired in unscientific terms: range finders provided ranges; elevation and training data came from the director and the HA control officer's estimate of height and speed of aircraft read off from his fixed binoculars amplified by what was known as the angle of presentation, obtained by lining up an engraved and arrowed graticule in the binoculars with the fuselage of the approaching plane. Connell continues:

'It was remarkable that these crude . . . systems produced any results at all. Until new guns, control systems and proximity-fused ammunition began to reach the fleet in new ship constructions and placed in older ships during refits, it was only because of superhuman efforts by ordnance artificers and torpedo branch seamen responsible for high and low power electrical gun circuits that any form of rough accuracy could be achieved . . . captains of guns and their crews fought their guns with superb elan using a special kind of disciplined initiative that has always been a feature of the British fighting man.'

*   Connell, op. cit, pp. 146–7.

30

But superb elan and disciplined initiative, both exhibited in profusion by the 'C' Class cruisers off Norway, were no substitutes for modern weaponry which all the ships lacked. It could well be argued, too, that off Norway the ships were hampered by lack of sea room, compelled as they were to operate in the confines of the fjords. Conversely, it could be just as easily argued that the terrain and conditions did not favour the attacking aircraft squadrons either.

Gauging the efficacy of a ship's AA fire power is at best an empirical decision and at worst a reasoned guess. On the face of it, it should be judged by the number of aircraft it can fairly claim to have shot down and destroyed. But this is too simplistic and is not the only criterion. Such a fierce barrage of AA fire can deter approaching aircraft pilots, impelling them to turn and fail to press home their attack or even to jettison their bomb load to make escape easier.

However, it must be a judgement of sorts when AA cruisers are sunk by attacking aircraft. And this statement alone implies, even proclaims, the inadequacy of the ship's AA weaponry or of its guns crews' skill.

A brief glance at Table No. 2* will underscore the fact that four of the six 'C' Class cruisers were sunk or virtually destroyed by aircraft attacks; one was sunk by a submarine's torpedo and the sixth, *Curacoa*, by collision.

Calcutta's loss was at the hands of a Ju 88: two bombs blew out the ship's bottom and she sank in about five minutes. Eighty-two of the ship's company died. Twenty-three officers and 233 men survived, being picked up by *Coventry*, her chummy ship.

Cairo's end came in a dramatic encounter off Cape Bon when the Italian submarine *Axum* (Lieutenant Renato Perrini) intercepted the embattled convoy to Malta in the operation known as Operation Pedestal on 12 August, 1942. Perrini fired a salvo of four torpedoes. All four found a target. One struck the 8,000-ton cruiser *Nigeria*, another hit *Cairo*, while the remaining two struck the oiler *Ohio*. None of the ships sank, but *Cairo's* quarterdeck and Y gun disappeared, twenty-three men were lost and the remaining 377 were transferred to the Hunt Class destroyer *Wilton* (1,050 tons). She must have been packed to the gunwales.

Cairo was eventually sunk by a Royal Navy ship. *Nigeria* and *Ohio* both survived their ordeals, the oiler's experiences providing one of the most dramatic incidents in the history of sea warfare.

Fifteen months later it was *Coventry's* turn, and her destruction also took place in the Mediterranean, during a futile attempt to retake Tobruk. Fifteen Ju 87 dive bombers came out of the sun and blew off her bows as far back as A gun. Another one or two bombs destroyed the boiler and engine rooms, which meant the ship was doomed, and the W/T and RDF or radar offices. The bridge party survived but Ordinary Signalman Peter Clay (later

*   See p. 33.

Lieutenant RNVR) is badly affected to this day over half a century later by the memory of the holocaust around him. The ship became a burning, drifting hulk. Sixty-four men died. All the survivors were picked up by the two Hunt Class destroyers *Beaufort* and *Dulverton*, both of 1,050 tons.

Coventry, the most famous of her class of cruiser, is reported to have brought down more German and Italian aircraft than any other Royal Naval vessel during the war. She refused to go down despite all the destruction. The Tribal Class destroyer *Zulu* had to despatch her by torpedo and, as if in some macabre retribution, she herself was sunk in the following attack.

★   ★   ★

Curacoa's bomb damage repairs and her refit following the Norwegian campaign were put into dockyard hands in May, 1940, and within a few days the cruiser had taken on the appearance of unashamed chaos. Holding the fort during the refit and endeavouring to keep a grasp on all that was going on was Number One, the First Lieutenant, Lieutenant-Commander L.H. Phillips, who had joined the ship during the previous year.

He was joined on 25 May by Lieutenant Clover, Sub-Lieutenant Lloyd and the fifty-odd Humber Division RNVR ratings drafted to RN Barracks, Chatham, and the Royal Marines to RM Barracks. Several of these ratings formed AA gun crews ashore, for the Battle of Britain was raging overhead in the clear blue skies of that hot summer. France was to fall, and soon Britain was alone to face the might of Germany, and England awaited invasion daily.

In July Captain Charles Hughes Hallett* took up his appointment to HMS *Curacoa* 'in command'.

Other officers joined: Lieutenant-Commander (E) T.S. Lee became the new Chief Engineer, and Surgeon Lieutenant C. (John) Rooke joined as an RNVR doctor.

Towards the end of this refit Sub-Lieutenant (E) Corlett joined *Curacoa*. He vividly recalls those days. He remembers in particular the unusual weapon that occupied 'X' gun site:

> 'It consisted of a group of mortar tubes on a mounting. Fired from these tubes were projectiles containing, amongst other things, a mechanism which, at the correct height being reached, released a bomb suspended by a parachute on a long wire. Whatever the merits of this device, these projectiles had an unbelievable attraction for their mother ship, and disaster was narrowly averted by the accurate small arms fire from the Marines. . . . Despite the fact that it was the brainchild of Winston Churchill, it was quietly removed and replaced by the trusty twin HA mounting.'

---

* Later Vice Admiral Sir Charles Hughes Hallett (1898–1985). Fought at the Dardanelles and at the Battle of Jutland 1916. Commanded HMS *Implacable* 1944. COS Home Fleet 1950. KCB 1954. His younger brother John also became a Vice Admiral.

FATE OF 'C' CLASS AA CRUISERS

REBUILT BEFORE 1940

1940   *Curlew*   Bombed and sunk by German aircraft off Ofot Fjord, Norway 26 May, 1940.

1941   *Calcutta*   Bombed and sunk by German and Italian aircraft NW of Alexandria, 1 June, 1941.

1942   *Cairo*   Torpedoed and sunk by Italian submarine *Axum*, N of Bizerta during Operation Pedestal, 12 August, 1942.

1942   *Curacoa*   Sunk in collision with *Queen Mary* off coast of Donegal, 2 October, 1942.

1942   *Coventry*   Bombed and sunk by Italian aircraft off Tobruk, 14 September, 1942.

1945   *Carlisle*   Bombed off Dodecanese by Stuka bombers. More awash than afloat, towed to Alexandria, 9 October, 1945. Constructive total loss. Scrapped 1949.

33

Corlett remembers the cruiser's engines with something akin to affection. The design of her machinery was quite advanced when she was built in 1917–18:

'Many ships at that time still had turbines driving directly onto the propellor shafts. This was rather like trying to harness a race-horse to a plough. The advantage of geared turbines was the greatly increased level of efficiency because both the turbines and the propellors could be arranged to run at their most efficient speeds. It was Brown Curtis geared turbines which were in *Curacoa*. The passing years had done nothing to quieten these machines and the ageing metal complained loudly when driven hard.

Steam for the turbines was supplied by six Yarrow water tube boilers. All the auxiliary machinery was driven by reciprocating steam engines – pumps, dynamos and boiler fans. It was necessary to lubricate the pistons of these engines and in doing so oil was entrained into the exhaust steam. All steam was condensed in order to improve the thermal efficiency of the machinery and to provide pure water for the boiler feed.

Now oil in the boiler feed water causes over-heating of the furnace tubes – quickly followed by an explosion. In order to avoid this situation the exhaust steam from the auxiliary machinery was passed through filters packed with towelling. Hardly sophisticated – but it worked well provided it was looked after and cleaned regularly. But it was also the source of some anxiety. Despite the layers of paint on the bulkheads and the wheezing pumps, the engine room crews tackled the job of getting the best out of the archaic collection of machinery with resigned determination. It was a case where horse-sense, experience and engineering know-how rated higher than equations.'

Corlett pays tribute to Warrant Engineer Aikman; it was he who had his finger on the pulse. He and the Chief Engine Room Artificers could coax the best out of the engines and machinery, but even they were unable to stop water mixing with the oil fuel and it getting into the burners. The burners go out. Without warning there is a resultant loss of pressure, and as Corlett puts it: 'Way off ship, irate Captain, not to mention Chief Engineer, added to which you make a lot of black smoke.'

The trouble was located – seawater leaking into the port fuel tanks by way of the propellor shaft; it was cured, but with the loss of endurance and range of action. And not before the cruiser approached the boom at Scapa with the flagship a few cables away. She emitted the densest cloud of black smoke imaginable, covering everything, including the flagship.

Another source of recurring trouble was a generator, and, with the ever-increasing electrical load due to more sophisticated weaponry and detection gear, the generating capacity was well stressed. It had never, it seems, been able to develop full power, or not until an enthusiastic ERA, Ted Beavis, tackled the problem. He employed some gadgetry for measuring cylinder pressures and produced sketches with little wiggly lines showing that the valve timing was wrong. This suggested that the piston valve had been fitted the wrong way round. It was changed. Tension grew as full load was applied. The needles crept through the scales. Full load was achieved.

*   *   *

Curacoa was shaping up nicely when the exigencies of the Navy demanded her presence elsewhere. When she sailed from Chatham's No. 7 dock barely 25% of her weapons were in working order, and dockyard maties sailed with her as far as Sheerness. There she was fitted with degaussing gear to counteract magnetic mines and the ship was swung to correct compass deviation. Gun crews' and director crews' drills were carried out, but a gunnery officer's dream come true was let slip. The Captain described the incident:*

> 'On the second afternoon at Sheerness a raid occurred by about 30–40 Messerschmitt 110s on the oil tanks at Sheerness, the ship at the time lying at a buoy just off them. None of the aircraft made any attempt to attack the ship, and during most of the final stages of the raid were flying around in mass formation within a few hundred yards of her . . . only a few spasmodic rounds could be got off, and they got away entirely unscathed.'

Curacoa finally left Scotland on 12 September, 1940, and she was never to put into an English port again. Paravanes were streamed, a zigzag was followed and during the next fortnight just before escorting her first convoy she improved her status enormously. She became based at Scapa Flow where the vast anchorage was filled with every imaginable type of ship. There she held sub-calibre shoots and, perhaps a little cruelly, exercised collision and abandon ship stations. ADP, director and searchlight crews carried out drills.

At exercise action stations the main armament shot at a towed battle practice target, while close-range weapons fired at a sleeve towed by an aircraft. Almost every aspect of activity was exercised in order to familiarize the crew in all their duties. Captain Hughes Hallett was demanding. He described the ship's duty in his article in *The Naval Review*:

---

* *The Naval Review*, No. 2, Vol 36, May, 1948. Magazine of the Association of Royal Naval Officers, 'Experiences with the Rosyth-North-about Convoys, 1940–42.'

'The convoy situation at this time was that the east coast portion of inward-bound convoys came round the north of Scotland and down to Methil where ships were dispersed to their ports or joined the south-bound east coast of England convoys. Outgoing convoys sailed from Methil north-about out to the Atlantic through the Pentland Firth. The timing of convoys was to ensure that they passed through the Pentland Firth in daylight with the tide; but . . . it was not always possible to stick to this. The disadvantage of this convoy plan from the point of view of the escorts was that we always found ourselves with a different A/S escort whom we relied on to supplement the AA fire, since the convoys came in or sailed with part of their ocean-going escort groups.

We joined our first convoy, a northbound one, off Aberdeen about 1600 on a late September afternoon. We zigzagged to seaward of the leading ships of the convoy until dark and then, as recommended, went to the rear. This was a great mistake. We had hardly been there more than a few minutes when, with absolutely no warning or indication of its presence, a very low-flying German aircraft hit the commodore's ship with a bomb and set it on fire. We steamed at high speed to the head of the convoy again; but it was too late to do anything, and nothing further occurred. . . . After this episode we took stock of the situation and decided the advice we had been given must be forgotten. The requirement obviously was to remain near the head of the convoy and at the same time to take anti-submarine precautions since there was not sufficient sea room inside the screen for manoeuvring, a requirement that was a bit of a problem to comply with.'

Captain Hughes Hallett, like all escort commanders at the time, did not appreciate that the U-boat peril on the east coast of Scotland was non-existent; consequently escorts still maintained a zigzag course which made station keeping after dark awkward, if not dangerous in bad visibility.

Soon HMS *Alynbank* joined forces with *Curacoa* and worked as an opposite number so that every convoy instead of only a portion had an AA ship in company. *Alynbank* was one of a class of vessel specially converted to AA ship for the aerial defence of convoys. She was regarded as equivalent to, though much slower than, an AA cruiser. She carried a main armament of eight 4-inch HA/LA guns and registered a gross tonnage of 5,150. She was a tribute to her builders, Harland and Wolff. At the age of nineteen she was expended as a blockship but salvaged and later scrapped.

But the association did not last long. Towards the end of the year *Alynbank* dropped out and *Curacoa* was left coping with all convoys. The routine was that the cruiser sailed from Scapa to escort all inward-bound convoys since they were obviously more valuable than the outward-bound empties. The routine was that two inward-bound convoys arrived on successive days followed by a gap of two days. *Curacoa* escorted these convoys southward until after dark or until Buchan Ness was reached, whichever occurred earliest. Convoys, curiously, were not usually attacked south of Buchan Ness.

'After a number of these attacks the pattern began to show up, a pattern which never varied throughout the whole of the ship's service escorting these convoys. Attacks always occurred within a few minutes (plus or minus) of one hour after sunset, and we dropped into the routine of going to action stations half-an-hour after sunset and falling out if nothing had happened one-and-a-quarter hours after sunset; and I take my hat off to him that he never once let us down over this.'

Captain Hughes Hallett related another incident when a convoy was attacked 'as usual' off Kinnaird Head at dusk by two Heinkel 115s. The first one made a mess of his attack; his torpedoes missed and in making his getaway he crossed *Curacoa's* bows. The cruiser let rip with all guns that would bear, and claimed hits. At that moment two Blenheims appeared and one shot down the Heinkel. Then two Hurricanes wrongly identified the Blenheims and attacked one of them. All turned out well but it had been an unfortunate incident, resulting in *Curacoa* being fitted with an RAF VHF set to enable her to control accompanying aircraft.

Another incident entailing natural perils of the sea occurred when an inward-bound convoy became storm-bound in the Moray Firth at night. The convoy's speed dropped to two or three knots, visibility was bad and lights specially exposed ashore were not seen. The Commanding Officer noted:

'The convoy more or less unintentionally dispersed and five ships ran ashore between Rattray Head and Kinnaird Head, of which two became total losses. It was quite beyond the escorts to prevent this disaster, as in the darkness you could only see a single ship occasionally and tell her where you thought she was; some ships were probably saved by these means. A further complication was that a north-bound convoy was rounding Kinnaird Head at the time, though, of course a few miles to seaward . . .

Soon after this, in the early part of 1941, the convoys were reorganized. All home-coming convoys went in to Liverpool or the Clyde and all ships bound for the east coast sailed from Clyde to Rosyth and *vice versa* in a series of what were known as WN and EN convoys. The close escorts of these convoys were a permanent force of trawlers and 'minesweepers' – the latter very international

– consisting of two British minesweepers (ex-surveying ships), one Norwegian destroyer and one Dutch gunboat. We thus had the same party always working together, and the efficiency of the escort increased by leaps and bounds.'

In the summer of 1941 *Curacoa* went to Rosyth for a refit and the opportunity was taken to improve her armaments and communications. Once this was done, she operated thereafter from Rosyth instead of Scapa, bringing her into line with the minesweepers and trawlers who were already operating from there.

Patrick Holmes has analysed *Curacoa's* periods of refit (see Table p.39). She had three refits of a major nature and two more minor ones in the two years she operated from Rosyth Dockyard, a shore establishment operating under the names HMS *Cochrane I* and *II*. Small wonder *Curacoa* became jokingly referred to as HMS *Cochrane III*.

A tabulation has also been compiled (see Table p.40) of the convoys *Curacoa* escorted: ninety-eight south-bound and seventy-one north-bound. They steamed along the swept channels between Methil and Rosyth, and on up to the fast-flowing Pentland Firth, the dangerous channel between the north of Scotland and the Orkneys. It must be some sort of a record for a cruiser to have passed through the Pentland Firth about 170 times over so short a period.*

The Table on p.40 also reveals that enemy aircraft were seen from *Curacoa* on seventeen days only during her Rosyth north-about stint, and on only nine of these occasions were attacks attempted on the convoy. Three ships were sunk and another three damaged during these attacks.

Seldom were there more than two German aircraft involved, but on 3 November, 1940, north-bound convoy WN24 was attacked by seven planes and many bombs were dropped. One ship was struck and had to be abandoned. This was probably the 3,877-ton *Kildale*. Ten days later, on 13 November, five aircraft, four Heinkel 111s and a Focke-Wulf 200, sank one merchant ship in another north-about convoy, WN33, and the Focke Wulf machine-gunned *Curacoa*. The merchantman was probably the *St Catherine* of 1,216 tons. She was hit by an aircraft torpedo and sank on the 14th about a quarter of a mile south of the Outer Buoy swept channel off Aberdeen. In both these dusk attacks *Curacoa* opened fire with her Pom Poms and used the 4-inch guns in barrage fire. No aircraft was shot down but had the cruiser not been in attendance several more ships are likely to have been sunk.

---

* Captain Hughes Hallett is probably wrong in stating in his article that the figure was 174 convoys in eighteen months. Patrick Holmes' figures were extracted from *Curacoa's* log books at the Public Record Office.

ROSYTH REFIT PERIODS 1940–42

No.	Dates	Days	Work done in addition to the numerous constant defects
1.	15–17 February, 1941	12	New W/T set fitted
2.	10 Apr – 30 June, 1941	81	Tank leaks. Two single Pom Poms added aft
3.	26 Oct – 1 Dec, 1941	36	SA gear repaired
4.	21 Jan – 8 Feb, 1942	18	Repairs to dynamo engine
5.	18 Mar – 15 Jun, 1942	89	4 x 20 mm single Oerlikons added, one either side of bridge & replacing some point fives. Radar added.*

Total days under refit equal 236 out of 647 days from 6 September, 1940, when *Curacoa* was moved out of dock at Chatham until 1 August, 1942, when she left Rosyth for the last time.

* *Curacoa* was now equipped with the following:

(a) Surface Warning (SW) RDF Type 273

(b) Aircraft Warning (AW) RDF Type 286 – at mastheads

(c) AR RDF Type 285 on for'ard and after HADCTs

(d) AR RDF Type 282 on the director for the quadruple Pom Pom mounting

39

CONVOYS ESCORTED & AIRCRAFT SIGHTED

Period	Dates	South Bound	North Bound	Aircraft*
A	26 Sept '40 – 10 Apr '41	50	31	14
B	30 June '41 – 26 Oct '41	25	20	1
C	1 Dec '41 – 18 Mar '42	18	16	1
D	15 Jun '42 – a Aug '42	5	4	1
		98	71	17

169

* Number of days on which German aircraft were sighted, either shadowing or attacking.

Most of the shadowing for these attacks was carried out in the afternoon by Dornier 17s or Heinkel 115 floatplanes. The attacks themselves were usually made by Heinkel 111s and Junkers 88s. When fighter aircraft were provided as air escorts – and in 1940 and 1941 these were few and far between – they were Blenheim fighter-bombers; they were too slow to catch Ju 88s and could barely deal with He 111s, but they were suitable to deal with enemy floatplanes. Occasionally Hurricanes were provided for air cover, but ten out of the seventeen days when the *Luftwaffe* paid attention to *Curacoa's* charges were in late 1940, long before patrolling fighters became generally available.

The drab monotony of routinely escorting these Rosyth-north-about convoys was lightened by two forays towards Norway. The first was in July, 1941. *Curacoa* joined company with the new Colony Class cruiser *Nigeria* of 8,000 tons and the 1,870 ton destroyer *Ashanti*. The foray has been described as an attack on the Norwegian coast but *Curacoa's* log gave a furthest position from Scapa as 62 deg 15' N and 0 deg 15' E, about 100 miles west of Statlandet on the Norwegian coast about half way between Bergen and Trondheim.

Tony Corlett, an engineering Sub-Lieutenant at the time recalled the episode in an article:[†]

† *Sea Breezes*, May, 1990.

*'In 1941 we were accompanying HMS *Nigeria* and HMS *Ashanti* on a raid on the Lofoten Islands, which for some reason was aborted. The sea was calm, visibility was good and the pressure to get the most speed out of *Curacoa* was great. [Her maximum of 25 knots was no match for the 30 plus of the modern consorts.] In the engine-room we were constantly being asked for more revolutions and by superhuman efforts we managed to get 29.1 knots out of the old girl. Twenty-three years before she had done 29 knots on four hours overload. The *Nigeria* could do 32 and the *Ashanti* 36 – but they were new ships. Our limiting factors were the forced draught fans driven by steam reciprocating engines. They were situated above the boiler-rooms on the upper deck level and we just could not get any more air to the furnaces to burn more fuel. To nurse these fan engines I stationed an ERA on the fan flat.'

The ERA Corlett stationed there was Bob Gornall, who for several years after the war was responsible for putting an In Memoriam notice in the *Daily Telegraph* on 2 October every year. Corlett wonders whether the reason Bob survived the collision with *Queen Mary* was because he was not far below decks, nursing those fan engines, and was thrown clear.

The second occasion *Curacoa* ventured towards Norway was a year later when Captain Boutwood took his cruiser to join a decoy convoy which spent two days and nights steaming back and forth, NE and SW between latitudes 61 deg N and 61 deg 30' N and longitudes 1 degree W and 1 degree E.

Further north a major fleet operation was in progress, attempting to pass a convoy to north Russia. This convoy was the ill-fated PQ17 comprising thirty-six merchant ships, twenty-three of which were lost in the ensuing battles. Vice Admiral B.B. Schofield described the ploy to use a mock convoy:

'In an attempt to deceive the enemy into thinking that a raid on the Norwegian coast was intended, a dummy convoy consisting of the five ships of the First Minelaying Squadron and four colliers escorted by the cruisers *Sirius* and *Curacoa*, some destroyers and trawlers left Scapa on 29th June and steered to the east. If it had not been sighted by reconnaissance on reaching 1 degree E, it was to turn back. . . . The ruse failed as the enemy did not observe it.'*

★   ★   ★

* See *The Arctic Convoys* by Vice Admiral B.B. Schofield, Macdonald & Janes, 1977, p. 49.

The gods smiled on John Rooke. He was another man destined to escape the disaster. As an undergraduate he had contracted jaundice and this made him wary in later years of drinking too much alcohol. During parties aboard ship he used to slink off early and turn in. Many a time his absence was noted by his colleagues, his cabin invaded and the young doctor carried, mattress and all, into the wardroom to rejoin the fun.

John Rooke admits to his duties as a medico aboard the cruiser being a sinecure. It certainly was not arduous for two doctors to look after 450-odd men, most of them young and healthy. Nor were the doctors' other duties of censoring letters, wardroom catering and cyphering overtaxing. Rooke recalled, too, the great part played by the Caledonian Hotel in Edinburgh for those on shore leave. Curacoans were allowed to have mess bills there with the accounts sent to the ship monthly. On such occasions when the last train to North Queensferry was missed, the somewhat over-indulgent naval officers were put up in a suite for which they were never charged more than a single room's price. The hotel also sold a splendid gin called Old Tom which resulted in monumental hangovers. The Caledonian became a home from home.

By contrast, Doc Rooke had this to say about Belfast where *Curacoa* was based in September, 1942:

> 'Even in those days we were told not to go ashore in our great-coats as they were very like those of the Royal Ulster Constabulary, and we might get a knife in our backs. . . . Belfast was a miserable place. There seemed nothing to do there and I don't think anyone enjoyed his stay there.'

He is wrong about that. Pat Holmes, John Maxwell, Philip Brocklesby and Eric Vaughan had the time of their lives there.

CAPTAIN OF HIS MAJESTY'S CRUISER

'Wind and sea had been increasing. . . . At 0915 an exceptional sea broke over HMS *Curacoa's* forecastle shattering four of the bridge windows.'

Commanding Officers's Report of Proceedings Convoy TA 19, 12 August, 1942.

Captain John Wilfred Boutwood joined HMS *Curacoa*, in command, in June, 1942. Since Hughes Hallett had left in February a new Commanding Officer, Captain S.W. Paton, had been appointed – for just four months. There is no explanation for this brief spell in command. Both Hughes Hallett and Paton, incidentally, were to achieve flag rank, the right to hoist an admiral's flag in their ship. The rank of Captain in the Navy is a senior rank that equates to that of a full Colonel in the army; the step to flag rank is regarded as perhaps the greatest in a naval man's career. Only a chosen few achieve it.

John Boutwood was not to make it. This is no criticism. After all, the vast majority of naval officers, even those with a most distinguished career behind them, don't make it.

He was born on 30 March, 1899, so he was forty-three when he assumed command of the cruiser, an age probably reflecting the height of his powers. He did not come of a naval family, although his son Jeremy* later followed him into the Navy and retired as a Lieutenant-Commander. He retired in 1964 'after submarining and surveying . . . and since then got married and brought up five children . . . became an RC and an enthusiastic Franciscan. My links with the naval world that Father inhabited are tenuous.'

Boutwood's family background centred on straw hats in Luton, and later the interest was drapers – Plummers and Debenhams seem to have stemmed from that line. The family was non-conformist, church-going and teetotal. On the family's paternal side there was a religious philanthropist involved in

---

* Jeremy Boutwood has kindly written at length to Patrick Holmes about his father. He gave up the Navy for 'an existence as social service community-builder'.

soup kitchens 'or whatever was the role of the well-endowed Christian lady for trade and chapel'.

Boutwood's elder brother became a dentist and his elder sister married into an artistic household. Annual family holidays on Dartmoor were enjoyable, with walking, fresh air, challenge. Jeremy writes of his father:

'So joining the Navy was not in any family tradition and it meant that Pa had to prove himself alongside the more natural young naval officers of the day from service and aristocratic backgrounds. He had an extremely good command of the English language, competing at The Leys School, Cambridge (Quaker) with James Hilton, later author of *Goodbye Mr Chips*. So at the intellectual level the naval life was not testing; but I think he put his whole energy into becoming the conscientious, loyal, respectful and thoroughly reliable young officer.'

Jeremy Boutwood believes that much of his father's philosophy of leadership stems from doing one's duty and being respected rather than trying to be popular. 'I should think he was, in fact, popular, just because he was open.'

There are doubts that his son is right about this. Research and enquiry suggest John Boutwood never sought popularity and, indeed, there is no evidence of anyone ascribing that quality to him. But what he did earn was respect. He was often described as a martinet and letters imply that he was a disciplinarian. Even his most ardent admirers, such as John Nicholas, never admitted to popularity:

'I met, indeed, served with [as a Sub-Lieutenant] some of the ship's captains of the 12th Minesweeping Flotilla [commanded by Captain Boutwood] later in the war. All of them had nothing but good to say of JWB and we were speaking man to man, as it were, and where criticism was acceptable. There were adverse criticisms of other people. RNVR Commander Norman Morley DSC and three bars was certainly complimentary as were Commander John Temple and Commander George Dibley.

He once said to me, "You like being at sea, don't you?" I made some fatuous reply about it being in my blood and being one of a long line of Merchant Navy officers and it being better than being alongside a dockyard wall. He laughed and said that a dockyard wall was a kinder taskmaster.'

There seems little doubt that Boutwood was a disciplinarian in the eyes of the ratings. Nicholas tells us that ratings told him that they had been reprimanded for things like putting their arms over the side of a whaler. Until

Nicholas explained that it was to prevent them getting a broken arm, they had not realized he was doing it for their own good.

> 'If those whom he had told off had a little more insight they would have understood that his strictures were meant either for the safety of the ship in the first instance – the collective safety – and secondly for the safety of the individual concerned. . . . I was carpeted twice and I must admit both were justified. Notwithstanding the fact that I had displeased him the ticking off was immediate, and then, if not forgotten, was never held against me. . . . I am sure he respected me for not cringing under the weight of his four rings. However, had I been either a whinger, or truculent, I'm sure he would have thrown the book at me.'

Another shipmate of Boutwood's early and later years at sea is Ordinary Signalman (junior bunting tosser) Tom McMeekin. He served in the heavy cruiser *Berwick* during her commission on the China Station in 1933–34 when Boutwood was a Lieutenant-Commander gunnery officer, and naturally had little contact with McMeekin. But it was about ten years later when both of them served in the minesweeper *Fantome*, when the officer was a Captain and the young signalman a Yeoman of Signals:

> 'From the very start JW and I hit it off well. . . . With being the leader of the 12th Minesweeping Flotilla it put an awful lot of work on the captain and my staff. Sometimes we were on the bridge from 3.15 a.m. till midnight. After six weeks him and I couldn't stand up and had to sit down on the catwalk to write down my signals.
>
> 'To show you the sort of man he was, one afternoon I called up the Leading Signalman to relieve me, and on leaving the bridge the captain asked me where I was going. I said to get my dinner. "Your dinner will be like a burnt offering," he said. He looked at his watch and said, "It's after 3 o'clock. Come down to my cabin and have half my lunch with me." That's the sort of chap he was. If I had my time to do again in the Royal Navy there is no captain I would serve under better than JW.'

Jeremy Boutwood writes with insight about his father:

> 'Reading into my own soul a bit, there may be a family inability to pass on orders to those below you in a manner that is both authoritarian and kind. Maybe the ratings picked up this lack of rapport and so felt the barrier to complete communication. The weakness, I detect – possibly through a feminine intuition of a

daughter-in-law – is an inability to convey human warmth in the necessary authority to be shown to the "lower deck".'

A less charitable view of the Captain was taken by John Tether, a leading signalman on *Curacoa's* bridge, watch on/watch off, with a privileged view of the ship's watch-keepers and commanding officer. Tether had joined the ship in the autumn of 1940 after the refit following the bomb damage in Norway. Thus he had served under Hughes Hallett and Paton, for both of whom he had an enormous respect. Curiously, there was little respect for Boutwood. Tether referred to his 'inefficiency and unpopularity on the lower deck'.

Tether remembered Paton with esteem, describing him as a perfect gentleman, a view also held by Patrick Holmes. The leading signalman recalls having to deliver a signal to the Captain's cabin. Paton asked him to sit down and tell him all about his family: 'big men' do not need to stand on ceremony.

Boutwood, on the other hand, being less sure of himself, was abrupt and rude – and deaf. Patrick Holmes put on record:

> 'Once John Tether reported "Lights astern" one night to Boutwood who took no notice. He shouted it louder – still no notice, but Johnson, the navigating officer, winked at him and said, "OK, don't bother." A few minutes later Boutwood saw the lights and gave Tether a hell of a blast for not reporting them.
>
> 'However, the crunch story – literally – relates to when *Curacoa* damaged her port prop against the wharf at Belfast. We were due to set sail – I think to meet the *QE* – from the quayside at Belfast and we needed to go sideways really, as there was little room astern and a wall ahead. Two tugs were standing by. The tugmasters hailed the skipper who disagreeably told them to bugger off (I don't know his actual words). The leading tugman warned Boutwood of the dangers ahead and astern. Taking no notice, he promptly went astern and swung the bows out to starboard and rammed the quay on our port quarter. Going ahead from there, the ship shuddered mightily – gaining speed the shuddering died temporarily and B said, "I told you so: no damage done." But hell! When we really got going the ship nearly fell to bits and had to be towed home. I guess I was down below and didn't see all this, but I must have felt it. Those on the bridge thought the director and the ADP were going to fall on top of them.'*

---

* Letter: Patrick Holmes to his son, Marcus, September, 1989.

In all fairness this episode must be fairly typical of all commanding officers' experiences. Hitting a dockside wall or coming-to alongside a berth and causing minor damage were fairly mundane wartime misadventures.

Captain Boutwood's naval life coincided almost exactly with *Curacoa's*. His seniority as a midshipman dated from 1 September, 1917, a few months later than the cruiser's launching in May.

His First World War service was in the 17,250 ton battlecruiser *Inflexible* with the Grand Fleet Battlecruiser Force. In the twilight of his life, at the age of nearly 91, he revealed, in conversation with Patrick Holmes, that his happiest time in the Navy was his midshipman's days, an odd reflection after an active, worldwide career spanning more than thirty years.

Young naval officers whose training had been cut short by war service were offered the chance by a suddenly broad-minded Admiralty to attend university to complete their education. One of the earliest such candidates to attend Cambridge University was Lord Mountbatten in 1919. Boutwood followed in 1920 and during his year there he received promotion to acting Lieutenant.

The twenties were years of regular promotions, a variety of appointments, short and long courses and the offer to concentrate on the department of one's choice – gunnery, navigation, signals; Boutwood was to choose gunnery.

On 3 September, 1921, he was appointed to the Devonport ship *Campbell*, leader of the 3rd Destroyer Flotilla. It seems that he was ill ashore for much of the next year until reappointed to the 1,350 ton *Campbell* in April, 1922. As he had chosen gunnery as his specialist subject he was sent on the long gunnery course at the Royal Naval College at Greenwich.*

In June, 1923, he was appointed to the gunnery school at HMS *Pembroke* at Chatham as Lieutenant (G) and this was followed by his joining the 32,000 ton battlecruiser *Repulse* as assistant gunnery officer to the Lieutenant-Commander (G). By June, 1927, he was back again at Chatham and in August of that year joined the 3,750 ton light cruiser *Cambrian* as gunnery Lieutenant.

Boutwood got his half-ring on 15 February, 1928, and was appointed to HMS *Excellent*, the gunnery school on Whale Island in Portsmouth Harbour later that year. Also stationed at the gunnery school with him as Lieutenant-Commanders were W.G. Agnew, later to gain fame as commanding officer of the cruiser *Penelope* (dubbed HMS *Pepperpot* for the damage sustained in Force K during the Second World War), and C.C. Hughes Hallett, captain of *Curacoa* from 1940–42.

In February, 1930, Boutwood was appointed to the 1,480 ton destroyer *Broke* as Lieutenant-Commander (G) and as the 4th Destroyer Flotilla

---

* Long gunnery courses are traditionally associated with Whale Island, but the RNC Greenwich also undertook such courses.

gunnery officer in the Mediterranean Fleet. Two and a half years later he joined the three-funnelled, 9,750 ton heavy cruiser *Berwick* with her eight 8-inch guns, currently stationed in China. While in the far east Boutwood received promotion to Commander in June, 1934.

Those were heady days for a naval officer on a foreign commission. Jeremy Boutwood can remember when he was young:

'The cine would come out and we saw jerky black and white pictures of polo at Wei-Hei-Wei up country with the tea planters of Ceylon. . . . I think the commission on the China Station was a time when he rode on a crest of success and sheer enjoyment of the young naval officer doing the job of showing the flag to the world. It was there where he won trophies for winning rifle competitions on board, and the weekend ashore enjoying the colonial delights of polo must have been a far cry from the austere background of bourgeois Hastings. He was very much the dedicated young gunnery officer (and Whale Island traditions meant much to him). Those were the days when the gunnery officer was the élite of the élite.'

The same year as he was promoted to commander Boutwood married, at the age of thirty-six. Later, when complications set in for the birth of Jeremy, John Boutwood was flown home on compassionate leave from Ceylon where he was the commander of the cruiser *Emerald*, under the captaincy of Captain A.W.S. Agar, VC, DSO. Special flights were arranged. 'It seemed as if the journey was full of drama, changing many times from one small plane to another like some spy escapade.'

Boutwood was also a man of personal courage. Harry Ellis who was a stoker from *Curacoa* served with him in *Emerald* and he relates that when they were in a typhoon it was the Commander who went overboard to rescue the lower boom, an act of considerable courage.

In October, 1938, Boutwood got his first command when he became captain of the 1918 'V' and 'W' destroyer *Whitley* of 1,100 tons, recommissioning her as an escort vessel with four 4-inch HA/LA guns. Later she became one of the first casualties off the beaches during the Dunkirk evacuation. Just before the outbreak of war in 1939 Boutwood was appointed the commander in HMS *Iron Duke*. At the time she was a training ship under Captain R.D. Oliver, DSC, though she had seen finer days as Admiral Jellicoe's flagship during the First World War and especially at Jutland.

In 1941 he became head of the gunnery school in HMS *Pembroke* as acting captain and on the last day of the year his full captaincy was confirmed. The step from commander to captain in the Navy is almost as difficult as that from captain to flag rank.

Patrick Holmes, the only other officer to survive the cruiser's sinking, is generous in his praise of Boutwood. He interviewed his one-time captain in 1989 and noted to his son, Marcus:

'Slight, though with a bushy eyebrow, sparse hair standing vertical, a twinkle in his eye, dressing-gowned, I found him drinking from a great bowl of tea. He called me Holmes throughout and I called him Sir. He really didn't seem to have much idea about things [he was recovering from a stroke] but nevertheless spoke sense (if rather indistinctly). I feel privileged to have known him, and forty-seven years after the collision when I met him again in his home at South Harting near Petersfield in Hampshire I looked upon him as a long-lost friend. Age had turned his ginger hair whitish. We chatted for two hours and I wasn't allowed to go until I'd had a gin.

'He had had his critics in *Curacoa* and was known by the crew as "the yellow peril" because of his somewhat parchment-coloured skin. He was brusque and something of a martinet, but brusqueness can often conceal shyness and his bark was often worse than his bite. Not being a watch-keeper on the bridge I did not know him as well as several of the other executive branch officers did and I suppose he was unlucky to succeed two such outstanding men as Hughes Hallett and Paton.'

Patrick Holmes always found Boutwood considerate and thoughtful and absolutely honest and fair-minded, observations which were shared by others who served under him later in the war. Holmes points out that the Captain was a gunnery specialist and perhaps this was held against him after he had rammed the dockside at Belfast, wishing to prove himself a good ship-handler:

'This was an unfortunate contretemps but at the court of enquiry held at Belfast he was excused on the grounds that he was a bit rusty, having been ashore for some time.'

Apparently diminished by age and the stroke, he was unable to recall many officers aboard the cruiser, hardly surprising as he had only served aboard her for fifteen weeks, though he did remember John Maxwell, the RN lieutenant who entered the water with Holmes. It was evident that Boutwood had really put the *Curacoa* versus *Queen Mary* incident out of his mind. There was no evidence whatsoever that he bore any guilt for so many lives lost on that October afternoon.

This then was the man to whom had been given the captaincy of HM Cruiser *Curacoa* in 1942. He had served in twelve different ships and three different shore stations in the twenty-five years between 1917 and 1942. He had gained experience in battle-cruisers, light and heavy cruisers and had been the executive officer in *Emerald* and *Iron Duke*. He had commanded HMS *Whitley* and had been captain of the gunnery school at Chatham. It was a proud if not dazzling record.

Captain Boutwood was to survive the war, distinguishing himself by earning a DSO in the Mediterranean. His long life of ninety-four years came to a peaceful end even as this book was being produced. He had declined to be formally interviewed by his only surviving officer, Patrick Holmes, but this was consistent with his attitude of being 'tight-lipped' about the *Curacoa* incident as one of his obituarists expressed it. On the rare occasion he spoke on the subject he claimed he was blameless and he stood by the Admiralty's original enquiry which exonerated him. It has been reported that in the early 1980s he allowed a tape recording to be made on which it is alleged he said 'he could sleep at nights without any feeling of conscience or shame' about the *Curacoa* disaster.

★   ★   ★

It is appropriate now to take a brief look at some of the ship's officers and men whose destiny became totally enmeshed with Boutwood's, whose lives were put in his hands, and hundreds of whom were to die that October afternoon in 1942.

Such are the fates of men and the exigencies of the Navy that many officers and men, after spending months and even years aboard the cruiser, were given a new appointment or a draft to a new ship and thus were spared the agony of the collision. One such was Commander (E) Lee.

Lee had had a chequered career. He became an engineer lieutenant in the Royal Navy in 1927 and served in the large submarine *Parthian* from 1930–33. In the thirties he left the Navy and became a stockbroker. He was recalled to naval service at the outbreak of war and served in the destroyer *Electra*★ as Lieutenant-Commander (E). He joined *Curacoa* after her post-Norwegian refit in 1940 and two years later put up his third ring as a commander. He left the doomed cruiser just a few weeks before the collision to become the chief of HMS *Montclare*, the former Canadian Pacific liner converted to an armed merchant cruiser, since when she had been converted to a submarine depot ship.

Tom Lee was a larger than life character. He had the physique of a rugby player and had represented the Navy as a forward. Surgeon-Lieutenant John Rooke†, another officer to leave the ship a few weeks before the tragedy, recalls Tom Lee as being the life and soul of every party. He was above standing on ceremony, was a born leader, with a devilish sense of humour and was a skilled cartoonist. John Rooke classified him as 'endless trouble'

★   She was one of many Allied warships to be lost in the forlorn naval battles of the Java Sea when striving to halt the Japanese invasion of the East Indies early in 1942.
†   He died in 1991.

with a 'gang of loose, vulgar and dissolute friends, the bane of Rosyth dock-yard.' There was the incident of the motorboat. *Curacoa* needed one. Tom Lee discovered one 'lurking' and put in a request for it as no one seemed to own it. He filled in all the forms but his application was refused. The night before *Curacoa* sailed Tom took a party ashore and 'borrowed' the boat. No more was heard of the incident.

Another assessment of Tom Lee is given by Sub-Lieutenant (E) Tony Corlett, yet another officer who left *Curacoa* before the sinking. He was one of Lee's junior officers and he acknowledges his debt to his old boss:

'Tom was a big man in every respect. He would have a go at anything and expected the same of his staff. To him I owe much. He it was who fostered my interest in submarines and enabled me to join what the Navy has always called the submarine service, "the trade", a decision I have never regretted and an experience which has stood me in good stead all my life.'

Tony Corlett was to go on to win a DSC when, after many hours in a submarine lying at the bottom of the Malacca Straits in 1945 being depth-charged by Japanese patrol boats, he got the machinery working and so enabled the submarine to crawl away to safety.

* * *

The First Lieutenant in a ship the size of *Curacoa*, usually a lieutenant-commander, was the second in command of the ship. It was he who ran the daily routine of the ship, but like the Staff Captain in *Queen Mary*, or the Commander in a battleship, was not a watch-keeping officer. The First Lieutenant in a destroyer, on the other hand, was. Lionel Phillips had been in *Curacoa* since November, 1939. He saw her through her conversion to an AA cruiser, survived the Norwegian campaign and her subsequent refitting and repairing in Chatham.

He seems to have been something of a stickler for etiquette, as Tony Corlett recalls, when he joined at Chatham in August, 1940:

'. . . then came my first brush with protocol. Officers were expected to dress for dinner – at least to wear wing collars and ties. Was this how we were to fight a war and defeat a ruthless enemy? I had not come prepared for such gracious living. However, a quick sally ashore by my stalwart Marine Stewart Marriott soon kitted me out – for dinner at least.'

A kinder story about Phillips – he was known as Captain Bligh by the crew – is told by John Rooke. A trawler signalled to *Curacoa* to ask for any spare small arms ammunition and, after coming alongside and receiving this, the skipper asked how many men were aboard. On learning there were 420 or so he asked Phillips if he would like that number of fresh cod. But the cod would have to be gutted. It so happened that among the many Hull lads aboard there were two on a charge. It was suggested that they could do the gutting better than most, if let off the charge. Much to his credit, Number One agreed. Doc Rooke says Phillips may have been a martinet, but when he left the ship and got command of one for himself, he was a changed man. He also escaped the sinking.

Phillips was succeeded by Lieutenant-Commander A.Y. (Gus) Spearman, much less of a disciplinarian; he was an easy-going president of the wardroom, but he did suffer from the habit (there is a medical name for it) of suddenly dozing off. Rumour had it that he sometimes went to sleep with his soup spoon in hand between plate and mouth. On one occasion he nodded off reading the paper propped up before him. Tom Lee could not resist setting fire to it.

Along with Spearman, another twenty-four *Curacoa* officers were to lose their lives in the depths of the Atlantic.

The gunnery officer aboard the cruiser was Lieutenant (G) Douglas Bodger RNVR. He had taken up his appointment to her in June, 1941. Three years previously he had joined the London Division of the RNVR and received his commission as a Sub-Lieutenant in October, 1938. He was called up on the approach of war in August, 1939, and was appointed to HMS *Cairo* along with gunnery ratings from HMS *President*, the London Division RNVR ship.

Douglas Bodger is described as having been 'an organizing and persuasive powerhouse' when he produced a pantomime in Loch Ewe during the chilling December weather of that foul winter of 1939–40. The show was such a success that several performances were put on, including one aboard the battleship HMS *Nelson*.

Bodger served throughout *Cairo's* ordeals in Norway during which time she fired 5,700 rounds of 4-inch ammunition, was hit by bombs from a Ju87, when nine were killed and twenty-one injured, picked up survivors from *Curlew* at Hardstad and, after returning them to Scapa Flow, steamed to the Tyne for repairs and three weeks' well-earned leave to each watch.

He was aboard *Cairo* in October, 1940, with the destroyer *Broke* when they tried to save the Canadian Pacific liner, *Empress of Britain* (42,348 tons). The liner had been set ablaze by a bombing attack from a FW200, and was then struck by two torpedoes fired by Lieutenant Jenisch in *U-32* in the Western Approaches. The *Empress* refused to sink and it fell to *Broke* to sink her when hopes of salvaging her faded. She was the largest British merchant ship lost during the war, and the sinking occurred in the very waters through which the *Queens* passed on their trooping runs.

That winter Douglas Bodger left *Cairo* to undertake the long gunnery course at HMS *Excellent*, Whale Island. His promotion to lieutenant came through in April, 1941, and he must have been one of the first RNVR officers

1. HMS *Curacoa* at Pembroke Dockyard in 1918. She was built here and had just finished being fitted out. *(P. E. M. Holmes)*

2. HMS *Curacoa* dressed overall on Empire Day at Gibraltar,
   24 May, 1932.
   (*J. W. Honey*)

3. King Carol of Rumania is greeted by Rear-Admiral Tottenham
   aboard the cruiser, up-river at Galatz on 26 September, 1932.
   (*J.W. Honey*)

4. The serenity of a
   Norwegian fjord in
   April, 1940, belies
   the severity of the
   bombing and the
   naval losses.
   (G. Moore)

5. Bomb damage
   sustained at
   Andalsnes, Norway,
   in April, 1940. View
   looking aft on the
   port side of the
   fo'c's'le.
   (Don Marshall)

6. The twin guns of 'A' turret largely awash and guns elevated to a high angle, seen from 'B' gun deck with its quadruple Pom Pom guns. *(A. E. Corlett)*

7. These quadruple point-fives, abreast the fore funnel port side, were replaced with single Oerlikons. *(A. E. Corlett)*

8. HMS *Curacoa* at Scapa Flow, 1940-41. The topmost structure is
the Director. Below it is the Air Defence Position (ADP) and
below that the bridge. Clearly visible is one of the twin 4-inch
High Angle/Low Angle guns. *(A. E. Corlett)*

9. Captain C. C.
   Hughes Hallett
   in his cabin.
   (A. E. Corlett).

10. The AA cruiser soon after her March-June refit in 1942. Her
    eight 4-inch guns are clearly visible. The lone officer in the bows
    is Lieutentant Robin Clover who transferred from the ship a few
    weeks before her sinking.
    (P. E. M. Holmes)

11. Aircraft lookouts on the crowded Air Defence Position. This picture shows nine out of the fourteen who kept watch at any one time. *(P. E. M. Holmes)*

12. Looking down on the bridge and the multiple Pom Poms from the ADP, 1942. Note the rolled-up flotanets and the Carley float. On watch are Lieutenant John Maxwell and Gunner James Frost, both lost in the collision. *(P. E. M. Holmes)*

13. The First Lieutenant, Lieutenant-Commander A.Y. (Gus) Spearman, Sub-Lieutenant P.W. Brocklesby, Sub-Lieutenant S. B. Caldwell and the Principal Medical Officer, Lieutenant-Commander M.Cay, watching cricket at Belfast. They all lost their lives shortly after this. *(P. E. M. Holmes)*

14. Wardroom Party, 1942. Three officers are not recognized: of the rest only Holmes survived, The ten who died were Brocklesby, Johnson, Cay, Cole, Howland, Bodger, Maxwell, Vaughan, Woodcock and Frost. *(P. E. M. Holmes)*

to become a cruiser's gunnery officer when he joined *Curacoa* that summer. While in *Cairo* he received a mention in despatches. He was not only a dedicated officer, but was much liked by his colleagues.

He was also much loved by a ten-year-old sister to whom he wrote the occasional letter. A few days before the tragedy Douglas wrote to young Olive who treasures the letter and sketch to this day:

'HMS *Curacoa*, c/o GPO, London, 27.9.42.

My dear Great Big Beautiful Doll,

I am so sorry to hear from Nina that you are in bed again. Whatever are you up to? You can't go on doing this, you know.

'How is Victor these days? I suppose he is quite a big dog now. Hope you've brought him up nicely. We have no animals in this ship at the moment except for a few rats. We had a couple of kittens but apparently they didn't come from a seafaring family and walked ashore at the first opportunity. Very unfriendly, I call it.

'The old *Curacoa* is still pushing along although I think she is beginning to feel her age – she gets tired quickly and creaks a bit as she goes along! But she gets there sooner or later.

'Here is my idea of the cats leaving the ship. Our guns are not quite so imposing as those I've drawn but never mind – I'm not an artist as you may have gathered.

'Hope everyone else at home is well – please give my love to them all.

'Incidentally, I got into a frightful row for sending that last lot of chocolate home – we are not supposed to send it out of the ship. Nevertheless, I hope it arrived safely.

Goodbye, my beautiful doll – do please hurry up and get well again.

With very much love from   DOUGLAS'

By the time Olive received the letter Douglas was dead.

The senior doctor aboard *Curacoa* – he was known as the PMO (Principal Medical Officer) – was Lieutenant-Commander M. Cay. Pat Holmes remembers him best for his prowess at cricket. *Curacoa* sported a cricket XI which Holmes captained. Cay was one of the two opening bowlers in the matches in Fifeshire, Greenock and Belfast. He was in his early thirties and had just married a twenty-year-old girl.

Sub-Lieutenant P.E.M. Holmes RNVR joined *Curacoa* at Methil, the small seaport on the northern shore of the Firth of Forth the chief coal port feeding the coalfields of Fifeshire. It was the end of February, 1942. He was to be the aircraft recognition expert aboard, watchkeeper in the Air Defence Position, responsible for the dozen lookouts on watch with him.

Pat Holmes was born in Monmouth, the son of two artists. He joined the Navy as an ordinary seaman in 1939, saw service minesweeping in Belfast Lough before being commissioned as a Sub-Lieutenant at the age of twenty-two in 1941. He joined the destroyer *Duncan* operating out of Gibraltar before joining HMS *Curacoa*. Apart from Captain Boutwood, he was the only officer to survive the sinking, a fact attributable no doubt to his being in the ADP, a lofty platform, higher than the bridge, from which he clambered down the ladder to the iron deck and 'walked into the sea'. Pat explains about his ADP:

> 'There were six pedestals each supporting a pair of binoculars numbered P1, P2, P3 and S1, S2 and S3. There were two lookouts per pedestal and during the four-hour watch they would switch being on watch every ten minutes.

[from a drawing by Fred Dennis]

Ordinary Seamen Vic Jones and Ted King manned P1. Able Seaman Bushell and Shropshire were on P2. Ordinary Seaman Murley and Able Seaman MacIver were on P3. On the starboard side, S1 was manned by Ordinary Seaman Bruckshaw and Able Seaman Abbot. On S2 were Ordinary Seaman Eager and Able Seaman Cottam. On S3 were Fred Dennis and Ordinary Seaman Brownsett.

'Able Seaman Jimmy Green as communications number and I, the Air Defence Officer, made a total of fourteen. Action stations would normally bring a senior ADO to join me so that both the master sights which automatically brought the close range weapons to bear were manned.'

The routine for lookouts was to sweep their arc of 60 degrees (right ahead to green 60 for S1: Green 60 to Green 120 for S2: Green 120 to right astern for S3 – and so on for the port side), firstly at sea level, then 5 degrees up, 10 degrees up, more quickly up to 30 degrees and then back to the horizon again, repeating the sequence all over again, all with the objective of sighting an aircraft as soon as possible. Anything sighted was reported to the ADO whose responsibility it was to decide friend from foe, and to use the communications number to alert the bridge and close range weapons.

Pat Holmes explained that out of the fourteen men on watch in the ADP that afternoon of 2 October six survived. In addition to himself, there were Fred Dennis, Ted King, Vic Jones, Buchell and Eager. Six out of fourteen was a higher proportion than 101 out of 439. 'In fact,' Holmes concludes ruefully, 'we were luckily placed.'

Lieutenant (N) A.P.C. Johnson, DSC, was the navigating officer in *Curacoa* from February, 1942. Courteous, debonair, suave, he was a typical 'pilot'. Navigators were known as the gentlemen of the service and Tony Johnson was certainly one of those. He was a midshipman in 1937 and by 1939 was a Sub-Lieutenant in the old 'V' and 'W' destroyer *Wolverine*. In 1940 he received promotion to Lieutenant and won the DSC before going on the long navigation course in 1941. Pat Holmes remembers him as one of the party who enjoyed Verdi's *Il Trovatore* in Edinburgh. Pat's last memory of Tony Johnson was catching a glimpse of him on the bridge stuffing confidential and secret books into leaded canvas bags. At that moment their worlds turned upside down. Pat emerged. Tony was never seen again.

Captain John Cole, Royal Marines, was in charge of the Marine contingent aboard *Curacoa*. He had joined the cruiser from the aircraft carrier *Furious*. He was Pat Holmes' opposite number (that is, he shared watches) in the ADP at defence stations; thus he was off watch in the afternoon of 2 October. At Belfast Holmes had introduced John Cole to a Jean Beath whom he had met there in 1940 when Holmes was serving as a signalman in the minesweeping drifter *Gloamin*. In the short time before Coles' death, the Marine Captain and Jean became engaged.

Of the twenty-five officers who were to lose their lives that day there were two that Pat Holmes recalls with affection:

> 'My two best friends in the ship were Lieutenant John Maxwell – always known as Max – and Sub-Lieutenant Philip Brocklesby RNVR. What can I say about these cheerful and humorous young men I only knew for eight months? . . . We played cricket and golf together. We sang songs and generally played the fool together. Our girlfriends were from Athol Crescent, the Domestic Science School in Edinburgh. The cheerful times we experienced there were continued at Greenock where we got to know some Wren officers. And more fun was experienced at Belfast, where I had been two years before.
>
> 'We had an old 78 portable gramophone in Philip's and my cabin which was in constant use, and to this day I can never hear the tenor aria from *Martha M'appari tutt' amor* (*How Like a*

Dream) without a pang, for it was – for all three of us – our favourite song. The musical repertoire, however, was not limited to opera and I well remember those friends of mine and Lieutenant Eric Vaughan coming aboard in the small hours in Belfast having taken over the entire band at a night club, with Eric knocking all hell loose out of the percussion.'

THE SUPERLATIVE
LINER: CUNARD
CAPTAIN

'No opportunity should be lost of impressing on the officers of the escorted ship the necessity for their own ship to keep the sharpest possible lookout.'

Captain J. W. Boutwood, Report of Proceedings, 12 August, 1942.

The first of December, 1930, was a raw, dark, foggy winter's day at John Brown's shipyard on Clydebank. The weather reflected the sombre mood of the nation, gripped as it was by the world's economic depression. However, a feeling of optimism uplifted the workers' spirits as hundreds of numbed and coarsened hands began labouring on the first hull and keel plates of Job No. 534.

The men of John Brown's had begun the construction of one of the world's greatest ocean liners. The *Queen Mary*, first of the legendary *Queens*, began to take shape. She had been conceived four years earlier when Cunard management concluded that *two* powerful, speedy super-liners could provide a regular, weekly, trans-atlantic service, instead of the three ships then required to provide such a service.

Each of the twin liners would need to be capable of making the Atlantic crossing in five days, sailing each week from alternate sides. Such a service in the Twenties required *three* ships. It was a lucrative trade and the prospective financial rewards for a two-ship schedule looked glittering. The concept of speedy floating hotels on the Atlantic run was not new. Cunard itself was operating eighteen liners, including splendid ships like the 45,647-ton *Aquitania*, but none of them had the power to give the speed and turn-around service that Cunard envisaged.

True, the French were designing the *Normandie*: at 82,799 tons she was bigger than *Queen Mary*, without doubt would be the most luxuriously appointed liner, and she was a year ahead of the British ship in terms of completion. But her French owners were not planning a two-ship service across the Atlantic: *Normandie* was to sail independently without a consort, so would not enable the French line to give the weekly service that Cunard proposed.

The perception of *Queen Mary's* designers was visionary. Almost everything about her had to be expressed in superlative terms.

But within a year of work starting on the ship all the hopes of the Cunard Company, of John Brown's and all their employees came to a grinding halt. The depression struck deeper than ever. The world needed ships. but there was no money to pay for them. The shipyard stopped work on Job No. 534 on 11 December, 1931, and 3,200 men were laid off. It was a disastrous Christmas for many thousands on Clydebank.

A moribund government would not or could not give aid until induced to do so by a merger between the Cunard Steamship Company and the White Star Line. It was implicit, if not actually spelled out, that the government made the merger a pre-condition for aid; certainly matters were expedited after the merger. The government advanced £9.5 million to the new company at the end of March, 1934, and work recommenced within a week.

26 September, 1934, was the date of the great vessel's launching. And the ceremony was to be performed by no less a personage than the upright, imperious Queen Mary herself, with all due pomp and ceremony.

There is a delightful story, probably apocryphal, but worth repeating, based on the belief that Cunard wanted to name the ship *Queen Victoria*. Credibility is lent to this belief inasmuch as all Cunard's liners names ended in *ia*. The naming of Job No. 534 had been a closely guarded secret. The story suggests that King George V misunderstood Cunard's intention to name the ship after 'the country's most illustrious queen' – which he took to mean his wife, Queen Mary, rather than his grandmother, Queen Victoria. No one dared to correct him, it is asserted, and *Queen Mary* it became.

Launch day was a time for rejoicing, and no one who attended the ceremony would ever forget the sight of such a majestic symbol of Scottish engineering sliding down the slipway. It was also a day of sadness for the thousands of workers now thrown out of work in the shipyards. It would be some time before the *Queen Mary's* consort would create their re-employment. After the launch it took another eighteen months to complete the liner and to fit her out.

The ship was an engineering marvel and the statistics surrounding her were stunning. Although she was not quite the gross tonnage of the *Normandie* – 81,237 against the French 82,799 tons – her passenger capacity was greater – 2,139 against 1,972.

The most incongruous comparisons were made to illustrate her dimensions: the space in the first class lounge, for example, could accommodate nine double-decker buses placed abreast, with three Royal Scot engines superimposed on their roofs, and they could all drive through the lounge's archway. The ship was the greatest power station afloat; seven turbo-generator sets developed 10,000 kilowatts, enough for a small town.

Queen Mary was defined as 'long as a street and lofty as a tower, loftier and wider than many a country church'.

Her plates had been hammered together with no less than ten million rivets, collectively weighing 4,000 tons, every single one of which 'had a man's personality stamped on it'. With memories of the sinking of the *Titanic* in their minds, the naval architects had designed *Queen Mary* with an outer and an inner hull, and with 160 watertight compartments.

The giant rudder, the biggest ever built in maritime history, weighed 150 tons, and the four huge manganese bronze propellers weighed 35 tons each, manufactured with such precision they could be turned by the touch of a man's hand, and they were polished like a Life Guard's breastplate. 4,000 miles of electric cable went into her construction.

Before setting out on her maiden voyage she was fitted out with 30,000 electric lamps, 4,000 beds, ten miles of carpets and 200,000 pieces of china and glassware.

The completion of *Queen Mary* had been a statistician's dream and the shipbuilder's pride and joy.

At the end of March, 1936, *Queen Mary* was taken from the Firth of Clyde to dry dock at Southampton, and, when completed there, she was formally handed over by the proud builders to the equally proud owners on 12 May.

Command of the liner had been entrusted to Commodore Sir Edgar Britten, Cunard's most senior captain. To him went the honour of sailing her to a rapturous welcome at New York. Americans turned out in their thousands and in their hundreds of craft to greet the majestic visitor. New York had never witnessed such a reception of a ship before.

Expectations of her winning back the Blue Riband of the Atlantic from the *Normandie* were high, and when she failed to do so on her maiden voyage critics were quick to make their comments. But in August of that year she confounded her critics and captured the Blue Riband for the fastest crossing of the Atlantic at an average speed of 30.63 knots.

Queen Mary and *Normandie* then strove to beat each other like a tennis rally, until finally, in 1938, *Queen Mary* registered an average speed of 31.69 knots. Technically, this is how it was registered: it was on Sunday, 14 August at 2.42 p.m. that *Queen Mary* passed Bishop Rock, 2,938 miles out from Ambrose Light in 3 days 20 hours and 42 minutes, averaging 31.69 knots. This was 1 hour 25 minutes (or .49 knots) faster than the record passage set by *Normandie* in August of the previous year when she covered 2,936 miles at an average 31.20 knots.

*　　　*　　　*

By now, August, 1938, *Queen Mary's* consort, *Queen Elizabeth*, even grander than the *Mary* with a gross tonnage of 83,673, was building at the same John Brown's shipyard. She was programmed to join *Queen Mary* in the projected dual-liner, weekly service, in April, 1940. But by then the world would be in chaos, nations at war and the ships in peril.

Queen Mary entered the war while west-bound, in mid-Atlantic, en route to Manhattan, carrying a record number of 2,332 passengers. The giant liner secured alongside pier 90 in New York harbour, close by her old rival, the *Normandie*. She rested there awaiting orders while the opportunity was taken by hordes of workmen to over-paint her distinctive peacetime colours of black hull, white upperworks and red-and-black funnels with a uniform dull battleship grey. This was to give rise to her nickname of The Grey Ghost. From a glamorous, magnificent example of modern engineering, she now took on the appearance of a huge monster, the very word adopted to describe the two *Queens* – the Monster Liners. Yet still, underlying the obliterating grey, there could be discerned the graceful lines of the Cunarder; from her raking stem to her stern there was still something magical about her, as compulsive to look at as Concorde was forty years later.

Queen Elizabeth joined *Queen Mary* in her New York berth after a maiden voyage made in secret and at speed across the Atlantic. Her arrival, unlike the much-heralded one by *Queen Mary*, was a subdued affair, indeed almost to the extent of being ignored altogether. America, for one reason or another which has never been fathomed, simply did not welcome the world's greatest liner. The incident aroused this comment:

> 'Yet she received hardly a whistle of greeting from the many craft in the harbour. One sensed a feeling almost of reluctance to admit that she was visible at all. In that intensely pro-Allied city it seemed as if the recognition of her arrival might somehow count against Britain.'*

For a rare moment in maritime history the world's three greatest liners all lay alongside adjoining piers in New York harbour only a few hundred yards apart.

On 1 March, 1940, Cunard was officially informed that both liners had been requisitioned for military service. On the 21st *Queen Mary* slipped her moorings and left New York. Soon *Queen Elizabeth* would follow. The *Normandie* was commandeered by the US authorities after the attack on Pearl Harbor and was made ready for trooping duties like the *Queens*. But a few weeks later, whether by arson or carelessness, she caught fire and blazed away to total destruction, filled with fire-fighting water until she heeled over at her moorings and sank. Her partially salvaged remains lay rusting for years before she was finally demolished and scrapped.

Queen Mary's first voyage was to Australia via Cape Town where she was seen in Table Bay, thence to Sydney, New South Wales. Sydney had seen no liner greater than the 45,000-ton *Aquitania*. The sight of *Queen Mary* was

* *Ocean Liners of the Past: Queen Mary*, Patrick Stephens, 1972, p. 201.

out of this world. One of the world's largest and most beautiful natural harbours presented a splendid backdrop for the majestic liner.

Unceremoniously the Cockatoo Dock and Engineering Company transformed the enormous liner into a monster troopship in a matter of fourteen days. Out came all the trappings of luxury, all of them labelled, listed, packed and sent for storage somewhere in northern Australia. In this one stupendous effort the ship was refurbished to carry 5,500 troops instead of her certified 2,139 passengers. Tiered bunks by the hundred were bolted to bulkheads and very soon 5,000 Australian troops were loaded aboard en route to England via Fremantle, Cape Town and Freetown.

This was the start of one of the world's great wartime enterprises, the transportation of about one million people to various theatres of war, covering hundreds of thousands of miles: 5,000 troops to the Middle East; trooping trips from Sydney; Italian prisoners from the Desert War to imprisonment in Australia; soldiers from America via Rio de Janeiro and Cape Town to Fremantle; back across the Atlantic to Gourock; German prisoners of war with Polish guards to America from Suez.

Throughout something like six years of war and post-war trooping, through dangerous seas, her only asset was that of speed, for she carried virtually no AA guns to start with, although later she became fitted with both HA and LA guns. During all these years of thousands of miles travelled, not one man was lost due to the action of the enemy.

It seems cruel to add a jarring note to this claim. On one October afternoon in 1942, 338 British seamen aboard a cruiser perished when their ship was in collision with *Queen Mary*.

*   *   *

The wartime need for super-troopers, liners capable of transporting large numbers of personnel at once over long distances and at speed was self-evident. But the risk of doing so had to be faced. Later in the war *Queen Mary* carried life-saving equipment sufficient for the numbers of people aboard, but this was misleading. Theoretically thirty lifeboats would accommodate 3,000 people, and there were enough life rafts for another 17,000. But these simple facts presuppose all the lifeboats and rafts, or at least the great majority of them, being satisfactorily launched. The reality of disaster at sea is demonstrably to the contrary. The mere prospect of abandoning ship was awesome.

The matter had arisen in discussion between the British Prime Minister Winston Churchill and the US General Marshall,* a man of great courage and vision. Soon after the Japanese attack on Pearl Harbor the *Queens* had gone under direct US control, although Cunard continued to own the ships, and their crews were paid by the shipping line. During Churchill's visit to

---

* George Catlett Marshall (1880–1959). US Chief of Staff 1939–45. Originator of the Marshall Plan for European reconstruction. Nobel Peace Prize 1953.

Washington at the end of December, 1941, Marshall asked the Prime Minister about the possibility of modifying each ship to carry a complete division of about 15,000 men, considerably more than the 5,000 certified after the Cockatoo refit.

Marshall was concerned that in the event of one of the liners being sunk, there would only be lifeboats for about half the people. Churchill made this observation:

'I can only tell you what *we* should do. You must judge for yourself the risks you will run. If it were a direct part of an actual operation, we should put all on board they could carry. If it were only a question of moving troops in a reasonable time, we should not go beyond the limits of lifeboats, rafts etc. It is for you to decide.'*

General Marshall received this advice in silence. He visited New York and inspected *Queen Mary*. He asked Harry Grattidge, Staff Captain of the liner, for his opinion of the 15,000 plan. Grattidge saw only one problem: the possibility that the great weight of men would cause the ship to list. If all the men up top gathered on one side for a last view of New York the great liner would list, say just 5 degrees, and cause *Queen Mary* to foul the top of the Hudson Tunnel, such was the narrowness of the clearance, as she made her way downstream to the Atlantic. Grattidge gave approval so long as the army disciplined its troops to stay put until given the green light to move freely up top.

The orders went out to convert *Queen Mary* to maximum troop-carrying capacity. Later the ships were filled to the brim and, as Winston Churchill commented, 'Fortune stood our friend.' In *Queen Mary's* case it was an incredible example of good fortune. In over five years of war service steaming hundreds of thousands of miles *Queen Mary* never saw a U-boat or enemy submarine, was never fired on from the air, from sea or from land, never had a bomb dropped on her and was never placed in a situation to fire a shot in anger. The only blemish on her escutcheon was the *Curacoa* Incident.

The *Queens* were under strict orders, regardless of the situation, never to stop. Their safety lay in speed. At a speed of something like 30 knots they could out-range a U-boat, whose maximum surface speed was, typically, about 17 knots, and submerged was about 7½ knots. High speed and a zigzag course were their two greatest anti-submarine assets, plus the injunction not to stop under even the most humanitarian interests. To do so would be to expose the ship and all the thousands aboard her to attack by a U-boat. Such a risk was totally unacceptable. Just how dangerous were the

---

* Winston Churchill, *The Second World War*, Vol III, 'The Grand Alliance,' 1950.

circumstances in the depths of the cruel sea can be appreciated by an understanding of the state of the Battle of the Atlantic.

*   *   *

1942 was a momentous year in British history and its main elements need mentioning briefly if only to give a historical perspective to the *Curacoa* Incident. The early months of the year saw our eastern colonies and possessions overrun by invading Japanese forces. The whole of the Malay peninsula fell and the surrender of the bastion of Singapore in February stunned the world. In Libya Rommel drove the British Desert Army into withdrawal while the island of Malta lay under siege, isolated and exposed to constant bombardment from the air.

February also saw the ignominy of the Channel Dash which burst upon an unsuspecting public and allowed *Scharnhorst* and *Gneisenau* to cock a snook at Britain's defences.

The clash at sea between Germany and the USA led to the wholesale sinking of unconvoyed ships off America's seaboard. Convoy battles raged in the North Atlantic and the battling through of PQ convoys to northern Russia – especially the calamitous PQ17 and the gruesome PQ18 – took on the stature of major fleet operations.

By 1 August, 1942, Admiral Dönitz had a fleet of 342 U-boats in commission, almost 300 more than at the outbreak of war nearly three years earlier. The Wolf Pack technique of attacking convoys in force was registering a peak of success for the U-boat service.

Worldwide, August, 1942, saw the sinking of 131 ships totalling more than two-thirds of a million tons of shipping, all this achieved at the cost of twelve U-boats. 'Stragglers and independents, without the benefit of escorts, were picked off like ducks in a shooting gallery.'*

In the same month there came the disaster of Dieppe. And September saw the *Laconia* Incident whose repercussions were to rumble on for years and would finally help convict Dönitz of war crimes at the Nuremberg Trials. The troopship *Laconia*, sailing independently in relative safety of the West African coast was torpedoed and sunk by *U-156*. She had nearly 2,500 people aboard; ironically this included 1,800 Italian prisoners of war being transported from the Middle East via the Cape of Good Hope to America. All told, about 1,400 people perished. The incident showed what happens when great numbers of people fight for survival in a disastrous sinking at sea. The prospect of this happening to either of the *Queens* was beyond belief.

But 1942 was not all gloom; unknown to the Allies, this year also marked the end of the beginning. In many ways the worst of the war was over, although another two and a half years of bitter ordeals in the Atlantic still had to be endured.

---

*   *The Atlantic Star 1939–45* by David A. Thomas, W.H. Allen, 1990, p. 139.

64

It was through these treacherous waters that the *Queens* travelled – independently. But one concession was made. In the waters from the Clyde to about 12 degrees west where the threat of air attack from long-range patrolling aircraft was very real, an AA cruiser and destroyers with AA armament would be provided as escorts, meeting the home-coming troopship somewhere to the north-west of Ireland, and for outward-bound *Queens* escorting them to a similar location, about 12 degrees west.

The conversion of *Queen Mary* to 15,000 capacity was largely brought about by what were called standee bunks, made of tubular steel, positioned in every conceivable space, even including the swimming pools. When the bunks were not in use they were hinged upwards and secured. A canvas base was laced to the tubular rim of the bunk, making it lightweight yet strong, easily cleaned and perfectly comfortable.

The First Class Smoking Lounge was converted into a hospital. Extra galleys and heads were provided. The huge Observation Lounge and Midshipman's Bar became filled with bunks. Austin Reed's tailoring shop in the Main Hall became a detention centre. Elsewhere, in every possible location, 12,500 standee bunks, designed by Americans, made the whole exercise possible. In addition another 3,500 troops were allowed to be carried as a special dispensation, 'overload' passengers who would sleep on deck during summer crossings.

The US Secretary of the Treasury, Henry Morgenthau, visited *Queen Mary*. According to Staff Captain Grattidge* he asked to see the worst living conditions aboard and was shown the swimming pool where some bunks were stacked *seven* tiers high.

Captain James Bisset[†] took over command of *Queen Mary* at the end of February, 1942, and maintained a meticulous record of the ship's achievements in his memoirs. He records, for instance, the outward passage from New York starting 2 August, 1942, en route for the Clyde when 15,125 troops were loaded aboard, plus 863 crew, making a total of 15,988 persons, then by far the greatest number of people ever transported in a single vessel. It also marked the first time that an entire American division – the First US Armored Division – travelled in one shipping movement.[‡]

Shift systems had to be introduced, especially for meals, Bisset recorded the mealtimes:

---

* Captain Harry Grattidge OBE (1890–1979). Joined Cunard 1914. Captain of *Queen Mary* 1949–52. Captain of *Queen Elizabeth* 1952–53.

[†] Later Commodore Sir James Gordon Partridge Bisset (1883–1967). Commanded a destroyer in WWI and the *Queens* in WWII.

[‡] Even this number was exceeded. On 25 July, 1943, she sailed from New York with 16,683 souls aboard, the greatest number of human beings ever embarked in one vessel.

'Only two meals a day were served, each of six sittings. Breakfasts were from 6.30 to 11 a.m., and dinners from 3 to 7.30 p.m.

'The officers' dining room – which in peacetime was the tourist-class lounge – seated 350. The troops' mess hall – which was the three-deck-high first-class restaurant – seated 2,000. The mess tables – of metal, with wooden benches – seated an average of eighteen men, with two orderlies to each table. The orderlies formed queues to the kitchens, drew the food in large metal containers, then carried it into the mess hall and dished it out to the tables. Every sitting lasted forty-five minutes. Every soldier carried his own knife, fork, plate and spoon. The men entered the mess hall at one end and left it at the other end, to avoid clashing with the queue waiting for the next sitting. The utensils, known as 'eating irons', were well designed to be hooked together and held on a wire handle. Each man, on filing out of the mess hall, swizzled his gear in a battery of four tanks in succession holding soapy water, boiling fresh water, boiling disinfectant and finally boiling sea water, and then took it to his quarters to drain dry.'

Bisset also put on record the enormous complexity of an operation involving the transportation of tens of thousands of troops in such congested conditions, unparalleled since the infamous days of slavery decades previously. The crowding of the transatlantic liners, however, had been designed with

'a sensitive understanding of the limits of human tolerance and a meticulous and imaginative knowledge of household economy on a colossal scale afloat. As a result . . . hundreds of thousands were brought through their hard experience physically whole, sane, well-fed, accepting a strong but necessary discipline.'*

Captain Cyril Gordon Illingworth assumed command of *Queen Mary* in June, 1942, the same month that Boutwood took command of *Curacoa*. Illingworth had had a long and distinguished career at sea. During the First World War he served as an RNR officer in the 10,850-ton cruiser *Argyll* in the Third Cruiser Squadron until October, 1915, when the cruiser was wrecked on Bell Rock off Dundee. He served at the Battle of Jutland in 1916, then gained experience in convoy and patrol work. He also served in a trim, innocent-looking little topsail schooner, in reality a submarine decoy or Q ship, able to sink a U-boat in a ship-to-ship engagement.

The inter-war years gave Illingworth another two decades of experience at sea. The Second World War saw him in command of the troopship

---

* *The Cunard White Star Quadruple Screwed Liner*, No. 6 in 'The Shipbuilder & Marine Engine-Builder', p. 203.

Laconia, a near-20,000-ton Cunard White Star ship. He had commanded her some years earlier when she was a luxury liner. In December, 1940, he received an appointment well suited to his experience as Commodore of ocean-going convoys, until his appointment in command of *Queen Mary* in June, 1942.

Illingworth was not a popular master. One RN officer remarked that he was not respected among Royal Navy men, but this probably only reflected the age-long rivalry between the Merchant and Royal Navies. What mattered was that he had the confidence of Cunard and the ability to compensate for his lack of physical stature with a booming voice, likened by some to a foghorn.

ESCORTING THE QUEENS

'Operations, Admiralty, agree that this type of escort is mere eyewash. Suggest matter might be taken up . . . with a view to these ships sailing independently so far as surface escort is concerned.'

C-in-C Western Approaches Staff Minute 19 August, 1942.

By the time Illingworth assumed captaincy of *Queen Mary* in the summer of 1942 a routine for the liner's movements had been established. The liner would leave New York alone and unescorted, then increase speed to 28½ knots and adopt a zigzag. A preference was for the one known as No. 8. (see p.83) Every few minutes course would have to be changed to conform to a set pattern, sometimes changing to port, other times to starboard.

There were a wide range of patterns or zigzags to choose from, each lasting different lengths of time, after which the quartermaster at the wheel would repeat the zigzag pattern all over again. To aid the man at the wheel a clock would give an audible warning for every turn or change of course. Each zigzag and each course alteration had been carefully designed so that a mean or average course would be the result of all the course changes.

It can be understood that the speed of advance of a ship along her mean course would be less than the speed at which the ship was travelling, the extent of this reduction depending upon the zigzag number adopted. In the case of No. 8 the reduction would be two knots.

The employment of such a zigzag was considered sufficient to confuse a U-boat commander because the frequency of course changes, coupled with a high speed of advance, should make it virtually impossible to get in a successful torpedo attack.

The passage of the liner across the Atlantic would continue like this for about five days; then the liner would be met, as we have seen, by an AA cruiser and destroyers for the last dangerous leg for the Clyde.

Captain Boutwood of *Curacoa* was more familiar with this home-waters aspect of the procedure than Captain Illingworth. In the two months prior to the tragedy Boutwood had escorted *Queen Mary* four times on either outward or return crossings, and he had escorted *Queen Elizabeth* twice.

QUEENS ESCORTED BY *CURACOA*				
1942	Ship	Convoy	Commander	Destination
7 Aug	*Queen Mary*	AT19	Bisset	The Clyde
11 Aug	*Queen Mary*	TA19	Illingworth	New York
5 Sept	*Queen Elizabeth*	AT21	Fall	The Clyde
8 Sept	*Queen Elizabeth*	TA21	Fall	New York
5 Sept	*Queen Mary*	AT22	Illingworth	The Clyde
14 Sept	*Queen Mary*	TA22	Illingworth	New York
27 Sept	*Queen Mary*	AT23	Illingworth	The Clyde

The fast convoys bringing troops over to Britain from 1942 to 1945 were coded AT for those travelling east and TA for those returning west. Each were followed by a number.

Curacoa first escorted *Queen Mary* – convoy coded AT19 – on 7 August when Captain Bisset brought over 15,000 troops into the Clyde.

Four days later on 11 August Captain Illingworth sailed for New York in *Queen Mary* as convoy TA19 with *Curacoa* in attendance as escort to about 12 degrees W.

Both these convoys were interesting. In naval terms the first one, AT19, was the cruiser's most successful. Boutwood took her from the Clyde on Wednesday, 5 August for Moville on Lough Foyle downstream from Londonderry. There she joined HM destroyers *Newark*, *Lancaster* and *Broke*. The first two were old (1918 construction) ex-USN destroyers of just over 1,000 tons lent to the Royal Navy in exchange for bases throughout the British Commonwealth; *Broke* was built in 1920, was 1,480 tons and was lost in the Mediterranean a few weeks after the *Curacoa* loss. These escorts left at noon on the 7th and steamed at 17 knots into the North Atlantic on what was thought to be the reciprocal course to that adopted by convoy AT19, the unescorted *Queen Mary*, commanded by Illingworth.

The visibility was poor at first. The story is told graphically if sparsely by *Curacoa's* log for 7 August:

0700   HMS *Curacoa* obtained an RDF contact ahead 9 miles whose rate of closing indicated the probability of it being the convoy. Visibility was still very poor.

0710	In position 56 5ON, 14 37W *Queen Mary* was sighted.*
0712	AT19 bearing 278 degrees distance 3 miles. Our course 270 degrees at 15 knots. Altered course to 090 degrees. HM ships *Lancaster* and *Newark* formed a close screen ahead.
0740	Speed 21 knots.
0805	Altered course to 111 degrees.
0815	23 knots. Astern of convoy 5 cables.
0825	HMS *Broke* was detached to meet SC94 in accordance with C-in-C Western Approaches 0246Z/7.
0839	25 knots to maintain speed of advance of convoy at 27 knots and in zigzag.
1340	Aircraft at 100 degrees.
1415	An aircraft was picked up by RDF at a range of 20 miles
1428	and identified as a Liberator escort. It did not start to show IFF [Identification Friend or Foe] until 1445. Visibility was still low.
1502	Sighted land 145 degrees.
1515	Altered course to 108 degrees.
1600	Longitude 8 degrees 30W crossed about now. VHF watch was set at frequency for 82 Group.
1722	Convoy ceased zigzag 8.
1732	Speed 25½ knots to take station ahead of convoy.
1816	4 Spitfires believed to be from 82 Group took up fighter patrol around the convoy and close range fighter patrol was thenceforward maintained.
1830	Altered course 115 degrees. Speed 26 knots (290 revs.)
1847	Altacarry Head 2 miles on port beam.
1929	25½ knots.
1945	HM ships *Lancaster* and *Newark* were detached to their respective bases when 2 miles distant from the Clyde Light Vessel.
1950	Clyde Light Vessel 1 cable abeam to starboard.
2005	Contact was obtained with 13 Group fighters who remained in company until 2215.
2130	HMS *Curacoa* with *Queen Mary* passed the Cumbraes into the Firth of Clyde.
2146	Toward Point bearing 290 degrees distance 1 mile.

*   *

Not only was Captain Boutwood no stranger to these escorting duties, he was a critic of some aspects of them. The second convoy, TA19, in partic-

---

*   For a full explanation of direction, distance and speeds see Appendix E (p.174).

ular, and his subsequent *Report* of 12 August made it clear that all was not well. Visual signalling arrangements were quite inadequate and slow ships (by implication his own ship, too) found it difficult to provide proper protection.

Queen Mary, as convoy TA19, had disgorged her 15,000 troops after arriving off Gourock late on 7 August and a few days later set sail from Gourock for New York under Captain Illingworth's command.

Curacoa slipped from the Flagship Buoy at Greenock late on Monday evening, 10 August, and by 0600 next morning sighted *Queen Mary* seven miles to the south, both ships by now having rounded the Mull of Kintyre and on courses between west and north-west.

Within half-an-hour *Curacoa* had worked up to 25 knots, a creditable performance against a force 6 to 7 westerly wind, but on a short sea without much swell.

At 0730, with *Queen Mary* still one to two miles astern and just starting her zigzag, *Curacoa* reduced her speed since the troopship did not appear to be gaining on her. By 0815, with *Queen Mary* now ahead, speed was increased again, but by 0830 at 23 knots the sea had lengthened so that to exceed 23 knots would have been dangerous. *Queen Mary* was about two miles away on the port bow and still going ahead. She was informed of *Curacoa's* reduction and at 0840 signalled a reduction in her own speed to correspond.

A further reduction in the cruiser's speed became advisable, but to reach *Queen Mary* by visual signal was getting more and more difficult.

At 0909 the RDF plot in *Curacoa* picked up an aircraft bearing 132 degrees ten miles off and approaching the convoy. It was not showing IFF and it became imperative for the escort not to slow down until a message was passed. No answer could be obtained by light. Spray and funnel smoke must have made signalling difficult. At 0911 *Curacoa* sighted the aircraft bearing 180 degrees, seven miles. It was closing *Queen Mary* from her port quarter at about 100 to 150 feet. Spray made identification of the aircraft by binoculars impossible. It appeared to be big and unfamiliar and did not correspond with the air escort mentioned in C-in-C WA's and FOIC Greenock's signals of the 10th. It seemed probable that *Queen Mary* had not observed it.

The 4-inch guns manned in *Curacoa* had been trained onto the lookout bearing and at 0912 the order was given to open fire, the main objective being to attract *Queen Mary's* attention to the bearing, but fire was checked as the bearing began to endanger the liner. The aircraft proved friendly.

Wind and sea had been increasing every moment and at 0915 an exceptional sea broke over *Curacoa's* fo'c'sle, shattering four of the bridge windows. Speed was reduced at once to 19 knots and when the bridge and lookout personnel could see again properly the aircraft had disappeared.

There then followed cyphered signals from Admiralty, received in *Curacoa* at 0922, which took 1½ hours to decypher. It reached the bridge at 1050. Trying to pass this message to *Queen Mary* by 20-inch signal projector failed through *Queen Mary's* inability to read it, but at 1055 *Curacoa's* 'Close me' signal was successfully passed and at 1125 the liner began to comply.

While this was going on the cruiser had steamed at speeds of between 12 and 19 knots and on courses to help the use of the 20-inch SP. At 1130 Boutwood turned about and set course for the Clyde, speed 18 knots before the sea.

Captain Boutwood was unhappy with several aspects of this convoy and he conveyed this displeasure in his *Report*.* In particular he highlighted paragraph 20:

> '20. From consideration of experience with convoys AT19 and TA19 (a) the importance of good visual signalling arrangements in the fast liner and (b) the difficulties of providing proper protection for a fast big ship by slower ships with comparatively poor sea-keeping qualities at speed are emphasized.'

Paragraph 21 underscored this inadequacy in visual signalling procedures: referring to (a) above he comments:

> 'The impression was received . . . that the efficiency of the naval signalling staff in *Queen Mary* might have been improved if the senior rating (at present believed to be a Leading Signalman) was replaced by a higher grade rating with plenty of experience and confidence to qualify him both to make use of his equipment to pass messages to all the escort force with the minimum delay and repetition, and to advise the officers handling his ship how he could best be assisted without prejudicing the progress of the convoy. On the forenoon of Monday, 11 August, it took HMS *Curacoa's* utmost continuous effort considerably longer than two hours to effect an exchange of vital communications with *Queen Mary* which need not have occupied more than twenty minutes assuming normal vigilance and the handling of the faster ship in a manner appreciative of the limitations of the V/S equipment available and the conditions prevailing. The provision of a specially selected Chief Yeoman or Yeoman of Signals for supervision of Naval V/S work in *Queen Mary* and similar ships on convoy duties is recommended.'

Captain Boutwood went on to comment upon the relative speeds of the liner and the cruiser, pointing out that to maintain a speed of advance of 25 knots

---

* *Letter of Proceedings with Convoy TA19*, ADM217/3, 12 August, 1942.

Curacoa could not zigzag as this was her top speed for prolonged periods. He then added a small historical note in parentheses:

'It is of interest to observe that HMS *Curacoa's* highest revolutions recorded were 317 rpm for four hours with light draught in February, 1918. On 2 August, 1942, her revolutions averaged 284.1 over twelve hours with average draught 17ft 5ins, i.e. 22 ins extra mean draught. 280 rpm drive *Curacoa* at 25 knots in smooth water. In anything of a seaway HMS *Curacoa's* low free-board necessitates early reduction of speed to avoid weather damage.'

Paragraph 23 of this report pointed out that in an average zigzag the lateral distance of a ship at the end of her zig from the mean line of advance will certainly be in the nature of 1½ miles and may well be considerably more. Since, therefore, it will very often be the best general policy for a fast escorted liner to zigzag while the slower AA cruiser maintains the mean course, Boutwood concluded:

'No opportunity should be lost of impressing on the officers of the escorted ship the necessity for their own ship to keep the sharpest possible lookout and to establish the closest co-operation (probably including closest company also) with the AA escort at the first suspicion of enemy air activity.'

Some of these observations deserve attention. The need to spend two hours or more to pass information was a sad reflection of the communications system. The provision of a Yeoman or Chief Yeoman of signals might certainly have helped improve matters, but who can say whether such an experienced man on *Queen Mary's* bridge prior to the collision would have changed the situation materially?

In commenting on the relative speeds of the two ships Boutwood provided a critical analysis of the need for high speed, stable AA ships as escorts for the *Queens*, and by definition eliminated *Curacoa* herself.

Paragraph 23 has more than a hint of prescience about it when he propounded the need for the sharpest lookouts in *Queen Mary*. But this really has no relevance to the disaster because long before, and at the actual moment of collision, of course, both ships were abundantly clear to each other. Sharper lookouts would have done nothing to save *Curacoa*. The sinking of the cruiser had very little to do with visibility and with lookouts. It had more to do with tactics than anything else.

Boutwood's *Report* on TA19 is subscribed with a Staff Minute Sheet bearing comments by various hands, some of which have been quoted as chapter headings. One is dismissive of the Chief Yeoman suggestion:

'With present state of drafting I think it is useless to ask for a CYS to be appointed to the *Queens*.'

Another observation suggests it be made 'quite clear to the *Queen* that she must conform to the speed of the escort until the prearranged point when she becomes an independent.' This is a somewhat curious and unhelpful suggestion which seems to ignore the use of very old cruisers and destroyers incapable of high speeds in anything of a sea.

A final observation on the Staff Minute Sheet commented:

'I have already remonstrated . . . about the futile practice [of providing "useless" escorts for the *Queens*] but I gather it is a matter of high policy connected with the possibility of questions in the House in the event of any "Monster" getting into trouble.'

*   *   *

In August, 1942, perhaps the height of Dönitz's U-boat campaign in the Battle of the Atlantic, *Curacoa* was to change her base from Greenock in the Clyde to Belfast, and in doing so became engaged in giving escort to three convoys. She left Greenock on Saturday, 15 August and joined convoy DS31, bound for Reykjavik, Iceland, with A/S escorts, HM Ships *Lancaster* and the lightly-armed 1919 destroyers of just over 900 tons *Saladin* and *Shikari*. As the weather worsened, speed was reduced from 15 to 12 knots since the two old 'S' Class destroyers had fixed Asdic domes which made them a little unseaworthy. Both a Sunderland flying boat and a Fortress joined the convoy as anti-submarine escorts during the forenoon of the 16th.

Convoy AT18 from New York was sighted when about 250 nautical miles west-north-west of the narrowest part of the North Channel between the Mull of Kintyre and Fair Head on the Antrim coast, and very impressive it looked. It was an American-controlled convoy with the Senior Officer of the Escort in the very elderly 26,100-ton battleship USS *Arkansas* acting as Commodore of the Convoy as well.

Acting Captain Sir Archibald Cochrane, who commanded the Armed Merchant Cruiser HMS *Queen of Bermuda*, had some revealing things to say about AT18. To start with, in New York troops bound for Iceland got separated from their equipment and some of the same party went to Ireland instead. The Commodore of the Convoy, in the 27,000-ton troop transport *West Point* (formerly the USS *America* of the America Line), had all his duties taken from him by the Admiral in *Arkansas*.

Cochrane, who was Vice Commodore of the Convoy, headed the column on the port side of *Arkansas*. He reports that in nine days 380 general orders were given, most of them entirely unnecessary. It was early days in the war for the Americans; they still had a lot to learn. Reductions of speed signals and alterations of course invariably led to difficulties if only because the old

74

battleship (completed in 1912) lost way much quicker than the sleeker ex-passenger liners in the troop convoy.

Cochrane was amazed to be told by the pilot taking him out of New York that a lamp signal from the New Jersey shore asking 'name of ship' (which of course he had no intention of answering) came from a signal station owned by some of the New York newspapers. It was a situation comparable with the glaring lights along the coast of Florida just after America entered the war; U-boats had a field day picking off un-convoyed ships at will, often aided by the shore lights silhouetting their targets. The doyen of US naval historians, Samuel Eliot Morison, regarded those weeks of blazing lights a national disgrace.

When the convoys DS31 for Iceland and AT18 for the UK (including Northern Ireland) parted, HMS *Curacoa* joined the latter, while HMS *Queen of Bermuda* (22,575 tons) and Poland's largest liner, the 14,287-ton *Batory*, joined DS31.

Eighteen hours later, at 0500 on the 17th in the North Channel, convoy AT18 began to disperse, having made a speed of advance of 12½ knots steaming at an average of 15 knots and zigzagging. *Curacoa* took over responsibility for the troopships *Barry*, which parted for Belfast 4½ hours later, and the sister ships *Uruguay* and *Brazil*, both of over 20,000 tons. They were former liners of the America Line on the New York to San Francisco service via the Panama Canal. *Curacoa* escorted them into the Bristol Channel, detaching *Uruguay* for Swansea and *Brazil* for Cardiff. She then returned to Milford Haven not far from where she was built twenty-five years before at Pembroke Dock. She left on the 20th and joined convoy ONM123 and reached Belfast on Saturday, 22nd. It had been a roundabout passage to Belfast.

In September *Curacoa* joined Western Approaches Command – Irish Sea Escort Force. Her log for this month went down with her and the only written records to be found are Captain Boutwood's further *Reports of Proceedings* to C-in-C Western Approaches.

His report of 7 September concerned convoy AT21 which comprised the troopship *Queen Elizabeth* under the command of Captain Fall. She had left New York on 31 August and was due at Gourock on 5 September.

Curacoa left Bangor Bay in Belfast Lough before dawn on 4 September, joining the anti-submarine escort force comprising the two Town Class destroyers *Castleton* and *Wells*, the 1,070-ton *Zetland* and the Polish destroyer *Blyskawica* off the entrance to Lough Foyle. The sighting of *Queen Elizabeth* was even more breath-taking than seeing *Queen Mary*, but locating her had been a trial.

September gales can be extremely daunting in the North Atlantic. C-in-C Western Approaches sent Boutwood a signal during the middle watch ordering *Curacoa* to return to base because of the weather conditions. At daylight, however, the wind and sea had moderated and Boutwood signalled to the effect that he was proposing to battle on. *Curacoa* and her consorts swept ahead of AT21's projected route at 16 knots trying to locate *Queen Elizabeth* in strong winds and heavy seas. The troopship signalled her position and speed of advance (27 knots).

Speed of the escorts was reduced to 12 knots. Just before 1430 AT21 was sighted about 11 miles astern. Speed was increased to 17 and then 20 knots so that when AT21 caught up with the escort at 1530 the escort force was in sufficiently sheltered waters to be able to provide a close screen and a speed of advance of 25 knots.

Zetland and *Wells* were detached for Londonderry while *Curacoa*, *Blyskawica* and *Castleton* escorted AT21 to the Clyde, passing the Clock Point Gate at 1941 on 5 September.

A feature of the last stretch of the passage to Greenock was the aerial activity. Between noon on 4 September and noon on the 5th aircraft were contacted on ten occasions. None approached *Curacoa* nearer than four miles. Only two displayed IFF. Only one, a Flying Fortress, was actually sighted. Just how fragile communications were between ships and aircraft is illustrated by the fact that in the hour between 1600 and 1700 on the 5th two Spitfires and one Beaufighter were sighted but no VHF communication could be established, nor with their shore station of 82 Group. After 1700 good communications were established with the shore station at 13 Group and their Spitfires when they gave escort up the Clyde.

The attempt to escort *Queen Elizabeth* back again at the start of her voyage as convoy TA21 was extremely difficult. Captain Boutwood in his *Report** regarding convoys TA21 and AT22 related the story.

Curacoa and *Castleton* left the Clyde at 0800 on 8 September some sixteen hours ahead of *Queen Elizabeth*; it was evident that the prevailing weather would prevent close escort. Four other destroyers from Derry joined up at 1330 and an anti-submarine sweep was carried out by them and *Castleton* at 12 knots, the maximum possible in the stormy weather prevailing.

At 1505 on the 9th, over twenty-five hours since the sweep west was started, *Queen Elizabeth* was sighted on the port quarter about fourteen miles away, some 300 miles west of the North Channel between Northern Ireland and Scotland. By 1645, an hour and forty minutes later, the liner disappeared ahead, having swung round the port wing of the escort.

The escorting of *Queen Elizabeth* outwards was followed by turning northeast to link up with *Queen Mary*. She had left New York for the Clyde on the 5th and was due at Gourock on the 11th. She was commanded by Captain Illingworth.

Curacoa and her destroyers had stopped following *Queen Elizabeth* as far west as 15 degrees 41 minutes at 1830 on the 9th. By about midday on the 10th they had reached *Queen Mary's* likely line of advance. The flotilla swept

---

* *Report of Proceedings*, 11 September, 1942, No. 0191/51.

the area first at 12 and later at 15 knots in order to allow *Queen Mary* to overtake them soon after daylight on the 11th. But by the end of the middle watch, at about 0400 that early morning of 11 September, the three old 905-ton destroyers *Sardonyx*, *Saladin* and *Sabre*, among the oldest in the Royal Navy, were detached for Londonderry for refuelling. The destroyer *Wells* had already left company to investigate an unidentified merchant ship. *Curacoa* was left with *Castleton* in company.

Half an hour later, when *Queen Mary* was sighted on the starboard quarter 6¼ miles away, it was still one and a half hours before dawn. Speed was worked up in *Curacoa* and *Castleton* and the troopship was escorted from astern past Rathlin Island, the Mull of Kintyre and the well-known craggy rock of Ailsa Craig, past Aran Island and so to the Clyde, passing the Cumbraes Light at 0805 on 11 September.

Noting that *Queen Mary* was not following the swept channel between Rathlin Island and the Clyde Light vessel, Boutwood twice signalled her before notice was taken of the warning. The sheep was reluctant to take much account of the sheepdog.

Nor had much notice been taken of Boutwood's concern over Coastal Command's anti-submarine escorts, Sunderlands, Liberators and Fortresses not showing IFF. Although these three types of aircraft should not be confused with Focke-Wulf 200s, so often, especially in poor visibility, all aircraft look alike to trigger-sensitive ships' gunners. It is only fair to record that during the last hour and a half a Beaufighter and some Spitfires established good communication with the escorts.

Curacoa's last voyage with *Queen Mary* before her final fatal one was on 13/14 September when, in company with the same destroyers as before – *Wells*, *Castleton*, *Skate*, *Sardonyx* and *Saladin* – she steamed slowly into increasingly bad weather which culminated in south-west winds of gale force and a beam sea. The force was acting as escort for *Queen Mary's* passage to the west; the ships had left Greenock sixteen hours ahead of the liner, but she was only sighted for about ten minutes around 1600 on the 14th. However, her range and bearing were known to *Curacoa* who held her on her RDF set and it was known she was making good a course of 330 degrees at 25½ knots.

In really bad weather there was never any chance of the destroyers keeping up, nor even *Curacoa* herself with her low freeboard; nevertheless, in sweeping slowly along the liner's track some slight deterrent was afforded against U-boats out into the Atlantic for about 300 miles. *Curacoa*, of course, needed to be within three or four miles of her charge to provide long-range AA fire of any effectiveness. It is significant that of the seven voyages from 2 August to 2 October, 1942, on which *Curacoa* was detailed to escort the *Queens* on only one occasion was she able to carry out close escort for more than a few hours. This was with *Queen Mary* under Captain Bisset (convoy AT19) on 7 August for fourteen hours.

Curacoa escorted the *Queens* seven times in all, and with her sinking the policy was abandoned. The Navy no longer had any old expendable ex-'C' Class cruisers converted to AA ships left – except *Carlisle*, and she was fighting for her life in the Mediterranean and was soon to be rendered a constructive total loss in the Dodecanese. True, *Caledon* and *Colombo*, converted in 1943, became available but by then the tide of war had changed and the likelihood of German long-range aircraft venturing into the North-West Approaches had diminished, especially since a possible successor to the Focke-Wulf 200, the Heinkel 177, had proved unreliable.

The fact is that *Curacoa* and her 'C' Class consorts simply were not seaworthy enough for the duties given them in the North Atlantic. This had already been established by HMS *Cairo* in May of 1942. She had been returning to the UK from Gibraltar as part of the US carrier *Wasp's* escort when she was detached with three destroyers to meet *Queen Mary* for the last fifteen hours of her transatlantic crossing. The destroyers and *Cairo* struggled to keep up.

The same deficiency was evident some days later when the AA cruiser and four destroyers accompanied *Queen Mary* out into the Atlantic again under the command of Captain Bisset on one of her voyages to Suez via Freetown and Cape Town carrying over 9,500 British troops to the Western Desert. Connell recalls the anecdote:

> 'This time *Queen Mary* headed straight into a force 8 western gale and heavy sea, her great hull riding high and dry through breaking seas that buried the cruiser and destroyers. After twelve hours of agony plunging into seas that smashed boats, guardrails and upper deck fittings, driving gun crews from their stations, the escorts were rendered impotent, incapable of protecting their great charge; the Master signalled down from his dry, enclosed bridge, "Thank you gentlemen, I must be off. You are holding me back." *Queen Mary* cracked on speed to disappear into the weather murk ahead of half-submerged escorts who thankfully turned back for the Clyde . . . all with upper and between decks a shambles of broken fittings and flooded spaces.'*

Cairo's next voyage was to Gibraltar and she was sunk shortly afterwards, escorting the most famous of all Malta convoys – Operation Pedestal – by the Italian submarine *Axum* off Cap Bon in the narrows between Sicily and Tunisia.

---

* Connell, op. cit.

THOSE IN PERIL ON THE SEA: DANGER LOOMS

'I think the answer is to struggle on with what we have, but make it quite clear to the *Queen* that she must conform to the speed of the escort.'

Admiralty Staff Minute following convoy TA19, 25 August, 1942.

The day dawned bright but chilly. The wind freshened as it progressed and brought with it a worsening sea, tending to make the cruiser yaw a little now and then, and more than somewhat in the heavy westerly swell that was running. She thumped through the sea, heading for the rendezvous, while the destroyers found it increasingly difficult to maintain speed. Indeed, the senior destroyer commanding officer in *Bulldog* signalled Captain Boutwood to say that the destroyer escorts could not exceed 20 knots. There were six destroyers, two being almost as antiquated as *Curacoa* herself. *Skate* was the oldest in the Navy, a 900-ton ship which survived the war and was scrapped in 1947 at the age of thirty. *Saladin* was another small ship of 905 tons; she was also scrapped in 1947. It is difficult to understand how two such inappropriate ships should ever have been assigned to a duty like this. Two Hunt Class destroyers of 1,050 tons were *Bramham* and *Cowdray*, handy, wartime-construction vessels produced in their dozens. A Polish-manned destroyer, *Blyskawica*, with a proud wartime record, and *Bulldog* completed the six escorts. *Bulldog* (1,360 tons) had been launched in 1930. She is remembered for her magnificent exploit in the North Atlantic when she captured intact an Enigma machine complete with its daily settings from *U-110* in May, 1941. Within a week British cryptanalysts were reading and decyphering operational U-boat signal traffic almost as quickly as the German recipients.

The Polish destroyer was British-built, at Cowes, and was launched in October, 1936. At 2,011 tons she was larger than the British Tribal Class and at full load she registered 3,383 tons. She was converted to four 4-inch and four 20mm AA guns at the end of 1941 and was often regarded as a light AA cruiser. With a designed speed of 39 knots she was the fastest destroyer in the world when built.

Captain Boutwood received another signal early that morning. It reported

Queen Mary being two hours behind schedule. This delay increased his concern for the destroyers, so he ordered them to turn about to an easterly course at 0800 and to screen ahead of *Queen Mary* at 16 knots. Thus the liner would be closing the escorts at a differential speed of something like ten knots.

It is evident, however, that Boutwood was concerned over his own cruiser's speed capabilities. It is reported that after detaching the destroyers he turned *Curacoa* about simply to satisfy himself that the cruiser could steam acceptably at 25 knots with a following sea, and having done so, turned about again to head for his 'convoy', *Queen Mary*, at 13 knots.

A little before 0900 one of the ADP lookouts reported an aircraft flying towards them. It was soon identified as a Flying Fortress which for an hour had been giving air support to the liner. The aircraft soon signalled the liner's position. *Curacoa* altered course towards – slightly to the north, and at about 0900 the great grey funnels were sighted at a range of fifteen miles, while the liner herself was still hull down over the horizon.

The ships were approaching each other at a considerable rate of knots and at 0925 Boutwood altered course 180 degrees, taking up an easterly heading, at the same time increasing revolutions to work up to 25 knots.

Matters were progressing as intended and by about 1000 *Curacoa* was nicely positioned about five miles dead ahead of *Queen Mary*. The cruiser was closely approaching 25 knots while the liner astern of her was on a zigzag course giving a speed of advance on a mean course of 26½ knots. The 81,237-ton super liner was steaming up towards her escort, overtaking at a rate of about 1½ knots. and it is arithmetically simple to calculate that by about 1400 the liner would have caught up with the cruiser.

Aboard the liner's bridge, from a seemingly Olympian height of 80 feet above the sea, all was calm and normal. It had been a safe and comfortable passage, the aircraft was a comfort now the most dangerous part of the passage lay ahead. And the cruiser, too, was a comfort, small though she appeared from the height of *Queen Mary's* bridge. The destroyers in the far distance seemed even more minuscule.

At 1130 Boutwood's signalman flashed a signal by hand lamp: 'REQUEST YOUR PRESENT COURSE AND SPEED MADE GOOD'. The reply from the liner was: '108 degrees, 26½ knots'. In point of fact this was not strictly true. The 108 degrees was wrong. *Queen Mary's* gyro compass was reading two degrees high, so her true course was 106 degrees.

The speed, of course, was the mean speed. We know that her actual speed was 28½ knots, but her speed of advance on the mean course of 106 degrees was 26½ knots.

Boutwood was aware, of course, that *Queen Mary* was operating Zigzag No. 8 without having to be told. On the liner's previous visit to Gourock Boutwood had met Captain Illingworth and the Master had expressed a preference for Zigzag No. 8. He considered it suited *Queen Mary* very well and it would be the one he would adopt. Thus, although only discussed in a fairly casual manner, there was no dispute between the captains as to which it would be.

What has not been made clear is whether Boutwood knew on which leg of the zigzag *Queen Mary* was engaged once the escort had joined the liner, although the cruiser's navigator, Tony Johnson, must surely have plotted the liner's course and satisfied himself and his captain on this point.

If we apply Zigzag No. 8 (see p.83) to *Queen Mary's* true course of 106 degrees we get this situation: this mean course would be adopted for four minutes, followed by eight minutes on 081 degrees (i.e. an alteration to port of 25 degrees). Then a large turn to starboard to 131 degrees for another eight minutes before resuming the mean course of 106 degrees for four minutes. Course was then altered to starboard, back to 131 degrees, for eight minutes, then a large alteration of fifty degrees to a heading of 081 degrees. All these alterations aggregated forty minutes, completing the zigzag. The sequence would be operated unremittingly, without alteration, three times every two hours, and repeated over and over again across the Atlantic.

Boutwood, meanwhile, had stationed *Curacoa* as close as safety allowed to the liner because experience during the war had demonstrated that closeness was one of the first requirements of such an AA escort. The position was to the south of the liner and the cruiser's course was 108 degrees.

It is apparent that Boutwood and Johnson needed to watch the situation very closely. They were not helped by the strengthening following sea which tended to increase yawing and made station-keeping tricky.

At 12.30 Boutwood signalled *Queen Mary*: 'I AM DOING MY BEST SPEED TWENTY-FIVE KNOTS ON COURSE 108. WHEN YOU ARE AHEAD I WILL EDGE IN ASTERN OF YOU.'

Illingworth was to remember this signal well. He was faintly amused at the expression 'edge in astern of you,' which is not a phrase he could remember being used in such a situation.

At midday the watches had changed on the bridge of *Queen Mary*. The Junior First Officer (who was also the navigating officer) was Stanley Joseph Wright. He had held the forenoon watch and was relieved by the Senior First Officer, Noel Robinson. Wright passed over the watch to him, giving details of the watch, courses, zigzag, position of the cruiser, which was clearly visible only a few cables away, fine on the starboard bow. He then went below to have lunch.

Robinson was a capable 34-year-old officer. He had with him on the bridge the Third Officer, Albert Hewitt, Junior Officer of the Watch, whose navigational duties confined him mainly to the charthouse. Also on the bridge was Junior Third Officer William Douglas Heighway, an Australian, who was engaged in his calculations for the noonday sun sight he had just taken. Heighway retired to the charthouse to work out the sight and fix the noonday position.

Two quartermasters were on duty, to take turns in steering the ship. Theirs was a disciplined and responsible job. The quartermaster on the wheel was John Lockhart. Every few minutes, as determined by the zigzag, an alarm bell on the zigzag clock would ring alongside the quartermaster to alert him to change course. The new course was displayed on the zigzag chart which gave in three columns the time, the number of degrees of alteration and the new course.

The quartermaster then buzzed the officer of the watch, and he would confirm, or otherwise, the alteration before the quartermaster would apply the change. This occurred, as we have seen, six times every forty minutes throughout the twenty-four hours of every day. It was repetitively tedious, but a valuable safeguard.

Also on the bridge were two ordinary seamen as bridge boys, a lookout and a signalman. And high up in the crow's-nest there was a lookout with an unmatched view of everything around him.

Captain Boutwood seemed content and at 1230 he went below for half an hour to take an early lunch. Some have expressed criticism of this action. One wrote bluntly, 'If I had been the captain I would have had sandwiches on the bridge.' But there is no hint of a suggestion that his leaving the bridge between 1230 and 1300 contributed in any way to what was to occur.

When he returned to the bridge the Flying Fortress was leaving, exposing the liner to further risk as the likelihood of air attack increased the closer the ship got to the Clyde. Understandably Boutwood wished to keep as close to the liner as he could. He realized that the course of 108 degrees his cruiser was steering was allowing her to drift too far to the south: the two ships were diverging slightly because of the extra two degrees. To rectify this he changed course from 108 to 105 degrees and when this seemed not to remedy the situation he came round further to 100 degrees. This had the required effect and he altered back to 108 degrees. Indeed, these 'touches on the tiller' took the cruiser, still a few cables ahead of the liner, across her line of advance. So much so that *Queen Mary* cut across the cruiser's wake, placing the cruiser fine on the liner's port bow.

In the *Queen Mary's* wheelhouse at 1332 the zigzag bell rang. John Lockhart had the wheel and reached to press the buzzer to let the officer of the watch, Noel Robinson, on the bridge above, know that the next alteration of course was due. He called out the course they were to come to through the voice pipe. Peter Padfield captures the scene:

> 'Robinson told him to carry on, and he swung the spokes over to port and watched as the lubber line on the gyro compass followed, clicking off the degrees as the figures wound off to the right.
>
> 'Robinson was staring ahead at the cruiser. They [the *Queen Mary*] had cut across her wake a minute before so that she was on the port bow, yawing wildly at times, rolling and plunging in the

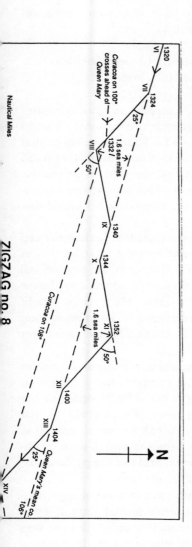

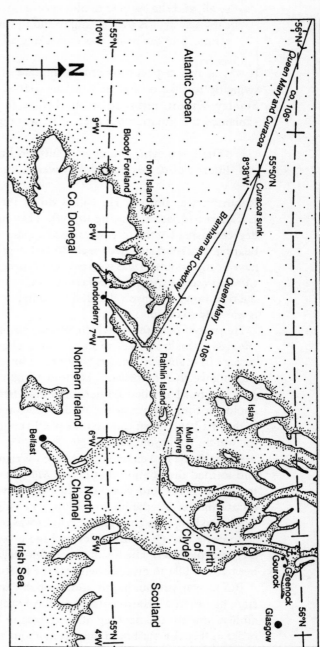

ZIGZAG no. 8

83

swell, and she seemed to him very close – only about three or four cables away – as they swung round towards her – well under half-a-mile, and the *Mary* was overtaking all the time.'*

It was at this critical moment in the fate of two ships, with *Queen Mary* swinging to take up her new zigzag course, that the Junior First Officer, Stanley Wright, returned to the bridge to relieve Robinson. Robinson explained the situation but even as he was doing so:

> 'The bows came round even further, bringing *Curacoa* finer and finer to port: he decided they were coming too close.'

Robinson was uneasy. He called down the voicepipe to Quartermaster Lockhart to check the swing to port. They had only turned some 25 to 30 degrees instead of the fifty prescribed and he told Lockhart to steady on that bearing. Lockhart steadied on about 101 degrees instead of the 081 it should have been. Robinson was worried about running into the stern of the cruiser. *Curacoa* was between one and two points (eleven or twenty-two degrees) on the port bow. Robinson decided to complete the turn when he judged that it was safe to do so.

He passed over the watch to Wright quite competently: he had noticed *Curacoa's* small changes of course as if she was keeping to some sort of zigzag. In reality, it was probably the cruiser's yawing in the heavy swell which gave this impression. He told Wright they were on the fifty degree port leg, but had checked her on course 101 degrees. He thought Wright could get round quite safely. And Robinson reminded Wright that as soon as they had overtaken *Curacoa* she would edge in astern. Having passed over the watch, Robinson went below.

Now that he had charge of the watch Wright looked intently at the cruiser and formed the opinion that *Queen Mary* could complete her swing round to 081 degrees and gave a rather tentative 'Port a little' order to the quartermaster. As the liner took up her swing again, Wright could see that Robinson had been correct: the cruiser was too close for comfort. Almost as soon as he had given the order and the bows began to swing, he immediately steadied her. The heading was 086 degrees. Still not happy, he eased her back to 081 to give himself and the liner a bit of searoom.

But he was still not happy and, probably with a rising sense of apprehension, he ordered, 'Hard-a-starboard!' Anyway, he comforted himself, it was almost time for the next leg of the zigzag to be implemented. But the very order of 'Hard-a-starboard' imparted a touch of emergency to the situation. Captain Illingworth was sitting in the chartroom hunched over the chart, plotting the noon position: the chartroom was at the back of the bridge on

* *An Agony of Collisions* by Peter Padfield, Hodder & Stoughton, 1966, p. 113.

15. One of the 170-odd North-about convoys escorted by HMS *Curacoa* 1940-41, taken from the cruiser. *(A. E. Corlett)*

16. Lieutenant Douglas Bodger RNVR, the gunnery officer who went down with the ship. He was previously aboard HMS *Cairo*, when he was mentioned in despatches.
(Mrs Olive Croft)

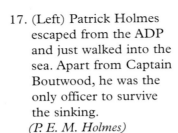

17. (Left) Patrick Holmes escaped from the ADP and just walked into the sea. Apart from Captain Boutwood, he was the only officer to survive the sinking.
(P. E. M. Holmes)

18. (Below left) Bill Woods (on the right) was lost in the sinking. Harry Bell (without jumper) and Bob Markham lived to tell the tale.
(R. Markham)

19. (Below) Electrical Artificer John Sewell was the only Electrical Artificer to be saved.
(Mrs Sewell)

20. 'Soldier' Cole was
Captain of Marines
aboard *Curacoa*. He
and Sub-Lieutenant
Caldwell were both
lost in the collision.
(*P. E. M. Holmes*)

21. Able Seaman Jimmy
Green was the
Communications
Number on the
ADP. He was
drowned on this
42nd birthday.
(*R. Markham*)

22. The massive bows of the *Queen Mary* in 1940.
(Frank O. Banyard Collection)

3. Boat drill aboard *Queen Mary* was largely a case of going through the motions. This is a view from the bridge. At the time of the *Curacoa* incident she had 10,239 people aboard, plus 900 crew. *(Cunard Archives, University of Liverpool)*

4. Bunks were stacked several high to accommodate the thousands of GIs packed into the one-time luxury liner. *(Cunard Archives, University of Liverpool)*

25. Captain C. G. Illingworth was Master of the *Queen Mary* at the time [of] the disaster. 'Ha[ve we] been bombed?' asked the Quartermaster. ['No,] Sir; we hit the c[ruiser.'] He later became [Sir Gordon, Commo]dore of the Cunard-W[hite] Star Line.
(Cunard Archive[s, University of Liv[erpool)

26. An early wartim[e] photograph of t[he] 81,000-ton Que[en] Mary in sombr[e] paint, displaying [none] of the splendou[r of its] five-star transat[lantic] passages.
(Cunard Archive[s, University of Liv[erpool)

27. Boutwood in the full dress uniform of a Royal Navy Lieutenant during the 1920's *(Peter Boutwood)*

28. Captain John Wilfred Boutwood, Commanding Officer of *Curacoa* at the time of the collision, photographed in 1942 with his son Jeremy. *(Jeremy Boutwood)*

29. This extraordinary photograph shows the for'ard two-thirds of HMS *Curacoa* immediately after she had been sliced in two by the *Queen Mary*. It was taken by an American GI. Only the cruiser's surface radar tower and mainmast are recognizable.
(*P. E. M. Holmes*)

30. The bows that cut through a cruiser. The result of the collision: the liner's stem was severely damaged for about 20 feet.
(*Cunard Archives, University of Liverpool*)

the port side. He heard Wright's order and with the innate sense of a responsible captain, captured the urgency:

'What's the matter, Wright?' Illingworth emerged from the chartroom and advanced to the front of the bridge.

'I don't like this cruiser, sir. She's a bit too close for me.'

'Well, let's have a look at her.'

Illingworth immediately went to the port wing, studied the cruiser for a moment or so and quickly formed the opinion that the *Queen Mary* could cross quite safely under *Curacoa's* stern. He judged that she was not as close as Robinson and Wright had imagined.

'No, that's all right,' he reassured the watchkeeping officer in his booming voice. 'Put your helm amidships and come back on the port leg.'

Wright gave the necessary order down the voicepipe to Lockhart, who reversed the wheel. Padfield reported:

> 'The great bows eased off their swing to starboard and came round again towards the stern of the cruiser. She came right ahead at between a third of a mile and half-a-mile distant and then the *Mary's* bows went past and left her well over to starboard as she settled on her proper course of 081 degrees. The time was one thirty-eight, six minutes after the alteration had become due.'*

After a short, desultory chat about general matters, Illingworth further assured Wright, 'You needn't worry about her. These fellows know all about escorting. He will keep out of your way.'

It was a confident, complimentary and well-intentioned comment. It is tragic that it was so wrong. But it was also a significant remark and incident which was to be crucial to the Admiralty's case in the subsequent litigation in the years ahead. It revealed, too, quite clearly Captain Illingworth's frame of mind. It was clearly evident that he believed *Curacoa* would 'keep out of your way'. *Queen Mary*, in his view, was the stand-on vessel, with right of way.

While the officers on *Queen Mary's* bridge were kept alert by their many mental calculations of time and courses, speeds of the two ships and their proximity, the men aboard *Curacoa's* bridge were probably similarly occupied.

Boutwood's tactics were dictated by circumstances, firstly by his lack of speed, secondly by the need to position his AA cruiser close to her charge, and thirdly by the weather and sea conditions. It was a tricky matter, but Boutwood had faced it many times before and he knew that the best position for defending the liner against air attack would be about half a mile astern of the *Queen*. But if he took up such a position *Curacoa* would soon be miles

---

* Padfield, op. cit., p. 113.

astern. Half a mile in naval terms, especially when involving a *Queen*, was uncomfortably close, indeed, with the seas that were running at the time, almost alarmingly so.

However, Boutwood was experienced in these matters and had long years of experience at sea to call upon. He had every reason to be satisfied with the morning's situation. The rendezvous had been accomplished satisfactorily. His tactics that morning were working out well enough. The liner was zigzagging astern, gradually closing the gap between the ships – all as planned. *Curacoa* was well stationed to give close AA cover if required. *Queen Mary* would soon be in a position to overtake her escort and allow Boutwood to 'edge in astern' while the destroyers were steaming some miles ahead giving distant cover. As *Queen Mary* would gradually pull ahead of *Curacoa* so she would close the gap to the destroyers who would then assume an AA protection for her.

At the very moment when Captain Illingworth was reassuring Junior First Officer Wright Captain Boutwood was on *Curacoa's* bridge looking astern at the huge mass of the liner.

On the bridge with Boutwood was his Navigating Officer, Lieutenant Anthony Johnson, the Officer of the Watch, Lieutenant John Maxwell, and the Principal Control Officer, Lieutenant Norman Brittain RNVR, along with bridge lookouts, a bridge messenger, Norman Good, and Leading Signalman Donald Eaton. The ADP above the bridge was fully manned and Patrick Holmes had the afternoon watch with his team of lookouts. Well aft a good number of off-duty crew men had assembled on the upper deck to gaze at the huge liner so close astern but gradually overtaking the cruiser, dwarfing her with the towering bows and superstructure, deck upon deck, on to which American troops crowded. Faces appeared at every porthole all anxious to get their first sight of a British warship.

Everything seemed to be progressing exactly as Captain Boutwood intended.

The officers on the cruiser's bridge were professionals, apparently unworried by the proximity of their charge, evidently in command of the situation, viewing the liner's movements closely, constantly taking bearings, unperturbed by their own ship's yawing, anything up to seven degrees either side of her mean course.

Boutwood viewed it all placidly enough, although he and his officers had some doubt whether *Queen Mary* was maintaining an absolutely steady course. Even the liner was yawing in the sea conditions that afternoon.

At 1340 *Queen Mary* straightened up on to her mean course, fine on the cruiser's port quarter. She maintained course and speed for four minutes before making an alteration to port on the next leg of the zigzag. She continued on this diverging course for another eight minutes. At 1352 she ominously turned fifty degrees to starboard, towards the cruiser.

By now *Queen Mary* was steadily overtaking *Curacoa*; she was coming up from the cruiser's port quarter until she was parallel, on the port side, practically abeam.

Close though the two ships were to each other no mental alarm bells were ringing. Boutwood himself was taking compass bearings and estimated that *Queen Mary* was overtaking at 1½ knots. He was to recall later that it seemed for much of this time that *Queen Mary* was roughly on a parallel course and appeared to have abandoned her zigzag in order to overtake *Curacoa*.

But Boutwood says he was content. At 1355 he signalled Illingworth: 'PLEASE GIVE ME YOUR ESTIMATED TIME OF ARRIVAL AT TOWARD POINT' [on the Firth of Clyde].

At 1400 *Queen Mary* was seen by Boutwood to alter course on to her mean course, parallel with *Curacoa*, her stern almost abeam, about five cables or 1,000 yards to port. This alteration of course was carried out by Quartermaster John Leydon, who a minute before had taken over the wheel from Lockhart. It would take a little while, probably three minutes, for the troopship to come round on to her new course, and almost as soon as this was effected, at 1404, a further alteration of 25 degrees to starboard became due.

Matters were now heading towards zero, the point at which a collision would occur, and with the benefit of historical hindsight it seems inconceivable that it should have happened under the prevailing conditions.

There seems to have been some slackness of a minor nature which is mildly disturbing. Captain Boutwood, it appears, was not even sure who was the captain of *Queen Mary* for this voyage. Neither did he or his navigator appear to have known precisely which leg of the zigzag the liner was following. Aboard *Queen Mary* Illingworth assumed Boutwood would know Zigzag No. 8 was being operated. It is a little disquieting to learn that Boutwood relied upon his own timepiece rather than the bridge clock, and that clocks between the cruiser and the liner had not been synchronized, or at least compared with each other.

More importantly, of course, is the direct conflict of opinion as to whose right of way it was. Illingworth felt convinced that as *Queen Mary* constituted the convoy then his ship was the stand-on vessel, with right of way.

Equally firm was Boutwood's conviction that *Curacoa*, being the over-taken vessel, had the right of way and it was *Queen Mary's* duty to steer clear. These represented two diametrically opposed views, held by two professional seafarers with thousands of men's lives in their hands.

Other factors were beginning to come together in a fateful fashion. On the cruiser's bridge at about four minutes past two the bridge messenger, Norman Good, was sufficiently awed by the proximity of the *Queen* that he had the temerity to report what to him appeared glaringly obvious.

Boutwood, Maxwell and Johnson now began to have stirrings of doubt. As the liner overtook *Curacoa* they were doubtful about the course she held.

Curacoa, we know, was yawing. Lieutenant Johnson, the navigator, observed at one stage:

'I think she's turning. Or is it only a yaw?'

The fact of the matter was that, at that crucial moment, the officers on the cruiser's bridge had no idea of the course the liner was taking, which leg of the zigzag she was on, whether she had abandoned her zigzag, whether any of these changes, if changes they were, were temporary or permanent.

No signals were passing between the two ships which might have clarified the situation, but by now it was too late to pass a signal and receive a reply.

Boutwood took the commonsense view of the situation – if, in the presence of an alarming closeness of two ships at sea, anyone can take such a view – that Illingworth (or whoever was captaining the liner) would be fully conscious of the fact that *Curacoa* must have held her course steady if she was to keep up. The master would be well aware that *Curacoa* was not zigzagging. Further, Boutwood knew with conviction, as all watchkeeping officers would know, even with a cursory knowledge of the Rules governing Collision at Sea, that no overtaking ship approaching from astern would ever alter course, as *Mary* seemed now to be doing, in such a manner as to endanger the overtaken ship.

At four minutes past two o'clock aboard *Queen Mary* Stanley Wright considered the cruiser uncomfortably close, on an approximately parallel course, but he was comforted somewhat by his Captain's assurance that 'he will keep out of your way'.

Wright had been told to keep to the zigzag, so when Leydon advised him of the need to alter course, Wright gave permission for Leydon to do so. Thus *Queen Mary* was brought round from the mean course of 106 degrees to the starboard leg of the zigzag with a heading of 131 degrees.

At that moment Albert Hewitt, the Junior Officer, returned to the bridge having had his lunch. Looking ahead to the far horizon he could see the masts of the escorting destroyers. He then saw *Curacoa* unnervingly close, hardly two cables or so away, on a converging course, indeed, so close that for a moment he thought she was approaching to use her loud hailer. He walked out on the starboard wing of the bridge with his telescope to see if he could recognize anyone on the bridge, but he couldn't, although he did see one officer operating a camera. He swept the telescope the whole length of the cruiser but, beyond the worrying closeness of the ships, saw nothing amiss.

William Heighway recalled these moments many years later:

'At 2.04 p.m. the *Mary* altered course twenty-five degrees to starboard from her mean course. The cruiser was now about a mile away, about forty-five degrees on our starboard bow and both ships on converging courses. About four or five minutes later an officer returning from lunch looked at the *Curacoa* through a telescope and said to the Senior Officer and me that there was an officer on the bridge of *Curacoa* taking photographs of us. . . . I have wondered many times what bearing, if any, the photographing incident had on the situation. Did the officer's comment tend to reassure us that the cruiser was only standing in to take photographs and that she would sheer away at any moment? Had it not been made would we have taken action that would have avoided the collision?'*

By the time that the new course of 131 degrees had been taken up one of those small coincidental but fateful factors occurred. Noel Robinson finished his lunch and walked through the wheelhouse to the starboard wing of the bridge ready to relieve Wright. At that moment Wright was leaving the bridge for the chartroom in answer to the Captain's call. It was eight or nine minutes past two.

The watch was passed over in a very perfunctory manner within a minute or two. Wright did not even refer to the cruiser, despite her proximity; presumably both took her for granted. William Heighway recalled the incident:

> 'The Captain called Wright from the chartroom. He was thus unable to hand over the watch. There would have been no collision had Wright been on the bridge! Hindsight: Wright should have remained on the bridge and sent me (the Junior Officer) into the chartroom with the appropriate explanation as to why he remained on the bridge.'†

Wright joined the Captain who was working on the message in response to Boutwood's signal about the estimated time of arrival in the Clyde. In the course of their conversation Wright made no reference to Illingworth about the closeness of *Curacoa*.

Robinson quite properly took stock of the situation. In fact he had inherited the responsibility of one of the world's greatest liners with more than 10,000 souls aboard converging at 28½ knots upon a cruiser barely two cables or 400 yards away.

William Heighway had finished taking his sight and was on the bridge wing looking at the cruiser far below in the turbulent sea. He reported to Robinson the earlier incident about the cruiser keeping out of the way and of Wright not completing the zigzag and the Captain's instructions: 'The Captain says the zigzag legs are to be carried out in full'.

Robinson checked in the wheelhouse to see that John Leydon was holding

---

*   *The Etruscan*, 2 December, 1969, Letter to the editor.
†   Padfield, op. cit. pp. 114–5n.

his course steady. He checked the repeater compass and the course was steady at 131 degrees. On the bridge again he reckoned *Curacoa* was about 45 degrees on the starboard bow, about 400 yards distant, unnecessarily close, and just to be on the safe side, he ordered 'Port a little'. So that *Queen Mary* would ease off away from the cruiser. It was a precautionary action: mental alarms were not yet ringing. The situation still appeared to be in hand. Robinson expected, anyway, that *Curacoa* would starboard her helm and she would swing clear. Hers would be a swifter response to a helm order than would be *Queen Mary's*.

Robinson strolled over to the wheelhouse door to see that Leydon had applied the wheel properly to port and, satisfied, returned to watch the cruiser. What he saw alarmed him. Suddenly she was dangerously close. As she rolled in the swell he could see down her funnels. She was still closing. He yelled the order 'Hard-a-port!'

Such an order always carries with it a sense of emergency. Leydon immediately swung the wheel over as fast as he could. But there was nothing in the world that he or anyone else could possibly do to avert tragedy. *Queen Mary* crashed into and through *Curacoa* with the finality of a guillotine.

We left the cruiser at about four minutes past two o'clock with the afternoon watch officers and lookouts closely observing *Queen Mary* come round on to her starboard leg of the zigzag to a heading of 131 degrees – and converging. She made a magnificent sight despite her battleship grey paint. So splendid was the sight that Leading Signalman Donald Eaton on the bridge spoke through a voicepipe to his friend Telegraphist Allin Martin who had just come on watch at 2 o'clock relieving the duty telegraphist on the lower bridge radio office. Martin recalls:

> 'Shortly afterwards the upper bridge speaking tube clanged and my "oppo" indicated that if any camera was to hand a particularly good view of the *Queen Mary* was available. Unclipping the bulkhead door, I stepped outside, where, to my horror, I saw the enormous bulk of the *Queen Mary* bearing down on our port quarter at about fifty yards range. Her huge white bow wave seemed as tall as a house and it seemed inevitable we were within seconds of being torn apart. I dived inside for my lifebelt.'*

Boutwood watched the approaching liner, wondering whether she was yawing or actually turning to starboard. As he himself explained later, just to be on the safe side, he ordered 'Starboard 15'. He still felt that the liner would keep out of his way – he had the absolute conviction of knowing he was in the right – that *Queen Mary*, the overtaking vessel should keep clear

---

* *Passenger Ships of the Cunard Line*, by Neil McCart, Patrick Stephens, 1989.

of the overtaken ship. He gave the wheel order 'in a moment of no concern'.

But the two ships still converged.

Robinson, on the liner's bridge, was waiting for some evidence that the cruiser would keep out of the way. But she held fast.

The realization of impending disaster must have struck everyone concerned at about the same moment. Boutwood suddenly saw the danger as the ships approached each other 'at a considerable and alarming rate,' and he formally took control of his ship from the officer of the watch.

Robinson probably realized the danger at the identical moment. By then it was too late. It did not matter now what Robinson or Boutwood did. The moment when likelihood of collision turned to certainty had passed some moments before.

The Quartermaster in *Queen Mary* kept the wheel hard over to port but it took what seemed an age for the huge bows to head round. The officers on the liner's bridge looked in mounting horror as it became evident *Curacoa* was holding her course and not attempting to give way. By then even Boutwood had given the emergency order 'Hard-a-starboard!' It would take a few moments for the cruiser to answer the helm in those seas.

Heighway could see the faces of the officers on the bridge, earlier gazing in wonder, but now staring with horror. And then Heighway could hardly believe his eyes. He thought he saw the cruiser begin to turn – *to port*.

Within seconds, they struck.

The mighty bows with 81,000 tons of ship behind them, speeding at 30 mph smashed into and right through the cruiser, scything the ship in two.

At that moment of hiatus aboard *Queen Mary's* bridge the zigzag clock rang. It was exactly twelve minutes past two. The time of the tragedy was fixed with navigational precision, although, curiously, Boutwood's timings are taken from his own watch whereas *Queen Mary's* are from her bridge clock. They differed. Seconds before the crash the liner's bows perceptively began to respond to her wheel) or was it another yaw? – but by then it was too late. Seconds before the collision Boutwood realized *Curacoa* had no time to respond to his helm order, that it had been too late, and that disaster was now inevitable.

The liner's bows had struck *Curacoa* about 140 – 150 ft from her stern (she was 450 ft long) on the port side at an angle variously estimated at between 20 and 40 degrees.

THE COLLISION: STRUGGLING FOR SURVIVAL

'Those on the bridge of the *Queen Mary* at the time of the collision will perhaps find some consolation in the thought that it had probably taken the efforts of the best legal brains engaged in the practice and administration of Admiralty law just about as many weeks as they had seconds in which to decide what was the correct action to be taken in the circumstances.'

Captain W.H. Coombs, President of the Merchant Navy Officers' Federation.

The gigantic stem had knifed through the three-inch steel armour of the cruiser, cutting her in half, allowing *Queen Mary* to bulldoze her way through, unchecked, with barely a jolt, shouldering aside the stern part of the cruiser to pass down the liner's starboard side, while the forepart passed down the port side like a huge mass of flotsam.

At the moment of impact *Curacoa* heeled over practically on her beam ends, the sternmost part floated away, the propellers pointing skywards, idly rotating while the stern was gently sinking.

The forepart slowly righted itself and for a fleeting moment Boutwood even thought there might be a slim chance of saving the ship. As he clung for dear life to the bridge, almost as quickly the thought evaporated.

The scene was one of indescribable chaos and the speed of events was breathtaking. The crashing roar of jolting and tearing metal joined with the screeching scream of escaping steam from severed steam pipes. What some people thought was smoke from fires was believed to be masses of soot blown out from the funnels: it enveloped everything.

Sailors from the severed parts of the ship were jumping, diving, scrambling, and even walking for their lives into the sea.

From their vantage point high above the liner's main deck American GIs were stunned by witnessing such a disaster. Many had the presence of mind to rush to the rails and cast overboard whatever lifebelts and lifebuoys they could lay their hands on. Others ripped off their life jackets and hurled them into the sea. Almost before this could be done the stern part of the cruiser, now some hundreds of yards away from the forepart, disappeared, and within five or six minutes of the crash, the forepart, too, with the majority of the ship's company, had sunk beneath the sea.

Eye witnesses aboard *Queen Mary* included an American sergeant major, Philip Levin of New York. He has left us with this account:

'October 2nd was a superbly clear day. We could just about see the Irish coast. . . . I was in the office on the main deck at the time and felt only the slightest rattle and vibration. Actually, it seemed quite normal. But word of the collision spread quickly, like wild-fire through the ship. I raced to the open upper decks and looked aft to see the two halves of the *Curacoa* drifting in our wake and then rather quickly sinking. . . . The *Mary* simply continued, unin-terrupted and at relatively high speed. We were twenty miles west of Bloody Foreland in Ireland. Word was that if the *Mary's* damage had penetrated another two feet some $2 million in gold bullion would have been lost. The valued cargo was in a forward compartment and was being delivered to General Mark Clark and was then to be paid to the French forces in Morocco. When we reached Gourock, concrete was poured into the great dent in the *Queen Mary's* bows.'*

The report is inaccurate in many respects but as a contemporary statement is worth reporting. The witness's conjecture about a U-boat scare has been deleted as totally erroneous, the position should read forty miles, not twenty, and the gold bullion story has not been verified.

A diarist, A.W. Masson, made this entry for Friday, 2 October, 1942:

'The cruiser took station ahead of us . . . at 2.10 p.m. when passing from starboard to port we rammed and sank her. She sank in less than ten minutes. Geordie Reed and I were just leaving the weather deck, when we felt the bump (which incidentally was very slight). We rushed out on deck, and I was just in time to see the cruiser's quarterdeck and after turret passing down our starboard side. It was covered in oil and there was no one to be seen. I rushed aft and saw both parts of the cruiser, her stern sticking up, looking for all the world like the *Indefatigable* at Jutland! The forepart of the ship was at a distance to the right. The cruiser had been rammed just aft of the after funnel. It was covered in a heavy pall

---

* *Transatlantic Liners at War*, W.H. Miller and D.F. Hutchings, David & Charles, 1985, p. 51.

of smoke and steam, then slowly it sank by the bows, then it reared its bow perpendicular – and with a little water foaming round her, she quickly sank. I did not notice what happened to the afterpart. Much later two of the escorts went racing towards the scene. We did not slacken speed at the time of the accident but later on we cut down to about 15 knots.'

Again, the errors do not detract from a useful contemporary document. Three escorts actually raced to the scene of disaster, and the liner did, of course, reduce speed, first to 10 knots and then 13. Masson is specific that Ireland was sighted at 4.30 p.m. whereas Levin implies it was earlier. A twenty-year-old GI has given a graphic account:

'I was below deck . . . slightly seasick, and lying in my bunk on 'A' deck when someone came in and said, "You guys ought to come up on deck and see the British navy escort we have picked up." In his words: "Looks like the whole British navy is out there."

'I put my heavy army overcoat on which happened to have my small folding "Jiffey Kodak" 620 camera in a pocket. I was standing at the rail or open window on the port side of the *Queen Mary* for only a few minutes when the *Curacoa* crossed very close in front of the *Queen* from port to starboard and disappeared [from view]. A short time later we felt a slight shudder and almost immediately the *Curacoa* appeared in front of us and appeared trying to right herself from the blow of the collision. From the height of our position standing on the deck we could look down on the *Curacoa* with the jagged, broken section toward us.

'After just a moment of stunned unrealisation of what had happened . . . I managed to take a picture. . . . I carried the film in my camera while we were in Northern Ireland until the next February and then sometime later took it out of the camera and kept it several months undeveloped, not wanting to have it confiscated – and I had no way to get it developed until later, after we had moved to North Africa.'*

It was the summer of 1943 before Olen Medley managed to get the film developed and he was rewarded with the dramatic, almost indecipherable picture of the forepart of the cruiser as she scraped and washed down the liner's port side.

As soon as the ships collided Captain Boutwood yelled to his officers to get the men up from down below and abandon ship, but no one could make

* Letter from Olen L. Medley of Oklahoma City to Geoffrey Carter, survivor, dated 7 December, 1989.

themselves heard in the cacophony. And anyway the cry to abandon ship was academic; it was evident to all but the blinkered that the ship was doomed and sinking fast. It was every man for himself from the moment of impact.

Down below in *Queen Mary's* between decks and in the engine room the tragedy had registered as a mere bump, like hitting a large wave.

In the liner's chartroom a few moments before the crash Stanley Wright had checked Illingworth's calculations for the liner's estimated time of arrival at Toward Point on the Clyde, in response to Boutwood's signal of enquiry. Wright agreed: 'I think that's about as accurate as we can get it, sir.' Illingworth replied: 'I think so, too. Send for the signalman and make the signal.' At that very moment there was a discernible bump. Illingworth immediately thought the ship might have been hit by a bomb from an aircraft. He and Wright hurried to the bridge and Illingworth paused at the wheelhouse. 'Was that a bomb?' he asked Leydon. 'No, sir,' the quarter-master replied, 'we hit the cruiser.'

When they got to the bridge Illingworth could see the enormity of the disaster, although both parts of the ship were enveloped in thick yellow-black smoke and funnel soot.

Rightly, Illingworth gave immediate attention to his own ship. His responsibility was enormous. The lives of more than ten thousand men rested on his decisions.

Asleep in his sea cabin was Staff Captain Harry Grattidge. He was awakened by the jolt of the collision. He wrapped himself in his duffle coat, rammed his tin helmet on his head and rushed to the bridge in time to see the two parts of the cruiser sink astern.

Queen Mary continued to steam ahead at full speed despite the risk involved because of unknown damage to the liner's bows. Almost immediately Illingworth received a damage report from the Bosun: the damage was not alarming although the stem had been pushed back considerably. Illingworth despatched Grattidge for a more detailed examination and report, then reduced speed to ten knots as a precautionary measure.

'The speed was still on the ship when I reached the forepeak. By the light of a torch I could see the water racing in and out of the forepeak, a great column of it forming a kind of cushion from the collision bulkhead, the water-tight reinforced steel wall that rises from the very bottom of the ship to the main deck. If that bulkhead were weakened I did not like to think of the *Mary's* chances of survival. I sweated through my silent inspection. But finally, not a crack. Not a break. The bulkhead had held intact. I turned to the Bosun and the carpenter: "Get every length of wood you can find, Bosun. Get it down here and strengthen that collision bulkhead as much as you possibly can. I'll report to the Captain." . . .

I was sick at what we had done, yet I marvelled, too, at the strange and terrible impregnability of *Queen Mary*. It came home to me that she had no equal anywhere in the Atlantic, perhaps not anywhere in the world.'*

The Bosun's damage control party strengthened the crucial bulkhead with strong timber props and for a moment the safety of the liner seemed to be under control.

Illingworth, of course, was concerned for the 439 men of the cruiser, their plight desperately cruel judged by any standards; it now became even crueller. Illingworth was faced with an agonizing dilemma. His instructions were crystal clear. He was not to stop the ship under any circumstances. To do so would endanger the lives of more than ten thousand men and such a risk was totally unacceptable. Rather sacrifice a few hundred men than suffer the very real danger of being torpedoed by a lurking U-boat commander as she hove-to and lowered lifeboats or even turned about and steamed through the wreckage and survivors at slow speed to cast overboard floats and other life-saving equipment.

Common humanity, compassion and the comradeship of the sea impelled Illingworth to turn about for a rescue operation. But in a sense Illingworth knew exactly what he had to do. His own ship and her thousands of passengers were his prime responsibility.

In a scene reminiscent of the drama in Nicholas Monsarrat's novel *The Cruel Sea*, Illingworth increased speed to 13 knots, abandoned Zigzag No. 8 and left to their fate the struggling mass of survivors, perhaps a couple of hundred men, for the rest were probably already dead. He directed that the destroyers, still far ahead, should return to carry out the rescue operation, even though it might take a few hours for them to reach the men in the water. The senior officer aboard HMS *Bulldog* despatched the two Hunt Class destroyers *Bramham* and *Cowdray*, together with the elderly *Skate*, to pick up survivors.

A few minutes later, at 1420, a coded MOST SECRET signal was radioed to the C-in-C Western Approaches in Liverpool, repeated to the Admiralty: 'HMS CURACOA RAMMED AND SUNK BY QUEEN MARY IN POSITION 55.5ON 08.38W. QUEEN MARY DAMAGED FORWARD. SPEED TEN KNOTS.'

Captain Illingworth seems to have made up his mind about the circumstances of the collision without great difficulty: at 1424 the signalman on the liner's bridge had flashed by signal lamp to *Bulldog*: 'IT WOULD APPEAR THAT CURACOA ATTEMPTED TO CROSS MY BOWS WHEN COLLISION OCCURRED. AM REDUCING SPEED TO ASCERTAIN EXTENT OF DAMAGE AND HAVE CEASED ZIGZAG. WILL KEEP INFORMED.'

It was nearly an hour later, at 1519, when he signalled: 'AFTER CAREFUL

---

* *Captain of the Queens*, by Captain Harry Grattidge, Oldbourne Press, 1956.

CONSIDERATION CAN ONLY CONCLUDE CURACOA PUT HER HELM WRONG WAY.'

By then *Queen Mary* was well on her way to the Clyde and the rescue destroyers were plucking the survivors from the sea.

From Ballykelly, the naval signal station in Londonderry, a MOST SECRET signal was sent to the Admiralty: 'CURACOA SUNK 55.50N 08.56W. SURVIVORS INCLUDING CAPTAIN PICKED UP BY TWO DESTROYERS RETURNING LONDONDERRY. QUEEN MARY DESCRIBES HERSELF AS SLIGHTLY DAMAGED IN THE BOW. PROCEEDING AT SLOW SPEED IN COMPANY WITH FOUR DESTROYERS. . . . CAPTAIN CURACOA DOES NOT CONSIDER THERE ARE ANY MEN STILL ON RAFTS. AIRCRAFT WAS DIRECTED TO POSITION OF SINKING BY DESTROYER WHICH ADDED "U-BOAT PROBABLY STILL THERE". ALL DESTROYERS HOMEWARD BOUND.'

It was this inference of a U-boat's presence which probably gave rise to the repetitive, and erroneous, references in later reports.

We have followed the fortunes of *Queen Mary* and her officers to a convenient point, but at the expense of chronology. We need now to cast a glance back to the luckless *Curacoa*, to the moment of collision so we can follow the fortunes of the 439 men in her.

ESCAPES FROM DEATH

'a disastrous collision . . . a collision which never ought to have been permitted to occur.'

Mr Justice Pilcher, 21 January, 1947.

Apart from Captain Boutwood himself, the man with the best view of the impending disaster was probably Patrick Holmes from his privileged viewpoint in the Air Defence Position high above the bridge. He shared watches, four hours on and four hours off, with Captain John Cole, the Royal Marine officer aboard. Holmes' report is compelling:

'I was the Air Defence Officer. . . . I was in charge of twelve lookouts and Jimmy Green, the communications number. He was a great character and a typical three-badge AB [i.e. a long-serving crew member with no pretensions to promotion, earning good conduct "badges" looking like army stripes: three represented fifteen years' long service and good conduct.] His brother, I'm told, was a Captain RN – but I have not managed to confirm this.

'I came on watch at noon. John Cole disappeared through the hatch in the ADP and descended the ladder to the after part of the bridge, then down again to the iron deck abaft the fo'c'sle. It was the last time I ever saw him. It was thrilling to watch the "grey ghost" as the *Queen Mary* was nicknamed because of her wartime camouflage. She gained on us slowly, sometimes over a mile-and-a-half away on our port quarter, and at other times more or less dead astern on the starboard leg of her zigzag. There is no finer sight in the world than a great passenger ship at full speed in a heavy sea, even if the passengers were closely-packed American troops – over ten thousand of them.

'By 2 p.m. (1400 hours) she was nearly level with us about a mile away on our port side and steaming parallel with us. Then she turned slowly towards us and that turn of 25 degrees was at first misinterpreted on our bridge as merely a yaw to starboard. We got a magnificent view of her as she approached – her bow wave gleaming in a slant of sunlight, her decks crowded with GIs, wisps of smoke streaming from her three funnels.

'Suddenly my admiration turned to fear, and looking over my right shoulder down to our bridge I saw the captain take over the conning of the ship. I saw him speak down the voicepipe to the helmsman below, look back at *Queen Mary* and speak again.

'By now the sharp bows of the *Queen* were heading directly at us in the ADP and a few seconds later before she crashed through a hundred feet abaft us I shouted "Hang on!" But even so two of the lookouts disappeared over our starboard side as we were knocked over 70 degrees or more. Vast quantities of black smoke and soot poured from our two funnels. The noise of escaping steam from severed steam pipes was deafening. The forepart of the ship slowly returned to nearly upright. As I looked astern I saw what I thought at the time was a U-boat sinking, until I realized it was our own stern about half a mile away.'

Such is naval discipline that Jimmy Green asked Holmes' permission to go below and get his life jacket. Holmes had never known him not to have it on before. And this had to happen at a time when it immediately became obvious that the ship was sinking. After all the remaining young lookouts had gone through the ladder hatchway with their 'Mae Wests' blown up, Holmes gave a final quick look around, saw *Queen Mary* already about a mile away, ploughing on, and what seemed like scores of the crew already in the sea. Holmes continued:

'Dazed and shocked, I made my way down the ladder. Glancing below I saw "Pilot" Tony Johnson still on the bridge dutifully stuffing confidential books into weighted bags to ensure their sinking. Reaching the iron deck which was already awash I walked uphill under the fo'c'sle to tell anyone there to abandon ship. Lieutenant John Maxwell, my best friend, who was officer of the watch, was yelling, trying to make himself heard over the cacophony of sound, telling everyone to jump. He and I entered the water together. But I never saw him again. I can only assume he scrambled back on board, perhaps believing he had left the ship too soon.

'To be in the North Atlantic ocean in October, in almost any sort of weather, with hundreds of fathoms of water beneath one, and forty miles from land is daunting; but when I was off the ship and "in the drink" I found the size of the waves and the height and depth of the swell quite fearsome.'

Holmes swam away from the sinking ship on his back and watched the forepart slowly assume a vertical position and then, slowly at first, disappear into the depths. He felt alone. Up came vast quantities of thick black fuel oil to keep him company. Keeping his mouth and often his eyes closed he found a rolled-up flotanet. The oil made it impossible to release the lashings which would have allowed it to open and float like a carpet.

> 'Heaven knows where the lanyard to do this was. I was joined by two other unrecognizable blokes and Petty Officer Saywell, whom I noticed before we were so completely covered in oil. The four of us hung on like grim death. The trouble was one's grip on the oil-soaked ropes and corks kept slipping and suddenly, to my dismay, George Saywell was no longer there: he had just slipped away.
>
> 'After what seemed hours we sighted the upperworks of a destroyer, and then, when on the crest of the swell, a whaler pulling towards us. I was bundled into the bottom of the boat. I recovered sufficiently to scramble up the net hanging over the quarterdeck of HMS *Cowdray*. In all over twenty of us were picked up . . . and nineteen survived. I was given a strong tot of rum. Later, wrapped in warm clothing, I was taken to see how the worst sufferers were faring. I fully recognized for the first time what a marvellous thing is the brotherhood of the sea.'

Holmes searched in vain for other surviving officers, especially John Maxwell, but was told that the only other officer alive was the Captain who was aboard *Bramham*. There were over seventy survivors aboard *Bramham*. *Skate* had recovered another ten. Holmes felt lucky and grateful to be alive, but deeply saddened by the loss of so many men, 338 out of 439. Holmes added: 'Especially Maxwell, Cole, Johnson, Vaughan and my cabin mate, Sub-Lieutenant Philip Brocklesby RNVR.'

Stoker 1st Class Allen Whalen, aboard *Cowdray*, recalls:

> 'By the time we reached the scene many were dead in the sea and the current was spreading them around for miles. They had died of hypothermia and choking by the thick oil fuel which had congealed like lumps of cart grease by the freezing water.'

We last encountered Telegraphist Allin Martin in the lower bridge radio office inflating his lifebelt after seeing *Queen Mary* about to strike the cruiser. The impact slammed him against the starboard bulkhead:

> 'I remember charging for the door through a mass of broken batteries, radio equipment etc, to reach the outer companionway

100

where I encountered my signalman "oppo" Leading Signalman Donald Eaton racing down from the upper bridge. At this time I remember seeing the starboard gun platform in seething water – this was normally about twenty feet above sea level – and it appeared that *Curacoa* had been rolled over on to her starboard side. Together we ran down to the main deck and picked our way aft to the foremost funnel where we located a wooden "paint ship" ladder which we hurled overboard and slithered after it. At this point I remember looking aft and seeing nothing beyond the after funnel. I reckoned that the stern had been sheared completely off and had already sunk. Scrambling down the sloping port side we grabbed the ladder, but so many other swimmers had the same idea that I decided to strike out and put my trust in my lifebelt. By this time the severed fuel tanks were disgorging oil so I aimed to make for clearer water. My oppo declined to follow and I never saw him again.'*

Martin swam away some distance from the scene of disaster, turned on his back to rest and survey the situation. The bow section of the ship pointed skywards, almost vertically. He reckoned perhaps thirty feet of the foredeck appeared to explode, hurling debris skywards. This was probably due to air being forced upwards internally by the pressure of the encroaching sea. As the bow section finally disappeared Martin saw a lone figure scrambling over the breakwater.

The sea was not particularly rough but there was a considerable swell running and each time Martin was lifted onto a peak he scanned anxiously for a sight of rescuing destroyers which he knew would have been alerted. After a short while the number of survivors had decreased appreciably. Floating debris littered the sea – oil drums, loose gear, woodwork, bodies and survivors, all in a welter of oil. He could see no Carley floats or lifeboats; there had been no time to release them:

> 'I recall the group nearest to me having several half-hearted attempts at community singing – I remember "Roll Out The Barrel". I remember an empty boot floating past, also an object the size of a football which I firmly believe to have been a disembodied head and which, in my blind panic to avoid, caused me to swallow a considerable quantity of sea water. I distinctly remember the dwindling number of swimmers, in particular a robust able seaman who just seemed to give up and quietly drown.'

* *Passenger Liners of the Cunard Line* by Neil McCart, p. 77.

Allin Martin was hauled aboard *Bramham* and remembers the lines of shrouded bodies ready for burial.

ERA Ted Beavis was off watch and alone in the engineer's workshop when disaster struck. Like many others he thought *Curacoa* had been torpedoed. Floodwater rose rapidly and Beavis merely waded into the sea, starboard side, waist deep in water, swam from the ship and hung on to a rolled up flotanet for what he reckons was two or two and a half hours. Such were the terrible conditions under which all the swimmers struggled for life that to this day Pat Holmes and Ted Beavis cannot say whether they were sharing the same flotanet.

One of the luckiest escapes was by Stoker Ken Huntley who was on watch in the after engine room with an ERA and Leading Hand. He managed to climb a series of ladders which led to a small compartment on the upper deck. He swam out of the door and was picked up by *Cowdray* about two hours later. He was taken down to the wardroom, temporarily converted to a sick bay, was checked over, washed down and given a stiff drink.

Kenneth Clarkson was asleep on the Stokers' mess deck table and when the collision awakened him his first reaction was that one of his mates was playing a prank. Still not aware of the true situation, he started to make for his action station aft. He was met by a rush of water in the port passageway by the boiler room. He made his way back to the sick bay flat where he was trapped until the door to the port waist freed itself as the ship righted herself. On reaching the upper deck he was washed overboard and swam away to avoid being sucked under. He was eventually picked up by *Cowdray* after hanging onto a flotanet.

Joe Murray was also asleep on a mess deck form when he awoke with a shock. Bewildered, but keeping his head, he was among those who slid down the port side of the fo'c'sle with his inflated lifejacket on. He hung on to a flotanet in the oily water and considers that several of those who climbed onto rafts suffered hypothermia. In his view it was warmer in the oily water. He was one of the few to be rescued by *Skate*. He was taken direct to Greenock, being transferred there to *Bulldog* on Saturday 3rd October, and on the Sunday to HMS *Argus* where the Board of Enquiry was empanelled. Murray was one of the very few who saw any of the officers. He recalls seeing a Lieutenant falling from the gun deck – presumably B gun – and a Sub-Lieutenant in the sea, neither of whom he can put a name to, and neither of whom survived.

Fred Woodger was another who walked down port side to the sea. He had been in the stokers' wash place and very nearly failed to make it when a broken companionway ladder blocked an escape route forcing him and others to get along to the sick bay flat, already under water. He got into the sea but was unconscious when picked up by *Cowdray's* whaler.

Another survivor who was practically unconscious when pulled from the sea was Able Seaman (Radar) Norman Blundell. He and Ken Cartright were the only two survivors of the twenty Portsmouth radar ratings in the ship. Blundell kept notes – staccato fashion – of his experience:

'Had the forenoon watch and after eating went out onto the fo'c'sle. Just arrived at the top of the ladder by the PO's heads when the wave hit me – waist high – and knocked me over. Looking astern – through the bulkhead door which was open, saw the stern of a ship sticking up out of the water . . . then looked down and realised it was the stern of our ship which now had nothing abaft B gun. Very frightened. We were listing to starboard about 30 to 40 degrees. Clambered (too steep to walk) up the port side fo'c'sle and stood by the guardrail for perhaps thirty seconds and remember:

(a) Jimmy (First Lieutenant A. Y. Spearman) trying to get people off ship (always wondered what his second name was). No way he was going to get off – should have got a medal.

(b) Clubs (PTI) doing the same thing – another hero. He got off, I thought. This was port side amidships.

(c) One flotanet spinning just off port side, and as some tried to get on it, it dragged others under – what bloody stupid things.

(d) The skipper climbing down the side of the bridge shouting "Abandon ship!" Bit late by then, but I was all for it.

(e) The ship was listing more this time and I couldn't jump out far enough to miss the side. Some were sliding down and getting caught by the armour belt – nasty!

(f) Blew up my lifebelt and clambered down to the lower boom, which was sticking out. Don't remember reaching it. I must have been washed off by the swell – very lucky – well clear of the ship. Swam like hell away and, by the time I took a breather and looked back, she had gone and the fuel oil was bubbling up to the surface. . . . I expected more drag when she went down. . . . Don't remember any noise apart from the shouting. A few of the swimmers seemed to stick their arms up and just go under. Bloody stupid. At least try!'*

Blundell described some of the difficulties with the flotanet – a large rope mesh 'carpet' supported by cork floats, able to support numerous men. Blundell reckons there were forty or fifty men trying to survive on his flotanet, but the thing developed a spinning action like a top. Disenchanted with this, he swam away to something he spotted about twenty yards away.

* *Transatlantic Liners at War*, pp. 52–57.

It was the seat out of a motor boat or cutter. He lay across it with his legs dangling and found it pretty comfortable. But after a while fears returned as he realized there was nobody very close. Fuel oil was the greatest nuisance. He tasted it for months afterwards and remembers its taste to this day. Perhaps his being seasick helped purge some of the oil from his system. Seasick? He always was anyway, every trip.

A moment of panic seized Blundell when he could see men being rescued from the sea, and he could actually see the destroyer *Bramham* which started to move away from him. He still felt all right, except for the sickness, the oil and the creeping coldness; he couldn't feel his legs at all. He yelled as loud as he could and was relieved to hear a voice through a megaphone, well-spoken, an officer saying something like, 'Hang on, we can see you.'

The voice may well have been that of Lieutenant-Commander Baines, commanding officer of *Bramham*, or the Marquess of Milford Haven, the First Lieutenant. Both had loud hailers to help them control the rescue operation.

Norman Blundell continues:

'They then backed this great destroyer just like parking a car and the second throw [of a line] landed across the seat. My legs wouldn't work and couldn't climb the scramble net. A big chap, Irish, came down and must have carried me up under his arm. Collapsed in a heap on the upper and a tot of neaters [neat rum]. Only out a few seconds and then felt marvellous. Later, on the main mess deck – shaking hands with chaps I knew and some I didn't, I expect. Tug Wilson was there, I was glad – a smashing chap . . . POs mess provided a smashing meal of bacon, beans and tomatoes – plenty of cigarettes and a game of crib – living again. Picked up about 5.30, I think – one of the last, I was told.'

The smashing chap that Blundell referred to was Edgar 'Tug' Wilson, a Hull reservist. He had come off watch at 12.30, had his lunch and had a bath before doing his dhobeying in the for'ard washroom. He had stripped to vest and pants – and heavy sea boots. He was sitting on a stool rubbing away at his clothes and rinsing them off as usual in a bucket:*

'The next moment there was a paralysing jerk, the stool shot from under him, the bucket crashed into a corner and all the lights went out. Wilson managed to crawl outside into the passage and scramble up to the deck. He was still in his underwear and had no lifebelt. When he got up on to the fo'c'sle head he made for the

---

* *Against the Sea*, by Ralph Barker, Chatto & Windus, 1972, p. 20.

boats. Wilson got into the port whaler which PO Downey was trying to launch or release, but it was impossible to shift it. He found some life jackets: When he heard the order to abandon ship Wilson hurried back to the fo'c'sle head. He had reached the guardrail when the ship went over for the second time, and he was able to crawl through and sit for a moment on the ship's side, which was not horizontal. Then he slid down her plates into the water, carefully avoiding the rolling chocks above the keel as he went. Once in the water he kicked off his sea boats and started swimming to get clear of the ship, which seemed about to capsize.'

After a short while Jack Swabey came upon Wilson and asked if he could hold on for a breather. He had exhausted himself swimming and had no lifebelt. They both managed to reach a flotanet and hung on.

The other radar survivor, Ken Cartwright, came to within seconds of death. Unconscious when hauled from the sea by *Bramham's* whaler, he experienced the near-death sensation of looking down on his own body being worked on by the crew once aboard the destroyer and heard a Chief Petty Officer say, 'Hold his bloody nose – he will drink it,' and this tot of 'neaters' did him a power of good, for as he says, 'I must have been close to the Pearly Gates.' Cartwright went on to relate that in a dormitory ashore in Londonderry that night the lads would not have the lights put out for fear of the dark, understandably so after their experiences.

A few days later, while on survivors' leave and enjoying a drink in a pub, he met a merchant seaman, a quartermaster from *Queen Mary*.

Curacoa's Royal Marine contingent suffered dreadfully: twenty-eight of them died that day, including the senior sergeant, Edward White, and Pat Holmes' opposite number, Captain John Cole: 'It was\ only due to the workings of fate that he was off watch,' Pat records, 'and I was on duty that afternoon.'

Sergeant Sid Dobbs was off watch in the Sergeant's Mess. His action station was as the Royal Marine AA gun crew captain. Raging floodwater washed him off the ship when he emerged from below. Like many others who were off watch Sid was sleeping off his lunch. He remembers dreaming: 'I was on a magic carpet going along nicely. Then the carpet suddenly collapsed into a river.' He woke up to find himself careering through the door, landing on the other side of the mess deck. He joined other off-watch marines scrambling for their lives to the upper deck. 'Before I had the chance to find out what had happened I was washed overboard. The next thing I remember is waking up on a Carley float.'*

---

* *Bingham News*, 27 September, 1991.

Another regular marine, the 21-year-old Eric Bower, spoke highly of the self-sacrifice of Engineer Commander Douglas Robertson RNR, who, without any thought for his own safety, enabled several others to escape.

Bower had been asleep on a mess deck stool, slightly aft of amidships close to the actual point of impact.

The collision threw him across the mess deck, a distance of about thirty feet. He told his story to Ralph Barker:

> 'The lights went out and as the ship went over everyone in the mess deck was thrown on top of him and he finished up in a tangle of arms and legs and bodies on the starboard side in complete darkness. To intensify the horror of it, a length of loose cable had been thrown into the same corner and was becoming intertwined with the men. Bower thought he would be either strangled or suffocated. There was a ladder leading to the upper deck, with a hatch at the top which was kept closed, locked by three cleats. Men were scrambling up the ladder as a column of water flooded the mess deck. Bower, strong and wiry, fought his way clear of the cable and the heap of bodies to the foot of the ladder, where he was up to his waist in water. Men behind him were shoving violently and shouting at those above them to hurry.
>
> 'At last they got the hatch undone, and one by one they clambered out onto the main deck. It, too, was awash. Waves were breaking into and over the jagged structure amidships where the *Queen Mary* had carved her way through. Above them a broken mast, smashed as the ship bent over, was swinging and banging against the superstructure. As Bower emerged from the hatch a huge wave broke over him and he was nearly washed overboard. He had no lifebelt, and he decided to climb up to the comparative safety of the gun deck. As the ship was still listing forty-five degrees, scrambling up the superstructure looked feasible.'*

From this vantage point Bower jumped back to the main deck. He clung onto a guardrail but sprained his ankle badly. Although he did not have a lifebelt he jumped into the sea and struck out for a liferaft. Just before he left the ship he was one of the last to see Douglas Robertson, the engineer commander, making his way through waist-high water, looking immaculate in uniform jacket, cap and gloves, still intent on saving men's lives.

Bower had a frightening experience as he plunged into the sea. He seemed to be dragged down and down, tumbling over and over in the turbulence, totally disorientated, until he broke surface gasping for breath. And then he

* Barker, op. cit., p. 21.

had to fight off another survivor, also minus a lifebelt, and swam away to relative safety.

He was not a strong swimmer and only managed to keep afloat by treading water, but he then found a flotanet and held on for two hours before rescue came.

Electrical Artificer John Sewell had the rare distinction of being the only *Curacoa* survivor from the electrical department, and, like so many, was trapped when the ship staggered over to starboard. He was alone in the electrical workshop but was able to escape once the for'ard two-thirds of the ship returned to a more upright position. After swimming away from the starboard side and gaining a piece of wreckage with two others he was eventually picked up by *Bramham*.

When *Bramham* arrived on the scene the First Lieutenant called for volunteers to man the whaler. All six CW (commission worthy) ratings stepped forward. The incident is recalled by Roger Barritt, one of the volunteers, an ordinary seaman aboard the destroyer:

'Thus it was that the whaler was manned by six very ordinary seamen, one general service AB, one two stripe leading hand and a young RN Sub . . . (Sub-Lieutenant E. Fawcett). He was only a youngster and when we had really got enough on board he should have gone back to *Bramham*, then come back for another load. However, there were still so many in the water that it was a difficult decision for him to make and in the event we carried on picking up people. We got lower and lower in the water and eventually we could not row. . . . We all had our seaboots on when we left *Bramham*. The leading hand was rowing in front of me. When we got rather low in the water I saw him kick his boots off and I thought he must fear the worst, and kicked mine off too.'*

Len Clarke was a supply assistant in victualling. This included the general issue of 'two water rum' (that is two measures of water and one of rum) for ratings, and 'neaters' (undiluted or neat rum) for Chiefs and Petty Officers. Clarke was on X gun supply at action stations, but at the moment of collision he was in the issue room on the stokers' mess deck. The ship heaved over onto her side and the lights went out. The emergency lights came on as *Curacoa* righted herself and Clarke made his way to the funnels. When on deck he saw rollers coming up where the after third of the ship should have been. The main (i.e. the aftermost) mast was broken and lying flat over the sea. He climbed along this, dropped off and swam to a rolled up flotanet with a marine. They were joined there by others and two hours later he was pulled aboard *Cowdray* where the crew, in Clarke's own words, 'were fantastic'.

* Letter to John Tether, 5 November, 1985. He died during the preparation of this book.

The survivors mention various forms of flotsam to which they owed their lives. Indeed, just about all survivors had found something to hang on to for the one and a half to two and a half hours while they were rising and falling in the big swell and being buffeted by continual waves. Rafts, Carley floats, flotanets – most of which were still rolled up, but a few were spread out – all saved lives. Leading Seaman Jess Turner hung on to a whaler's oar with three others until picked up by *Bramham*, where the tot of rum given to him made him sick – a common reaction, it seems, especially if any oil had been swallowed.

Dennis Hearn was a signalman, only eighteen years old, asleep on stools with the rest of the watch in the for'ard mess deck, starboard side, when what he thought was a torpedo struck the ship. His lifebelt was stuck fast in his locker so he abandoned it and, like many others, entered the water on the port side of the fo'c'sle. Fortunately he found a Carley float on which he was joined by three or four others. He survived the experience and was rescued by one of the destroyers. It is somewhat ironical that a year later he took passage to New York to help commission a new frigate – in the *Queen Mary*.

Geoffrey Carter, telegraphist, was on watch, on aircraft-listening-out duty on the bridge, and was one of the very few survivors who actually saw *Queen Mary* slice *Curacoa* in two. With lifebelt on and blown up he slid down a rope on the port side and, after some minutes alone, climbed on to a Carley float containing a number of oil-covered men. He recalls his rescue vividly:

'After what seemed like an eternity, but in fact was only two and a half hours, I sighted the foremast of a destroyer headed towards us. My excited shout was greeted with some scepticism by those around me, but very soon the destroyers *Bramham*, *Cowdray* and *Skate* hove-to close by and commenced rescue operations. *Bramham* dropped her seaboat which pulled towards us alternately rising on the crest then disappearing from view into the troughs of the swell. I was fortunate in being one of the first to be picked up and was dumped unceremoniously over the gunwale and into the bilges to sprawl on top of a groaning figure who I recognized as our erstwhile Captain.

'The whaler continued to scour the wreckage, picking up survivors until we were almost gunwales under, and in this condition I helped support Chief Yeoman Rogers who semaphored *Bramham* to come alongside us. She complied very carefully so as not to swamp us, but her scrambling net was wildly rising and falling some fifteen feet in the swell. I recall grabbing the net and hauling myself up to her guardrail where her deck party dumped me aboard.'

Carter recalls his arms and legs feeling as heavy as lead. His clothes were cut from him and he was provided with a survivor's kit of woollen socks, sweater and trousers. There followed a warming tot and the hospitality of *Bramham's* W/T office staff. After a rest he remembers experiencing a wonderful feeling of elation and of coming down to earth on walking *Bramham's* deck to see the lines of shrouded bodies being conveyed back for burial.

Leading Signalman John Tether was on watch during the forenoon that day and he passed signals backwards and forwards between *Queen Mary* and *Curacoa*. As he went off watch at midday he looked at *Queen Mary*:

'She looked just as impressive and well worth another look before I went below to get some sleep. I had been on watch from midnight till 4 a.m. and then had the forenoon [8 a.m. till midday]. No sooner had my head hit the mess deck bench than I was fast asleep.

'When the crash came I was hurled into the scuppers and came out of my sleep in a befuddled state. Obviously something was wrong. A torpedo? A bomb? I had to get out on to the upper deck to see what had happened. Once outside I could see the ship was foundering badly. The stern appeared to be below the waterline (I didn't know it had sunk half a mile away) and the bows were obviously going to follow suit shortly. There was no sign of *Queen Mary*.

'There was no time to lose. I had heard about the suction that ships made as they sank and I didn't want to be caught in that. I could swim reasonably well and if she didn't go I could always swim back aboard. She was listing badly to starboard and, letting go of the door frame that was holding me up, I ran down the sloping deck and dived over the side. I don't think I have ever swum in such cold water and wearing such heavy clothes, but fear lent me power and I swam as hard as I could away from our sinking ship.

'She started to come right over on her side. The two masts came down either side of me as I swam frantically away to avoid them, and the aerials and rigging which came crashing down at the same time. She partly righted herself just enough for thirty feet of the bows to come out of the water, almost vertically: a last figure ran up to the stem as, with a final plunge, she went. Three minutes had passed.'

John Tether, like so many of the survivors, found the sudden spread of the up-welling, thick, treacle-like black fuel oil from the bursting oil tanks particularly difficult to deal with as it was completely enveloping and made hanging on to anything doubly difficult. However, Tether found a rolled up flotanet to cling to. It saved his life. Only then was he told, '*Queen Mary* hit us.'

Ordinary Seaman Fred Dennis was one of the twelve lookouts with three-badge AB Jimmy Green as communications number and Patrick Holmes as ADO in the ADP. After being rescued he had the good sense to sketch a plan of lookouts and their positions in the ADP on the label of his survival kitbag next day in Londonderry. Fred Dennis described his ordeal:

> 'We came on watch at 1200 hours and closed up on our respective pedestals. I closed up on S3 with my opposite number, Frank Brownsett. At 1410 [two hours and ten minutes after coming on watch] I came off the pedestal and my mate Frank sat down and took over. I was now able to move about and saw *Queen Mary* heading towards us. I remember looking astern and our ship's wake was straight and true. I also remember saying, "if she doesn't turn to port she will go straight through us". The gap between us was closing fast so I went to the port side and looked over. Men were running from the stern of our ship along the portside upper deck trying to reach the safety of the fo'c'sle. Some had already stripped off and were diving over the side. Realizing that *Queen Mary* was about to ram us, our ADO ordered us to remove our seaboots and blow up our lifebelts. There was no panic; everyone seemed to accept it, and again I looked over the portside of the ADP to see *Queen Mary's* towering stem racing at us like a giant guillotine. There was no chance of her avoiding us now. Then came the impact – crash – she hit us at an angle of about 30 to 40 degrees on the port side just abaft the after funnel – over 80,000 tons at 28½ knots – she scythed through us like a knife through butter. The time was 1412.'

As the ship went over to starboard at a terrific angle Dennis found himself lying on the side of the tin hat locker in the middle of the ADP around the mast. He reckons this stopped him being flung over the starboard side of the platform; he saw some of his shipmates hurled over the side, including Frank Brownsett. The ship seemed to stay on her side for some time before she recovered. Dennis recalls:

> 'The noise of escaping steam and the tearing of metal was terrible, and as we came up further the steam seemed to engulf those of us still in the ADP. How I got down the hatch and the mast ladder I have no idea. However, I remember reaching the upper deck, portside, and grabbing the guardrail as she started to list heavily to starboard again I went through the rails and slipped down the ship's side and my feet came to rest on the bilge keel and then I

froze. It could only have been seconds, but it seemed ages, and all the thick oil was coming up the hull as I felt her going lower in the water. Then I was thumped on the shoulders and somebody said, "Make up your mind, mate – are you going to jump or not? You haven't much time." I didn't have to jump, she was so far over I just got to my feet and ran and slipped into the oil and water.'

Dennis managed to reach a raft which had probably floated off the ship; he hung on desperately, but it became so heavily loaded with survivors that he left it and soon found himself alongside four others holding on to a boat's oar. He could not recognize anyone because of the oil. One of the four told Dennis to grab hold in the middle, but it became slippery and insecure. One oar hardly gave a chance to five men and they began drifting away from the main body of survivors. People on the raft began singing 'Roll Out The Barrel'.

'Then I saw a box floating towards me; it was upside down, so I left the chaps with the oar and swam for the box. It had four small blocks, one at each corner, so I guessed it was a ready use locker and handy for me to grab. The base was not very wide so I was able to hook one block in the crook of my left elbow and hold the other with my left hand, and I hung on for dear life. One moment I was in a trough and the next I was on top of the swell and was able to see what was going on around me. It was then that I got my last look of *Curacoa*. She was up and down, her bows high in the air. The men trapped in the for'ard mess decks must have opened the scuttles in an effort to get out because as she slipped back into the water there was a deep roar of air, something like the bass notes of an organ being played out of tune – then she was gone. At this point I got company on my box, a shipmate floated near and asked if the box could hold two of us. I told him to hang on to the other end and I think they were the only words I said the whole time I was in the water.

'As we rose to the top of another swell I noticed we were well away from the rest of the crew, and far away to our right I saw a destroyer going towards them. Then all of a sudden a rope landed across the box. I heard someone shout, "Grab the rope," and my companion was gone like a monkey up it. He hadn't said a word to me and he must have seen the destroyer coming towards us. She was the *Bramham*. I had my back to her, and as I turned my head I saw the scrambling net over the side. Then my locker and I bumped the ship's side and I was told to let go of it. I was unable to do this as my arm had locked with the cold, and two ratings came over the side to assist me. One of them kicked the box from my grasp while the other chap grabbed my collar, and between them they lifted me over the guardrail on to the deck, face down. I remember someone cutting off my boiler suit, then I must have passed out.'

Fred Dennis was soon brought round, restored with neat rum and given a full survivor's kit.

The Commanding Officer of the rescuing destroyer HMS *Bramham* was Lieutenant-Commander E. Baines. When he received the signal of *Curacoa's* collision he turned his ship about, housed the Asdic dome, increased speed from 18 knots (the maximum when using Asdic) to 20 knots and headed into the heavy swell. Baines is critical about the use of *Curacoa*:

> 'I have always thought that the whole thing was simply a PR exercise to impress 10,000 Americans. . . . She [*Curacoa*] was carrying so much top weight over her designed displacement tonnage that her freeboard was reduced by about 3 ft – and her trim altered. In addition, of course, her engines were clapped out.
>
> 'The effect of the extra top weight, extra displacement tonnage and lack of freeboard – particularly when steaming at full speed – had a dire effect on her handling in a stern sea.'

It is to Baines' skilled shiphandling and *Bramham's* whaler's crew that most credit is due for saving about seventy lives that afternoon.

One of the most miraculous escapes was that of Ronnie Heavens, the Captain's steward. He had just finished helping serve the officers' lunch when the massive bows of the liner sliced through a few feet from where he was working. The deck fell away from him and he dropped straight through into the water. He managed to struggle clear, although seriously injured. Ted Beavis later described the huge wound down his back as 'split open like a peeled banana'.

Captain Boutwood tried later to recall the sequence of events when he gave evidence before the Court of Appeal nearly three years later:

> 'As soon as I appreciated a dangerous situation was developing I myself went to a position at the gyro compass which indicated to myself and everybody else that I had taken control of the ship. From then onwards until the time of the crash I cannot say with any assurance of any order I may have given.'

Boutwood described what happened after the collision in a curious reference:

'She heeled over to certainly her beam ends. I formed an opinion that she heeled over more than that, and for a moment I thought she would never recover. On the bridge we were hanging on. The forepart of the ship. which formed the major part, then righted to within not very many degrees from upright, and I formed an instant opinion that there was a chance to save the forepart.

'Very shortly after that, within perhaps a minute and a half or two minutes, I realized that there was no chance of saving any part of the ship, and in a very short time it was quite clear to me the forepart must go down. The noise of escaping steam and other things was deafening. After I gave up hope of saving the ship, I instructed the officers who were with me to go down and take charge of what ratings they could get hold of and to get the life- saving equipment down for use.

'I did not myself actually give the order "Abandon ship!" because there was no hope of getting the order carried out in all that noise. But then I think I heard somebody below shouting "Abandon ship!" and whoever gave that order was justified in giving it. My officers had gone below with the impression that that was to be done. I did nothing to countermand the order. The ratings got into the water, or a good many of them did, as quickly as they could, but within the space of five minutes the ship sank. I can say that because I referred to my watch. I was standing on a portion of *Curacoa* until she dipped – and then I dipped too.'

After two hours or so in the water John Boutwood was unceremoniously dragged aboard *Bramham's* whaler and finally got aboard the destroyer.

The commanding officer of *Bramham*, quoting his Sub-Lieutenant, Teddy Fawcett, who had charge of the rescue whaler, reports that the first thing Fawcett saw of Boutwood:

'was an arm with four rings on it and that there was some very hostile remarks which culminated in the suggestion that he should be left to drown. Teddy threatened to clobber anybody who made any move to throw him back with a boat stretcher he had armed himself with.'*

Nor was this an isolated incident. When the overloaded whaler came along- side, gunwales awash, the first thought of everyone was to grab the scrambling net, 'so we all went over to the starboard side of the whaler and it simply turned over.'

As the survivors scrambled up the netting an eye witness saw Captain

* Letter, Lieutenant-Commander E. Baines to R. Barritt, 3 June, 1991.

Boutwood dragged aboard and the shout was heard, 'Throw the bastard back', which seemed a bit unkind.*

While the hundreds of *Curacoa* sailors endured their personal ordeals in the Atlantic, from which just 101 men were to survive, the super troopship with her 10,239 people (plus about 900 crew) aboard steamed away towards the Clyde with the carpenters still fashioning structural support for the collision bulkhead until the Captain judged it safe to increase speed to 24 knots. *Queen Mary* arrived in the Clyde safely. On further detailed inspection of her stem, a huge casting, it was seen to be fractured and the bows crushed for a length of perhaps twenty feet. It was decided that the several weeks long repairs should be carried out in Boston, so temporary repairs were effected in the Clyde by the addition of several tons of cement. A few weeks later the new stem had been fitted and the bows looked as good as new. Every trace of the sinking of HMS *Curacoa* had been expunged.

The three rescuing destroyers, *Bramham*, *Cowdray* and *Skate*, had reached the scene of the disaster in a little under two hours and had then started the difficult task of rescue. All told they collected two officers, Boutwood and Pat Holmes, and ninety-nine ratings. *Bramham* had saved over seventy, *Cowdray* twenty and *Skate* ten. The ships had also collected a number of dead bodies and men who had subsequently died after rescue, all of whom were buried at sea. The ships were unable to rescue 338 men. Twenty-one of their bodies were later washed up on the Isle of Skye and the nearby mainland, their graves still standing, fifty years later, as silent testimony of a day of disaster.

It was realized immediately at the Admiralty that the Germans would have no knowledge of the sinking of the British cruiser. There were no German witnesses of the loss, and consequently all survivors were ordered to say nothing of the sinking lest the circumstances of the incident should leak to the enemy. Thus, the sinking of *Curacoa* became a secret and her loss was not officially announced until May, 1945, at the end of the war in Europe.

Yet, curiously, it is reported that at least one person, a member of the liner's crew, listening to a German radio broadcast, heard of the tragedy with details of the collision.

★　　★　　★

With almost indecent haste a Court of Enquiry was empanelled aboard HMS *Argus*† two days after the disaster. On the Sunday the destroyer *Saladin* took the survivors to Gourock where some of them had to attend the enquiry.

---

* Letter, 11 June, 1991.
† She had been adapted from the incomplete merchant ship hull of the liner *Conte Rosso*. She became the 22,600-ton flush-decked aircraft carrier launched in 1917. But she was too slow. In World War II she was used for training purposes, deck landings and, later, as an accommodation ship.

Bodies of men from *Curacoa* were washed ashore probably two hundred miles from the position of the cruiser's sinking. They lie in carefully tended graves in three cemeteries, two on the Isle of Skye and another on the nearby mainland.

ASHRAIG CEMETERY, STRATH			STRONUIRINISH CEMETERY, PORTREE		
GARGET	Sydney	Blacksmith			
GOZZETT	Alfred Henry	Coder	BROWNSETT Frank	OD	
CLARK	Patrick Frank	AB	DEAN Harry*	AB	
ANGER	Harold	CPO Tel	DUNNING R.	OD	
BEATON	Peter	ERA IV			
EGAN	Harold	AB			
HOOPER	James Thomas	AB	RC CEMETERY, ARISAIG		
WELLS	Frederick James	AB	BREWER A.A.	OD	
BARRATT	Kenneth Reed	OD	CALDWELL R.	AB	
CORNELL	Percy Victor	Yeo Sig	COX C.H.C.	Ch	Ord Art
HAWKINS	Henry Munro	SBPO	GOWER L.F.	CPO Cook	
COX	A.H.S.	OD	WILLMOTT A.	Ord Art IV	
WHITELAW	G.A.N.	OD			
3 UNNAMED GRAVES					

* This was the nineteen-year-old radar rating, P/JX304317, sometimes incorrectly listed as Robert F., Stoker II.

In the motor boat going out to *Argus* Patrick Holmes remembers Captain Boutwood asking him if he had noticed *Curacoa's* turning to starboard just before the crash. Holmes answered 'No sir, nor to port.' Holmes later wrote:

'Our wake was perfectly straight, to the best of my memory of it. Whatever helm orders were given seemed to have little effect.'

CAPTAINS IN COURT

'It is difficult to imagine an ordeal more trying than that through which Captain Boutwood must have passed, and if I feel myself unable to accept his recollection on certain matters of fact that is not because I formed an unfavourable view of his demeanour in the witness box.'

Mr Justice Pilcher: Judgement 21 January, 1947.

In mid-June, 1945, continental Europe lay in ruins, the smoke and dust barely settled since hostilities had ended only five weeks earlier. Thousands of miles to the east massive fleets of warships assembled for the final assault upon Japan. It would be another two months before two atomic explosions gave history the benchmark of Hiroshima and Nagasaki.

Meanwhile, in London some outstanding matters needed investigating and being brought to a proper conclusion. One of these was the question of responsibility for the sinking of HMS *Curacoa*. Her sinking had been announced officially on 2 May, 1945, after more than two and a half years of secrecy.

Almost immediately the Lords Commissioners of the Admiralty set in train an allegation of negligent navigation by *Queen Mary* against her owners the Cunard White Star Ltd of Liverpool. Cunard counter-claimed that the accident was caused solely by the negligent navigation or management of those in *Curacoa* while acting as escort to *Queen Mary*.

The hearing came before Mr Justice Pilcher sitting with two Elder Brethren of Trinity House acting as naval assessors, Captain W.E. Crumplin and Captain G.C.H. Noakes.

The date was 12 June, 1945, and the scene was set in No. 10 Court of the Probate, Divorce and Admiralty Division of the High Courts of Justice in the Strand, London. The panelled courtroom was magisterial, a little intimidating, appropriate to the solemnity of the matter to be examined. Ralph Barker gives a graphic description of the setting:

'The scene in that square drab courtroom off the Strand with its Victorian Gothic arches and grim oak panelling, its musty rows of law books and high canopied dais, seemed contrived and theatrical after the harsh realities of the Atlantic war. How could the frantic last few seconds before the collision, and the decisions taken in those unforgiving moments, ever be satisfactorily reconstructed and analysed in such an austere atmosphere? Yet the battle that was fought in that courtroom was scarcely less bitter than the wartime one, the collision of legal opinion almost as dramatic.

'The antagonists were impelled by the same deadly purpose – to seek out each other's weakness and destroy. The public gallery, packed with the widows and next of kin of the men who died, had far more than a morbid interest in the proceedings. If the Admiralty won their case, the relatives could sue Cunard for damages.'*

The hearing, which came two years and eight months after the disaster, got off to a good enough start, three days in mid-June before being adjourned until the end of November to allow William Heighway from Australia to attend.

Mr Justice Pilcher had an impressive background and he seemed well prepared to hear a trial of this nature.[†] He was painstaking, meticulous, finicky even, but highly respected by his colleagues and juniors.

As technical advisers he had two men skilled in the profession of the sea, able to guide and advise him on the intricacies of seamanship and ship handling. Both were master mariners. Captain George C.H. Noakes RNR was fifty in 1946 (he died in 1980). He started his service in the Merchant Navy in 1910. He served with the Royal Mail Steampacket Company and the Blue Star Line, transferring to the Royal Navy during both World Wars.

Captain W.E. Crumplin was even more experienced. He was fifty-five, had been with the Bibby Line all his professional life and had become one of the Elder Brethren in 1930. He died in 1974.

Perhaps justice would appear to have been served better had one of these officers been an RN officer.

Senior Counsel for the Admiralty was Mr K.S. Carpmael KC.[‡] He was assisted by Mr O.L. Bateson.

---

* Barker, op. cit., p. 28.
† Later Sir Gonne St Clair Pilcher MC (1890–1966). He served for years as Junior Counsel to the Admiralty. After the *Queen Mary* Appeal case he became Vice President of an international maritime committee, President of the British Maritime Law Association and retired as a Judge of the High Court of Justice in 1961.
‡ Kenneth Sydney Carpmael KC (1885–1975) spent most of his professional life in the Royal Navy and on maritime and Admiralty business.

The Cunard interests were represented by an equally distinguished KC, Mr R.F. Hayward* and by Mr Waldo Porges.†

During the first three days in No. 10 Court the one and only witness from *Curacoa*, Captain Boutwood, gave evidence. Three of the four Cunard officers directly concerned also appeared; they were Senior First Officer Robinson, Junior First Officer Wright and Senior Third Officer Hewitt. Another crucial witness was Junior Third Officer Heighway, the Australian, but he was unable to appear before the court until November. After three days of hearing evidence the case was adjourned until after the summer recess.

Captain Boutwood was the first and only witness on Day One. He carried himself well, smart in his naval uniform, the four gold rings on his arms nicely set off by the two rows of medal ribbons on his tunic, worn high as is the naval fashion, including the DSO, awarded for his distinguished service with his minesweeping flotilla in the Mediterranean.

But he was not to prove a good witness; he did not serve his own interests well by his answers to the questions, although the judge was complimentary enough in his judgement. Reading the court notes one forms the opinion that he answered adequately enough, but the feeling lingers that he could have supplemented what he said more helpfully. He gave the bare facts, but one fancies he failed to flesh out those bare bones.

Mr Carpmael led him quickly and smoothly through a series of non-contentious questions, setting out the basic facts: yes, there were six escorting destroyers; yes, he had escorted *Queen Mary* four times and *Queen Elizabeth* twice; and yes, he had met Captain Illingworth.

Boutwood explained briefly his plans for the defence of *Queen Mary*. Carpmael asked if he expected to keep up with *Queen Mary*. Boutwood explained that the liner was late on her rendezvous and from his knowledge of her in previous convoys, and the previous plottings of his navigating officer to gauge her speed, he concluded she was making good at least 26 knots. His own full speed was 25 knots. He knew the authorities in Greenock set great store by *Queen Mary* being on time so he did not intend to request her to keep down to 25 knots.

Asked if he intended to zigzag, he answered, 'No. I could not hope to live with *Queen Mary* if I did.'

Queen Mary's line of advance was 106 degrees, that is sixteen degrees south of due east (see pp.174–5) but her gyro compass was reading two degrees high and it was not until noon that this was corrected. This

* Richard Frederick Hayward MC QC (1879–1962). He served in the Royal Navy and the army, including the Royal Naval Division in France. Became a KC in 1936. Retired 1961.
† Waldo William Porges QC (1899–1976). Called to the Bar 1927. Bencher 1957. Joint editor *Temperley's Merchant Shipping Acts*.

information was never passed to *Curacoa*. So Captain Boutwood, who had requested course and speed in the forenoon when fine on *Queen Mary's* starboard bow steered 108 degrees as signalled. It is not surprising therefore that Boutwood had to adjust his ship's course between 100 and 108 degrees.

Carpmael asked Boutwood, 'What was the first thing you noticed with regard to *Queen Mary* which caused you trouble?' Boutwood gave a long reply:

> 'I have described the *Queen Mary* coming ahead on my port quarter until she reached a position which satisfied me; and she, as far as I could see, was on a parallel course to me with her stem practically abeam. It was just at this time that I myself and the other officers on the bridge had a feeling of doubt as to whether she was actually maintaining a perfectly steady course. It was natural at this time that we should all be observing her with the greatest interest.
>
> 'My officers, exchanging views with me, agreed that we were not confident that her course was perfectly steady and remained in this state of doubt for what I would think was a longish period when judging such periods. Again, I cannot bind myself to times, but I would estimate that for possibly something in the nature of a minute or a minute and a half we were in some doubt as to whether she was keeping a steady course, and I remember my navigating officer saying, "I think she may be turning, or is it only a yaw?"'

Neither Carpmael nor anyone else seems to have raised the question of whether it had been established by those aboard the cruiser which zigzag the *Queen* was following.

When it was clear to Boutwood that *Queen Mary* was turning to starboard, he gave the order 'Starboard fifteen'. His own course was then 108 degrees. The following sea at this time was dead astern and *Curacoa* was suffering from a yaw, three or four degrees either side of 108 degrees. Boutwood heard no siren from *Queen Mary* as she came on.

In answer to Carpmael's question, Boutwood elaborated: his 'Starboard fifteen' meant fifteen degrees of rudder. His 'Hard-a-starboard' would be thirty-five degrees. *Curacoa* did not respond at once. In a surprisingly short time from his order 'Starboard fifteen' he appreciated *Queen Mary* was continuing to turn to starboard.

This evidence seems to conflict with First Officer Robinson's, which, if accepted, asserted that *Queen Mary* was turning to port.

Boutwood continued with his evidence: 'The distance between us was becoming less at an alarming rate. By twelve or fifteen seconds after my starboarding had begun to have an effect I saw that a dangerous situation was approaching.'

Boutwood then made his most compelling statement: 'It seemed inconceivable to me that steaming at 28½ knots and knowing the cruiser to be steaming at 25, *Queen Mary* should make an appreciable alteration to starboard for any reason but mistake or mischance. I went at once to the conning position by the gyro compass to indicate that I had taken control of the vessel.'

He regretted that from that moment until the collision he could not be certain of any order he might have given.

It was an honest but somewhat unfortunate admission. 'All I can say,' he commented, 'and I am convinced of it in my own mind, is that from the moment of assuming command of the handling of the ship I did all that I conceived was for the best possible to avoid a collision between *Queen Mary* and *Curacoa*.'

Carpmael persisted: 'But you cannot remember what you did?'

Boutwood: 'I cannot now remember anything which I definitely said or did.'

Boutwood described the actual collision: 'After *Queen Mary* struck, she went over the top of and between the two pieces of my ship – she went on right through – and *Curacoa* heeled over on her beam ends, until I thought she could never recover. However, the fore end righted. I carried a good time-keeper and saw then that the hour was ten past two.'

He instructed an officer to go down and take charge of such ratings as he could lay his hands on and get out the life-saving equipment. In five minutes the ship sank. Again he consulted his watch. Ninety-nine ratings were saved, and one officer, Patrick Holmes, besides himself.

Carpmael finished his questioning with a point of drama: 'What did *Queen Mary* do after the collision?'

Boutwood: 'She steamed on.'

'Was that the proper thing for her to do?'

'I would say Yes.'

On that point, at least, all seemed agreed.

The 66-year-old Richard Hayward KC representing the Cunard Company rose to cross-examine Boutwood. The Captain declared he would find it difficult to believe as Hayward suggested that, shortly after the blow, the zigzag clock on board *Queen Mary* struck twelve past two.

Hayward questioned Boutwood as to why he had not asked *Queen Mary* at what times she would alter course on her zigzag.

Hayward: 'You say you do not think it a wise course to ask her what her zigzag was?' Then with a touch of theatricality he posed the simple view: 'At a distance of half a mile in daylight a couple of expert signalmen could pass this information, without even using flags, like tick-tack men on a racecourse, could they not?'

'I agree that expert signalmen could get a good deal of signalling done without trouble.'

'What did you mean,' Hayward persisted, 'when you say that you did not consider it wise to ask for this information? Were you thinking of any security measures when you said that?'

Boutwood answers at length:

> 'There were two or three considerations. The first was that I thought I had made it abundantly clear, and the master of *Queen Mary* knew from his experience of my practice, that I would not zigzag. I had been careful to give him no hint that I intended to zigzag. I thought if I asked plainly what zigzag he was doing that might lead him to suppose that I was willing to conform to it. It was perfectly clear in my mind that he knew that I was not intending to conform to any zigzag. I expected rather that any ship properly handled approaching me from astern would never alter in such a manner as to endanger another ship, at least without making a sound signal. Furthermore, this is a much smaller point, I regret to say that in my opinion the signalmen in *Queen Mary* were not very expert.'

Hayward pressed Boutwood on the issue of wheel orders immediately before the collision. 'You are meaning that although you do not remember doing so it is possible that you may have given another wheel order?' Boutwood responded quite openly:

> 'Not very long before the collision, I am strongly of the opinion that I had endeavoured to steady my ship, which makes me feel quite confident that I had at that time put my wheel amidships or possibly reversed my wheel in order to check my swing. I am quite confident and I am absolutely certain that not long before the impact I had in mind the possibility of averting disaster by going hard-a-port in order to swing myself clear, but it was not possible because the swing involved was quite out of the question in the time available.'

The judge intervened at one stage and referred to the time, about forty minutes before the collision, when *Queen Mary* was to turn fifty degrees to port at 1332. How far, he asked Boutwood, was *Queen Mary* as she crossed *Curacoa's* wake from starboard to port.* Boutwood answered, 'Four cables.'

The distance was queried later, as we shall see. The judge used a

---

* See position VIII of *Queen Mary's* track of Zigzag No. 8. p.83.

deceptively homely phrase in questioning Boutwood: 'It is easier to shepherd a ship if you know which way she is going?'

Boutwood could only agree with such a simple home truth.

But the judge could be irritable too: 'Having regard to the fine angle at which these two ships met, do you agree that until a very late moment your ship could, by a hard starboard wheel and reversing the starboard engine, have avoided the collision?'

Boutwood was thoughtless in answering: 'I do not agree that the initiative was left with my ship at all.'

'I am not asking you about the initiative,' Pilcher responded testily. 'Do you agree, as a fact, your ship was physically capable of being manoeuvred out of the way of *Queen Mary* until a very late moment?'

'I think it most improbable,' Boutwood replied.

Hayward put it to Boutwood that *Queen Mary* passed under the stern of the cruiser at between 1332 and 1340 much more closely than four cables. She passed so near, he suggested, that she had to interrupt her zigzag.

Boutwood said he would not have this. And anyway, what did it prove? He made the point again, that when the possibility of collision existed *Queen Mary* was willing to break the zigzag which thirty or forty minutes later she was not. It was a compelling argument in Boutwood's armoury, a great weakness in *Queen Mary's* case.

Captain Boutwood refused to accept Hayward's assertion that at the moment of impact *Curacoa's* head was at least thirty degrees to port of the mean course.

Mr Justice Pilcher asked the Captain, 'When you are escorting a vessel like the *Queen Mary* did you expect her to interrupt her zigzag manoeuvres for you, or do you keep out of her way?'

Boutwood gave an unclear response: 'I considered it the duty of the *Queen Mary* to interrupt her zigzag rather than take any action which would cause anything approaching a dangerous situation.' Then he added unhelpfully, 'I would prefer not to embarrass the steamer.' The meaning of this remark was not explained.

Mr Hayward clarified one persistent rumour about *Curacoa's* actions: 'Did you,' he asked, 'hear anything of a danger of a submarine?'

Boutwood laughed and replied dismissively, 'No, nothing of that sort.' The suggestion that *Curacoa* had sped across the liner's path in response to a U-boat alert had persisted despite there being no truth in the story whatsoever. Boutwood was able to lay the ghost of it once and for all.

Mr Justice Pilcher raised a question which brought forth an amazing reply from Boutwood. The judge asked whether Boutwood would have been happy had he known the liner's starboarding was a committal to an alteration of twenty-five degrees.

Boutwood asserted, 'I did not know she was doing Zigzag No. 8. I was never told that she was. She had no right to assume that I knew. And no right to starboard into her escort.' It was an extraordinary statement, and a powerful argument. It brought to an end the first day's hearing of evidence. It had been a long and tiring day for Boutwood. He had weathered it well enough, but had not overly impressed.

Captain Boutwood was the only Admiralty witness to give evidence. There were several officers from *Queen Mary* as well as Captain Illingworth who were called to put the Cunard case.

The first was appropriately the Senior First Officer, Noel Robinson. Senior counsel for Cunard, Mr Hayward, led Robinson through non-contentious questions, putting him at ease, gently establishing facts, figures and times. He had held a master's certificate since July, 1939. He had joined Cunard in April of the same year. He joined *Queen Mary* in August, 1942, as Junior First Officer. He received promotion to Senior First Officer in September, a few weeks before the collision.

Queen Mary was transporting American troops. She had 15,000 aboard, Robinson stated. [He was wrong, as we have seen; she had 10,239 aboard plus about 900 crew.] The liner's speed at the time of collision was 28½ knots. When he came on watch at noon she was two miles astern of the cruiser.

Patrick Holmes has studied carefully the two ships' track charts and it is useful to consider his comments before hearing the rest of Robinson's testimony. It needs to be made clear, he observes, that the major issue of the case centred on two quite separate situations. The first occurred soon after *Queen Mary* had for the first time crossed the wake of *Curacoa* when on her starboard leg (steering 131 degrees) between 1324 and 1332, and found some difficulty in re-crossing it on the following leg to port; and the second, on the next similar starboard leg between 1404 and 1412, when she sank *Curacoa*.

Coincidentally but perhaps not significantly, on both these occasions Robinson and his opposite number Wright shared responsibility for the navigation of *Queen Mary*. Wright, who had stood the forenoon watch from 0800 to 1200, relieved Robinson at about 1335 and handed back (after Robinson's lunch break) at about 1409, just three minutes before the crash.

Having got on to the starboard quarter of *Curacoa* for the first time at about 1330 the next course alteration, due at 1332, was a fifty-degree turn to port.

Robinson was on watch until relieved for lunch by Wright at 1335. He started the fifty-degree turn to port at 1332, but stopped it at 101 degrees, *i.e.* after only thirty degrees of the change of course of fifty degrees from 131 to 181 degrees. This was at about 1334.30 after 1.2 miles (12 cables) from the start of the turn at 1332.

Wright, at 1335, as we have already seen, went on with the turn to port, had second thoughts, stopped at 086 degrees and starboarded back to 091; he then ordered hard-a-starboard. Illingworth was alerted by this and brought him back to midships and told Wright to continue the zigzag to 081 degrees.

By the time *Queen Mary* was once more on course it must have been at least 1338 or 1339, and six or seven minutes of the eight-minute port leg was already up. When turning normally three minutes elapses for a fifty-degree change; in this case to port from 131 to 081 the leg is for eight minutes, so that five minutes of it are along 081 degrees.

With the dithering that went on after heading 101 degrees at 1334.30, porting further to 086 and then starboarding to 091 (1336.30), going hard-a-starboard and stopping at about 101 (at 1337), to get to 081 degrees (*i.e.* twenty degrees) would take nearly another two minutes (1339) and then there was only one further minute of the leg before the zigzag clock went off for the starboard turn onto the mean course at 1340. The position when finally on course of 081 works out at 3½ miles east-south-east of the 1332 position at about 1339 instead of 1½ miles east-south-east at 1335.

When *Queen Mary* crossed *Curacoa's* wake at about 1339 to 1340, Boutwood reckoned on being four cables ahead, and Heighway put it as close as one to two cables only. Captain Illingworth estimated it to be five cables.

Reverting now to the exchange of questions and answers between Hayward and Robinson, the Senior First Officer enunciated the gravamen of Cunard's case, that *Curacoa* would give way and stay clear.

Hayward asked, 'At the time you gave the order to your wheel "Port a little" did you or did you not anticipate the danger of collision?'

Robinson was positive: 'No, definitely not.'

Hypothetically Hayward asked, 'Had you at that time anticipated danger of collision, what would your action have been?'

'Hard-a-port.'

'Why did you not anticipate danger of collision? What did you expect would be done by the cruiser?'

Robinson then sated what was evidently the opinion of all Cunard officers: 'I expected that the cruiser would just keep off to starboard; that she would keep clear until we had made the leg of our zigzag.'

Hayward guided Robinson: What was the next thing that was done?'

Robinson decided that the vessels were getting much too close to one another.

'I checked that the quartermaster had put the helm the right way. I could only see that by going to the wheelhouse door, which was a matter of two or three steps. I then went back to the forepart of the bridge and saw the two vessels were closing very rapidly. I ordered the helm to be put hard-a-port. She was about two points on the bow and something less than a cable distant.'

'Was your order carried out?'

'Yes.'

*　　*　　*

The summer hearing was adjourned to allow for the presence of Bill Heighway who had to travel from Australia in time for the renewed hearing in the Strand on 23 November, 1945.

Captain William Heighway* was a key witness since he had a clearer view than any other one person in *Queen Mary* of what went on both at the time when *Queen Mary* altered course and broke her zigzag soon after the 1332 turn to port, and also just before the collision.

The transcript of the shorthand notes of his evidence, spread over twenty-four typewritten foolscap pages, includes no less than 426 questions and answers. There were 143 questions during Hayward's examination, 244 during Carpmael's cross-examination, and 39 more in re-examination by Hayward. Throughout, Heighway's evidence from the witness box was given clearly and sensibly; he was consistent in what he said, although it must have been a somewhat gruelling experience.

Heighway established his credentials: since the collision he had served aboard *Queen Elizabeth* and *Mauretania*. He was no longer employed by Cunard but since returning to the UK he had visited *Queen Mary* and made measurements and a plan of her bridge.

Heighway had been on watch from 0800 until noon, the forenoon watch, on 2 October, 1942, as Junior Officer of the Watch with 'Shiner' Wright as Senior Officer. The practice in the ship as regards lunch during the afternoon watch was for the officers of the forenoon watch to go down for their lunch at 1300 hours and, as soon as they had finished, to come up to the bridge again. On that day Heighway came up between 1330 and 1335 to relieve his opposite number, Albert Hewitt, who was in the starboard chartroom working out longitude from a noon sight of the sun, which by ship's time was at 1330.

Soon after this he heard Wright give the order 'Hard-a-starboard'. It was given because the chief OOW thought *Curacoa* was too close on the port bow for a continuation of the turn to port due at 1332 on the zigzag and started by Mr Robinson. On hearing this Heighway left the chartroom where he was working on his own sun sight taken a minute before, from the starboard wing of the bridge, and went to the port wing where he looked at the cruiser.

On hearing the urgency of the wheel order, Captain Illingworth also come out and asked Wright what the trouble was, and then, having satisfied himself that no danger of collision existed, told him to continue the zigzag by turning to port. He added that the cruiser would keep out of the way as

---

* Captain Heighway enjoyed a distinguished maritime career. He held the Extra Master's Certificate, was a Fellow of the Australian Institute of Navigation, a Member of the Company of Master Mariners of Australia and Head of the School of Navigation, Sydney Technical College. He died in 1992.

she was used to escort work. When asked how close *Curacoa* was as *Queen Mary* passed under her stern, Heighway said, 'Between one and two cables.'

He then went back to the starboard chartroom and worked out his sun sight. He was on the bridge next at 1355 and 1400 hours just before course had to be altered twenty-five degrees to port to come on to the mean course of 106 degrees which the ship steadied on for two or three minutes.

In answer to a question from Hayward, Heighway said that *Queen Mary* settled on a heading of 131 degrees at about seven minutes past 2 o'clock. It took 2½ to 3 minutes to steady her.

Question 102: 'Can you tell my Lord the sort of distance and bearing of *Curacoa* after you had steadied on 131 degrees?'

Heighway: 'She was about four points on the starboard bow then, and her distance would be about 4 or 5 cables.'

Question 104: 'What was the sort of heading of *Curacoa* at that time?'

Heighway: 'She was angled to our course – to port of our course – about 2 points approximately.'

Question 105: 'What did you expect she would do?'

Heighway: 'I expected the cruiser to go to starboard so that we could complete our leg of the zigzag.'

Heighway was asked to repeat his answer because the Judge did not hear it the first time.

Heighway was led through a great many more questions establishing the facts as he had seen them or heard them in those closing minutes in the life of the cruiser, giving his opinion as to distances, bearings, exact words spoken, orders given. In answer to further questions Heighway said he went into the wheelhouse, observed the wheel was hard-a-port, as it should have been, and then came out on to the starboard wing of the bridge again when the vessels seemed to close rapidly and the collision occurred.

Heighway continued to expect *Curacoa* to starboard and gave as his opinion that there would not have been a collision had she done so. But he thought that *Curacoa* altered to *port*, and that the angle between the ships when they struck was between two and three points (about 22 to 34 degrees).

It had been a long session in the witness box, but the examination had been friendly, by Cunard's KC, Mr Hayward. Heighway now faced cross-examination by the Admiralty's KC, Mr Carpmael. Most of Carpmael's questions were designed to make doubly sure that the evidence that had been accumulated was exact.

Heighway said that he first gave a statement to solicitors about the events leading up to the collision within a month of its happening and that it contained exactly the same information as he gave the court now.

Carpmael wanted to know precise details of events from 1357 to 1405 and, having established these, he then asked, 'And you were going at about 3½ knots faster than she was?'

Heighway answered with a precision which probably endeared him to Mr Justice Pilcher; 'I do not know what the speed of the cruiser was.'

Question 234, Carpmael: 'You have told me already that you saw the signal saying what her speed was.'

Heighway: 'The cruiser signalled that her speed was 25 knots. But I was not to know it was 25 knots. I could only assume it.'

Question 235, Carpmael: 'And did you assume it?'

Heighway: 'Yes.'

Question 236, Carpmael: 'Did you know what your own speed was?'

Heighway: 'Yes. 28½ knots.'

Carpmael changed tack with Question 238: 'Did the bearing of the cruiser broaden after you had got on to your mean course?'

Heighway: 'I cannot say whether it did or not.'

Carpmael: 'Why cannot you say whether it did or not?'

Heighway: 'I do not remember.'

Question 240, Carpmael: 'You were the junior officer of the watch?'

Heighway: 'Yes. But whether the bearing of the cruiser broadened or narrowed I cannot say.'

Question 241, Carpmael: 'Was that not a rather important matter from the point of view of the manoeuvres of *Queen Mary*?'

Heighway: 'Not at that time.'

Question 242, Carpmael: 'Were you not in the habit of taking bearings of the cruiser?'

Heighway was not to be badgered; not only was he not in the habit of taking such bearings, he did not think he ought to have done so. 'Why not?' pressed Carpmael. 'There was no danger,' Heighway answered simply.

Heighway agreed, when asked by the KC, that, after the alteration of course at 1404 towards the cruiser for eight minutes, a position of danger would possibly arise, although he did expect *Curacoa* to get out of the way.

Carpmael was persistent: 'The more you overtake *Curacoa* and then alter course towards her, the danger becomes greater, does it not?' And with Question 250 one senses he got the better of the Australian: 'In those circumstances I suggest that you ought to have been taking correct bearings of *Curacoa*.' Heighway's answer seemed weak: 'Not until we were on the next leg of the zigzag, anyway.'

Both Mr Justice Pilcher and Carpmael elicited from Heighway that during the starboard leg by *Queen Mary* towards *Curacoa* the bearing was narrowing and that, if this were so, *Curacoa* should have gone across *Queen Mary's* bows, and yet Robinson, in altering to port, made this less likely and the collision more likely.

Carpmael reiterated the point that it was inconsistent to allow the case that *Queen Mary* should be permitted to alter or interrupt her zigzag when a moment of tension arose earlier in the afternoon, but insist she should adhere strictly to the zigzag, without deviation, when the second emergency arose a short while later.

It would seem from the evidence that the moment when a decision should have been made by *Queen Mary* was at 1404 when either the zigzag should have been broken or at least *Queen Mary* should have sounded her siren indicating she was turning to starboard, thereby alerting *Curacoa's* officer of the watch of her intentions.

From 1404 on the die seems to have been cast. The substitution of Robinson for Wright at 1408 and the casual handing over of the watch made matters worse.

Nor was the situation eased by *Queen Mary* breaking the zigzag in the first instance, inviting *Curacoa* to believe she might do it again, and Captain Illingworth ordering his officer of the watch to reinstate the wheel order and to resume the zigzag, and in all good faith reassuring the bridge officers that *Curacoa* would keep clear.

But *Curacoa* steadfastly did not alter course nor feel obliged to keep clear, a view strengthened by *Queen Mary's* action in the first instance when *Curacoa* considered her to be the overtaking vessel and therefore required to keep clear. This terrible misunderstanding between the two captains ought never to have occurred. It is easy to enjoy the benefit of hindsight, but quite evidently both captains held strong, crucially opposed views and neither allowed the slightest doubt they might be wrong.

JUDGEMENT AGAINST NEGLIGENCE

'It is not the absolute duty of a naval vessel to keep out of the way of her charge – i.e. the sheep may be blameworthy if it allows the sheepdog to bite it.'

Captain W.H. Coombs, President of the Merchant Navy Officers' Federation. *

The resumed hearing in December, 1946, brought technical evidence about *Queen Mary's* performance from Mr John Brown, in charge of the ship designing department of the builders. The court learned that it took six and a half minutes to stop *Queen Mary's* engines and take way off the ship. It took even longer to go full astern. In ten years at sea in the *Queen*, the chief engineer stated, he had never been called upon to carry out such an order.

A further piece of statistical fact emerged: going ahead at 21 knots and putting the helm hard over, the liner took 4 minutes and 1 second to alter her heading 180 degrees.

The staff chief engineer, Thomas A.L. Bailey, responsible for 66 engineers and 24 electricians, was asked by Mr Hayward if he would welcome an order to go full astern from full ahead.†

'I certainly should not,' he replied.

Captain Illingworth was examined by Cunard's KC. Mr Hayward quickly disposed of all the well-known, undisputed facts. Temperatures rose somewhat when Mr Hayward asked the apparently innocuous question of the master, from his experience with convoys in two world wars, what he would say were 'the mutual duties of convoy and escort'.

Mr Carpmael for the Admiralty protested at the question. Mr Justice Pilcher reacted with a touch of asperity and answered the question himself:

---

*   On the face of it this is an amusing and graphic analogy, but on reflection its message is unclear.

†   A severe critic of the judge writes: 'Somewhere in the transcript there is mention of "putting the engines in reverse" as an option. That was Pilcher. I wonder if he had ever thought of changing gear in his Rolls flat out into reverse!'

'In the ordinary way the escorting vessel keeps clear of the vessels in convoy – that we have had hundreds of times in the Admiralty Court. I should think that it was common ground not only among the witnesses but with Elder Brethren, Court, Council and everybody. If that coincides with the master's view, so much the better.'

At one stage of cross-examination by Mr Carpmael it was stated that *Queen Mary* had forty guns mounted in her and carried 200 personnel to man them.

Illingworth also made the statement that he could not say whether Captain Boutwood knew that he himself was in command of *Queen Mary* on this voyage, but, whether he was in charge of her or somebody else was, there could be no ground for assuming that *Queen Mary* would make any other than a No. 8 Zigzag.

Mr Justice Pilcher intervened again after Captain Illingworth had repeated, 'I regarded it as the duty of the cruiser to give way, in accordance with the practice which obtains with convoys.'

The judge observed, 'Undoubtedly it was her duty to give way. If she had failed to give way, under the ordinary rules of seamanship, there would arise a point in time when it would be the duty of your ship to act to avoid colliding.'

Later the judge made the comment that there appeared to have been no Admiralty instructions to convoyed ships and escorts as to mutual duties in zigzagging and in possible emergencies. Mr Hayward, quoting a witness, stated, 'There are no regulations defining the function of the escort or the escorted ships.'

Mr Carpmael commented upon the numbers of American troops carried aboard *Queen Mary*. 'The statement had gone abroad that she carried over 15,000 American soldiers,' he declared. 'As a matter of fact one witness gave that figure in court. Counsel did not think it worthwhile to correct it at the time. There were times when she carried more than 15,000.'

Replying, Mr Hayward told the court, 'That we may have it correct now: the Captain of *Queen Mary* found from his records she was carrying 10,398.' (In fact, as we have seen, it was 10,239 plus about 900 crew.)

Another fact was established. The angle between the ships at the point of collision was stated by Mr Justice Pilcher to be not less than twenty degrees, but it was not more than forty degrees.

On resuming the hearing on Thursday, 12 December, 1946, Mr Justice Pilcher was able to display aspects of his pernickety nature. Mr Carpmael stressed the fact that a witness had said with her engines doing 28½ knots no way would be taken off *Queen Mary* until they had been stopped five minutes.

Mr Hayward said, 'One might assume that generally when steam was shut off the engines, the propellers would go on revolving in the water uselessly with no propulsive effect, but the *Queen Mary's* great powered engines continued to deliver thrust to the ship for a long time.'

The judge pronounced, 'If one has a ship which cannot stop in under five minutes, as to the duty of taking measures, you must take them earlier than a ship which can stop in two minutes. But no one will persuade me that with her 158,000 HP engines the *Queen Mary* will continue to go at the same pace five minutes after she has stopped them. If she can do that she has nearly solved the problem of perpetual motion. . . . The officer who said she would go as fast after five minutes was talking nonsense.'

At another stage of the proceedings Mr Justice Pilcher speculated, 'One could understand it if the *Queen Mary* had said she did not like zigzagging while passing up the port side of the *Curacoa*. She might have reasoned, "I will overtake and resume my zigzag when I have finished overtaking." But there is not a jot of evidence of that as a deliberate measure.'

John Boutwood had last given evidence about eighteen months before. He now returned to the witness box to give evidence of *Curacoa's* speed. He had already affirmed that her full speed was 25 knots. To achieve this the engine revolutions must be over 280 – between 280 and 285 – 'in proper conditions of still water'. Boutwood had ordered 280 revs.

In answer to Mr Justice Pilcher's question, 'Do you give your order in knots or in revolutions?' Boutwood replied, 'Revolutions.'

'Then you order "280" and not 25 knots?'

Boutwood agreed; when he said he ordered 25 knots, he ordered 280 revolutions.

Under cross-examination from Mr Hayward, Boutwood agreed he was unable to say exactly what speed 280 revs represented in the circumstances.

Scientific evidence was presented to the court by Dr Edmund Victor Telfer, consulting naval architect, called for the Admiralty, and Dr Andrew McCance Robb DSc LLD, professor of naval architecture at Glasgow University, representing the owners of *Queen Mary*.

Dr Telfer thought that to some extent 'interaction' came into play during the yaws of both ships, and that it affected the observation of the other ship when either was under some helm. But he thought it impossible that a navigator would not allow for such in his calculations.

Mr Hayward posed the question as to whether there would have been a collision had *Curacoa* at the end kept to her fifteen degrees of starboard wheel. Dr Telfer agreed that there would not have been a collision. Answering the judge, he explained that the starboard helm of fifteen degrees, beginning as early as it did, would have prevented a build-up of interaction and that the cruiser would have got clear of *Queen Mary*, even if the liner had taken no action at all.

The scientist underlined, of course, that he was speaking geometrically and according to technical expectations. He did not think both ships would have gone clear if *Curacoa* had had a yaw of seven degrees to port.

The theory that the immense volume of water thrust aside by *Queen Mary* had swung the light cruiser to port across her bows was tested in practice at the National Physical Laboratory at Teddington, Middlesex. The theory of interaction was examined and the *Curacoa* incident analysed by Professor Robb.*

Mr Justice Pilcher's prickly attitude emerged again when Dr Robb's qualifications were established. He had been invalided in 1916 in Mesopotamia, joined the Admiralty in the Department of Shipbuilding; then he was on the Constructive Staff.

The judge asked whether the word should be 'Constructive' or 'Constructional'.

Dr Robb said he thought 'Constructive' was right, but he could not say definitely.

Mr Justice Pilcher said he only wondered why the Admiralty adopted a different word from what he should have thought was adopted by the rest of the community.

Referring to the *Curacoa* Incident, Dr Robb commented in the *Transactions*:

'The problem in this case was really to determine the curious action of the cruiser just prior to the collision. To study the problem, the Admiralty, at my suggestion, agreed to special model experiments being carried out at the National Physical Laboratory. These experiments were carried out on self-propelled models one-fifty-sixth full size. Special delicate dynamometers held the *Curacoa* model forward and aft so that by the tension in the constraining springs the transverse force induced on the *Curacoa* by the *Queen Mary* could be measured accurately. Measurements of this kind were made with the two ships in various relative positions and at various distances apart . . .

'One particular test was carried out at the request of the judge, who, together with the Elder Brethren, the respective barristers and their juniors, witnessed some typical experiments before the final hearing of the case took place in the Admiralty Court. The test, of course, was not a fair one, as it did not represent a practical possibility.

'Actually, the *Curacoa* should have first started to yaw into the *Queen Mary* before the correcting rudder was put on; and in this case its effect would not have been nearly so rapid. However, it seemed fairly certain that if the captain of the *Curacoa* had appreciated that his vessel was in any – not to say extreme – danger from

* Dr Robb contributed a section in *Marsden's Collisions*, and the article 'Interactions Between Ships' in *Transactions* of the Royal Institute of Naval Architects, Vol 91, 1949.

133

the *Queen Mary* causing his vessel to swing across her path, he could probably have prevented the collision. This in fact was the decision of the judge, and because of this he held the *Curacoa* solely to blame for the accident. To comment on this judgement one can only say that it is practically certain that competent navigators who may have found themselves in the same position as the captain of the *Curacoa* with his ship running parallel to the *Queen Mary* and 150 metres from it would never have expected his vessel in such deep water to behave as did the *Curacoa*.'

Robb summarized his views with a question:

'What is the scientific lesson of all this experience? It is simply that when a ship moves through the water it sends out in front of it a field of excess pressure. A similar but not so intense field also exists behind the ship, but between its bow and stern the pressure is correspondingly reduced below the surrounding pressure. When one ship begins to overtake another their two fields begin to overlap and their steering is interfered with. This interference is much greater in shallow water since the pressures coming from the ships are absorbed by much less water and consequently greater local pressures are induced in the water. When the depth of water is not regular but is much shallower on one side than the other, the pressures on the bow of the ship will be greater and thus she will always turn away into deep water.'

Another view of this interaction, a less scientific view, is provided by Captain Harry Grattidge:

'I was always conscious of the need to keep a safety margin of between one and two miles away from every other craft . . . until the channel was widened at Cowes the pleasure boats skimming close to our bows were a nightmare; and the *Mary*'s bow wave was so great it sometimes sucked swimmers from the beach and into the water when she was seven miles from shore.'*

But the conclusions drawn from these scientific experiments and the technical evidence of Dr Robb, however well presented, did not unduly influence the judge. He relied much more heavily on the evidence of the witnesses.

He lamented the fact that, despite the production of several Admiralty Merchant Service Instructions (AMSIs), these were *post facto* and the crux

---

* Grattidge, op. cit.

of this case was that 'the poor fellows were left to their own resources; nobody knew what the responsibilities were'.

His Lordship observed that as there were no particular instructions for this convoy officers would tend to adopt the general rule that escorts kept out of the way of ships in the convoy. The case was not to be decided by the collision regulations or by rules in AMSI, but by a finding with the assistance of the Elder Brethren upon the obligation to give way. Further, he commented, if the cruiser had maintained her fifteen degrees of wheel she would have got clear away.

Mr Carpmael made a strong plea on the afternoon of Tuesday, 17 December. He clearly blamed the liner for not keeping a good lookout and for not taking steps to keep clear of the cruiser. Either she should have starboarded more, or earlier, or later, to go under the cruiser's stern. And she failed to port her wheel when she should have done. Further, she failed to announce her movements by whistle signals.

Mr Justice Pilcher said that the time would be reached when both ships would be in a position when one or the other would have to give way, but neither had instructions as to which was the give-way vessel. Usually the convoy would keep its course while the escort darted in and out among the ships like a sheepdog among the sheep. But this was a case, one of a minority, where the escort was slower than her charge.

In his final submission Mr Carpmael submitted that *Curacoa's* last actions came within the category known to the court as 'acts taken in the agony of collision'. The cruiser took the right action at the last, which, if maintained, would have avoided collision. *Queen Mary*, in contrast, did not take the right action at the last. It was wrong of her to alter course to starboard towards the cruiser. She had previously taken action to avoid getting too close to the cruiser, and her duty was to keep clear. She could have starboarded more and gone under the cruiser's stern, or have gone straight ahead.

During Mr Hayward's submissions he introduced the likely sums of money entailed in the possible court judgement. He calculated life claims at £3,000 each, aggregating over £1 million. The value of the cruiser was put at £450,000 and there would be other consequential damage claims.

His Lordship was surprised at the photograph of the damage to *Queen Mary's* bows. He said he had no idea such a bite had been taken out of her.

He rejected a submission by Mr Hayward that neither party was negligent. But for interaction neither ship had reason to anticipate collision, then claim and counter-claim failed.

Mr Justice Pilcher found it difficult to accede to this conclusion. He could not think it proper to allow vessels of this size and speed to get so close to each other as to bring the forces of interaction into play: 'Can you think it right to let these vessels get within 250 ft of each other?'

Mr Hayward offered the suggestion that *Curacoa* was coming to speak with a loud hailer and denied it was negligent for the two ships to get within 250 ft. His Lordship demurred.

Christmas, 1946, intervened and Mr Justice Pilcher gave his judgement on Tuesday, 21 January, 1947, nearly four and a half years after the event.

He said it was abundantly clear the collision was one which ought never to have been permitted to occur. He reviewed Captain Boutwood's evidence in some detail for two reasons. Firstly, he was the only witness from *Curacoa* and was on the bridge all the time after his lunch between 1230 and 1300. Secondly, because 'he gave his evidence with great care and with the obvious feeling of responsibility which one would expect from a witness of his standing and quality. It is difficult to imagine an ordeal more trying than that through which he must have passed, and if I feel myself unable to accept his recollection on certain matters of fact this is not because I formed an unfavourable view of his demeanour in the witness box.'

In his judgement, Mr Justice Pilcher commented upon other witnesses. Whereas he also approved of Mr Robinson's demeanour in the witness box, he considered Mr Wright a thoroughly unsatisfactory witness, dull-witted with poor powers of observation and a very poor memory. Some of his answers were such nonsense to show him to be either incapable or unwilling to visualize the situation. The judge found himself only able to attach importance to his evidence when it was corroborated by other witnesses. Of Mr Hewitt Mr Justice Pilcher found little to say, but he was exceedingly appreciative of Mr Heighway's manner of giving his evidence. He considered him to be very intelligent and to have thought a great deal about the case. He was not shaken in cross-examination and was not prepared to pledge his recollection to matters he did not remember even when they tended to advance the defendant's case.

In recent correspondence, Bill Heighway told Patrick Holmes how impressed he was when Cunard officials he talked to in no way wished him to colour his answers in any way to favour the defendant's case; nor did he see Cunard's counsel, Hayward, until he got into the witness box. He also wrote that in his opinion the judge was somewhat too harsh in his opinion of 'Shiner' Wright. Heighway had been impressed by Wright's competence.

The judge commented that it was on all these matters of fact that he had to determine where the blame lay for this collision. 'No specific instructions had been given to either vessel as to which was to regard herself as the give-way and which the stand-on ship. . . . It is axiomatic that under ordinary convoy conditions it is the duty of faster and more manoeuvrable escort vessels to keep out of the way of the units of the convoy.'

It was evident that throughout most of the hearing of this case the judge had little doubt that, if risk of collision developed, it was the duty of the escort, whose freedom of action was completely unfettered, to keep clear.

After the conclusion of the hearing Mr Justice Pilcher consulted the Elder Brethren who agreed with him that this was not a case to which the Collision

Regulations applied, and therefore not a case in which the overtaking rule should apply: that is, as a matter of seamanship the escort must be regarded as the give-way ship and the escorted vessel as the stand-on ship.

He also blamed *Curacoa* for not keeping close enough attention to what *Queen Mary* was doing during the half-hour before the collision. Accurate observation should have noted the continuation of *Queen Mary's* zigzag and if, indeed, Captain Boutwood did not know what the troopship was doing he should have signalled for information. It would also have been prudent to have synchronized clocks with *Queen Mary* as to be more properly aware of *Queen Mary's* zigzag alterations.

It was also the judge's view that until a very late moment the collision could have been avoided by the starboard wheel action of the *Curacoa* alone. The judge accepted that at the very last moment the cruiser's wheel was put to port:

> 'Whether the wheel of the cruiser was put to port at the last as the result of a panic order or as the result of the misinterpretation of some order given by Captain Boutwood will never be known. I am satisfied that the wheel was, in fact, put to port at the last, that the putting of the wheel to port was negligent and that it was this action which immediately brought about the collision. . . . I accordingly find that the *Curacoa* is seriously to blame (i) for a bad lookout, (ii) for failing to starboard in due time or sufficiently, and (iii) for putting her wheel to port at the last.'*

Mr Justice Pilcher then turned his attention to *Queen Mary's* part in the incident, to assess whether any blame rested with her. She was entitled to expect, he commented, that the cruiser would watch the zigzag and take steps not to interfere with it:

> 'His Lordship did not think there was any obligation upon her to sound a short blast on her whistle when she starboarded on to her 131 degree course, and, even if failure to sound was negligent, it did not contribute to the collision. . . . If the starboard wheel of the *Curacoa* had been persisted in, no collision would have occurred, even if the *Queen Mary* had taken no helm action. His Lordship thought it unlikely that the *Curacoa*, after correcting her port yaw, ever went off substantially to starboard of her 108 degree course under her starboard wheel.'

Mr Justice Pilcher concluded with a reference to Robinson's order 'port a little' given half a minute or so after the wheel of the cruiser was starboarded

---

* *Lloyd's List*, Law Report, 22 January, 1947.

and at a time when the vessels were still nearly two cables apart. Such an order was not accepted Royal Navy terminology and by the Navy's standard is regarded as sloppy. Robinson followed this order some half a minute later with the order 'Hard-a-port'. The judge considered that this was the first moment when the situation appeared to Robinson to be dangerous:

> 'He knew that the cruiser was used to escorting, that she was fully manned by highly-trained officers, and the fact is that when he took action, the cruiser had already taken action which, if persisted in, would by itself have avoided collision. In the circumstances, speaking for myself, I find it very difficult to say that Mr Robinson is to blame for not taking earlier or more drastic helm action. Whether he ought to have done so or not was, however, a question upon which I was entitled to ask the view of the Elder Brethren. I accordingly did so. They replied that they found it impossible to say that Mr Robinson ought to have acted earlier or differently.'*

Mr Justice Pilcher accordingly found the *Queen Mary* free from blame and the collision solely due to the negligence of those on board the *Curacoa*.

It was a harsh and, many thought, an unkind judgement. To find one party totally blameless seemed to do an injustice to the other, especially when the whole case revolved around the question of which ship had right of way. Both captains could claim, almost with equal persuasion, the strengths of their case, yet Mr Justice Pilcher settled heavily in favour of Captain Illingworth and his officers. Is there a detectable suggestion here that Captain Boutwood was being offered up as a scapegoat?

With the publication of his Lordship's judgement it may have seemed to be the end of the *Curacoa* Incident: far from it. The litigation was to drag on for over two years before being finally laid to rest.

* *Lloyd's List*, Law Report, 22 January, 1947.

COURT OF APPEAL

'His Lordship thought there was no reason why those in the *Queen Mary* should not have ported their wheel in ample time to avoid collision – and every reason why they should.'

Lord Justice Bucknill, Court of Appeal, 30 July, 1947.

Cunard's enjoyment of the Pilcher judgement was short-lived. The Admiralty lodged an appeal immediately, but as is so often the way with legal matters, the hearing did not come on for another six months. It was Tuesday, 19 July, 1947, when the case was brought to the Supreme Court of Judicature. Sitting in judgement were Lords Justice Scott,* Bucknill,† and Wrottesley,‡ with Rear Admiral H.D. Hamilton and Captain W.P. Townshend, nautical assessors, to assist them.

Mr Kenneth Carpmael KC again represented the Admiralty, with Mr J.V. Naisby KC replacing Mr O.L. Bateson KC. Cunard were again represented by Mr R.F. Hayward KC, Mr Waldo Porges and by Mr H.E.G. Browning.

Judge Scott made clear his view that the case did not rest on seamanship but on (i) a true analysis of the legal duties of the two ships and (ii) the last twelve, and especially the last three or four, minutes before the accident when Senior First Officer Robinson was on the bridge. It is unclear what he meant by this observation because the last critical few minutes had everything to do with good or bad seamanship on both sides.

The fact that Judge Scott's views differed from those of Judges Bucknill and Wrottesley make it important that his views should be considered

---

* Rt Hon Sir Leslie (Frederic) Scott (1869–1950). Solicitor General 1922. Lord Justice of appeal 1935–48. MP Liverpool Exchange 1910–29. Represented government at international conferences on maritime law.

† Rt Hon Sir Alfred Townsend Bucknill (1880–1963) KC 1931. Judge of High Court of Justice 1935–45.

‡ Sir Frederic John Wrottesley (1880–1948). KC 1926. Judge of King's Bench Division 1937–47. Lord Justice of Appeal 1947–8. Knighted 1937. PC 1947.

carefully, as he himself said, for the benefit of the House of Lords where he felt sure the case would be heard eventually.

Both Pilcher, at the main hearing, and Scott stated categorically that Article 24 of the Regulations for Preventing Collisions as Sea did not apply in this case. Article 24's first paragraph reads:

> 'Notwithstanding anything contained in these Rules, every vessel, overtaking any other, shall keep out of the way of the overtaken vessel.'

The argument that since *Curacoa* was the escort and *Queen Mary* the convoy, then, by some unwritten law, the overtaking rule no longer applied and that the troopship was the stand-on vessel and the anti-aircraft cruiser the give-way one was strongly upheld by Mr Justice Scott.

The two other judges also upheld this argument, but they brought into the debate the possibility of neither ship holding right of way, and they asked the two nautical assessors, 'What then?'

The function of the assessors was to give the Court expert evidence on technical matters of seamanship and navigation. The assessors commented that they found it impossible to say that Mr Robinson ought to have acted earlier or differently. The assessors were then asked by the Court to consider some specific questions and their written answers were given in evidence:

Q 1: Assume that the *Queen Mary* steadied on her course of 131 degrees at a speed of about 28½ knots when the cruiser was broad on her starboard bow and proceeding at about 25 knots, and on a course of 108 degrees and about three-quarters of a mile away. And assume that each vessel thereafter kept on their courses and speeds without any appreciable alteration of the bearing of the other ship: assume also that the overtaking and overtaken rules do not apply, but that the practice of good seamanship governed the navigation of each ship, then: (a) At what distance from the *Queen Mary* do you consider the cruiser should have taken action to avoid collision; and what action should she have taken?

Answer: Four cables, starboard twenty, at least.

(b) At what distance from the cruiser do you consider the *Queen Mary* should have taken action to avoid collision, and what action should she have taken?

Answer: Five cables; hard-a-port.

Q 2: Assume the relative positions and navigation of each ship as stated in Q 1, and assume that the primary duty was on the cruiser to keep out of the way of the *Queen Mary* in the execution of her zigzag leg of 131 degrees:

(a) Was it seamanlike of the *Queen Mary* to continue on her course at her speed until the cruiser was two cables away?

Answer: No.

(b) Was her action of porting a little then proper and seaman-like?

Answer: No.

If not: (c) What, as a matter of good seamanship, ought she to have done?

Answer: Hard-a-port should have been given at five cables because she would close two cables before any wheel action took effect.

Q 3: At what distance from the *Curacoa* do you consider good seamanship required the *Queen Mary* to take action to avoid colli-sion, assuming (a) the two ships were on converging courses of 131 and 108 degrees respectively with the *Curacoa* broad on the *Queen Mary's* bow for some four or five minutes before the colli-sion, speeds as before, and (b) at no time did those in charge of the *Queen Mary* observe any indication that the *Curacoa* was taking any steps to keep out of the way of the *Queen Mary*, and (c) that it was the duty of the *Curacoa* to keep out of the way of the *Queen Mary*, and (d) that it was the duty of the *Queen Mary* to keep her course and speed – (1) until there was serious risk of collision; alternatively (2) until those in the *Queen Mary* could see that a collision could not be avoided by the action of the *Curacoa* alone?

Answer: Five cables: (1) At anything less than five cables there was a serious risk of collision: (2) At anything less than five cables any action by the *Queen Mary* might negative the action taken by the *Curacoa* due to the *Queen Mary's* stern swinging out.

In giving his judgement Lord Justice Scott gave the opinion that Mr Justice Pilcher's conclusion six months earlier, that grave blame rested on the cruiser, was undoubtedly right. The only question of doubt he allowed was whether the liner was too late or too timid in her porting, and was she really to blame for not acting quite soon enough in the very special circumstances of the case.

Lord Justice Scott held that there was no duty on the liner to blow her whistle when she turned on her last starboard leg of the zigzag.

He thought Robinson (described later by a naval officer who knew him as 'that twerp') was consistent with good seamanship and even if he erred by not acting more strongly or earlier after his cautious 'port a little' he could not be blamed.

His Lordship was also satisfied that interaction had nothing to do with the collision.

Lords Justice Bucknill and Wrottesley were in agreement with their judgements. The significant parts of Lord Justice Bucknill's conclusions are summed up:

> 'To carry out her zigzag operation at full speed was the best safe-guard for the *Queen Mary* and those on board, and it was very desirable therefore that the *Curacoa* should not embarrass her in that operation by getting in her way. On the other hand, I do not think that that in itself was sufficient to release the *Queen Mary* from the obligation to obey the overtaking rule when approaching the *Curacoa*, unless there was either (a) a rule, or (b) a recognized practice or (c) a definite understanding between the captain of the *Curacoa* and the captain of the *Queen Mary* to that effect, or (d) the circumstances of the case were such as clearly to require that the *Curacoa* should keep out of the way and not keep her course and speed.'

In brief, Judge Bucknill's views on these four possibilities were that, as regards (a) Captain Illingworth said that no instructions were issued as to what was to take place and who was to give way if danger of collision arose.

As for (b) there was no evidence of any such recognized practice. Indeed, when first Robinson and then Wright manoeuvred the *Queen Mary* to keep out of the way of the cruiser at about 1335 they negatived any such practice.

As regards (c) when the captains met ashore in August only the likelihood of zigzagging was mentioned and nothing as regards the possibility of collision was mentioned.

To answer question (d) the Judge asked another one:

> 'Was the danger of hostile attack to which the *Queen Mary* was exposed such as to justify her in not complying with the overtaking rule, and was it the duty of the cruiser as an anti-aircraft escort to the *Queen Mary* to depart from obedience to the overtaking rule (which required her to keep her course and speed when risk of collision arose) and herself to keep out of the way of the *Queen Mary*? The answer to this by Judge Pilcher was categorically No. And supported by the views of the Elder Brethren, Pilcher said, "This is not a case to which the Collision Regulations as such apply. It is not . . . a case in which I should be justified in applying the overtaking rule even as a matter of seamanship . . . it is a case in which as a matter of seamanship, the escort must in the first instance be regarded as the give-way ship and the escorted vessel as the stand-on ship."'

142

The Court of Appeal asked their own assessors for their views on these matters and received this advice. The *Curacoa*, as an anti-aircraft defence ship, had every right to expect the *Queen Mary* to keep out of the way, and one of the assessors added that, in order to obtain the most efficient anti-aircraft visual look out, the cruiser should proceed on a steady course and that the *Queen Mary*, when overtaking, could and should have given way.

Lord Justice Bucknill considered that *Queen Mary* left it far too late to avoid *Curacoa* because Mr Robinson's hard-a-port, ordered when only 450 ft away, was far too late to have any effect, and he supported this contention by going back to the time when Captain Illingworth told Mr Wright to put *Queen Mary* back on her course and added, 'These fellows are used to escorting. They won't interfere with you.'

Paragraph 60 of Judge Bucknill's judgement reads:

> 'The judge [Mr Justice Pilcher] has pointed out in his Judgement that having regard to the distance at which the *Queen Mary* passed astern of the cruiser shortly before 1340, it was quite likely that when the *Queen Mary* on her next leg of 131 degrees crossed the course of the *Curacoa* between 1404 and 1412 there would be risk of collision. And so, indeed, the event proved. Under the circumstances it is remarkable that at the time of the collision Captain Illingworth was in his chartroom with Mr Wright, in connection with some message about the ship's arrival, and the first intimation he had of danger of collision was the shock of the collision itself. Mr Wright did not warn the captain that a dangerous situation was arising. I doubt if Mr Robinson had sufficient time to send a message to the captain about it.

Lord Justice Bucknill continued in paragraph 61 of his conclusions:

> 'Mr Wright admitted that the *Curacoa* when two cables away was very close, but he also said that the cruiser was heading parallel with his course and that he had no occasion to be worried about her at all. There he was wrong. Obviously wrong. He would have known if he had watched the cruiser that the ships were on converging courses and rapidly closing since he gave the order to starboard to 131 degrees at 1404. I think it probable that Mr Wright, having had his discretion as to the manoeuvre to take in order to avoid collision with the cruiser interfered with by Captain Illingworth half an hour earlier, paid no further attention to the cruiser and continued to navigate the ship as if the cruiser was not there.'

Judge Bucknill continues in the next two paragraphs:

'The effect of Captain Illingworth's directions to Mr Wright was to reverse the Collision Regulations and to make the overtaking ship the stand-on ship, and the stand-on ship the give-way ship; and this without any rule or clearly recognised practice to that effect.

'If Captain Illingworth had been on the bridge of his ship at the critical time I feel confident he would have ported and got on to a parallel course with the cruiser when the vessels were about four or five cables apart.'

It had become clear that whatever action was taken by either ship, once they had closed to four cables apart, it would not then avoid a collision.

As with *Queen Mary*, so with *Curacoa*. Action taken was too little and/or too late. Mr Robinson's hard-a-port was too late. His 'port a little' was absurdly too little. Captain Boutwood's 'Starboard fifteen' was, in all the judges' opinion, applied later than he stated it was; the porting of *Curacoa's* wheel to swing her stern clear, if it happened, was too late and too little.

Boutwood spoilt his case by admitting that he would have altered to starboard had he realized that what he thought was a yaw was the 1412 turn of twenty-five degrees to starboard by *Queen Mary*. It seems he did not realize at what stage on her zigzag *Queen Mary* was, because he had come to the conclusion that the liner had given up Zigzag No. 8. However, his argument that *Queen Mary* was the overtaking vessel suggests that his alteration to starboard, which was little and late, was based on the note to Rule 21 of the Collision Prevention Regulations whereby 'when the keep-on vessel [in Boutwood's opinion *Curacoa*] finds herself so close that collision cannot be avoided by the action of the giving-way vessel alone [i.e. *Queen Mary* in Boutwood's belief,] she also shall take such action as will best aid to avert collision.'

Because Judge Bucknill concluded that the overtaking rule in this case did not apply, a view in which he was supported by the Trial judge and by Judge Scott, it is not surprising to find the blame being apportioned two-thirds on the *Curacoa* and one-third on the *Queen Mary*.

Lord Justice Wrottesley agreed basically with almost all of Lord Justice Bucknill's findings, but he added a few telling points. How would things have been had there only been one witness from the *Queen Mary* instead of five officers and two helmsmen? No officers aboard *Curacoa* other than Captain Boutwood and Pat Holmes were saved, and Holmes was not on the bridge and therefore not privy to the comments made by those who were: Lieutenant Johnson, the navigating officer was there, and the Principal Control Officer who was the senior officer of the watch, Lieutenant Brittain. He and the junior officer of the watch, Lieutenant Maxwell, were also on the bridge when the collision occurred; none was saved. However, Pat Holmes did have a ringside view of the approaching calamity from his Air Defence Position.

Lord Justice Wrottesley underlined the following points. He did not believe that *Curacoa* at any stage turned more than ten degrees to port; he was sure that Robinson went hard-a-port far too late and that the order had no time to take effect; that from 1340 to 1344 with *Queen Mary* on a mean course of 106 degrees the two ships must have been very close to near parallel courses. He also concluded scathingly that Wright's opinion that from thereon *Curacoa* zigzagged with *Queen Mary* was, of course, pure rubbish. He found Boutwood's memory at that time also very hazy, but found this failure not at all surprising considering what he had been through.

From 1340 to 1400 aboard *Queen Mary* only Wright can speak with authority as neither the captain nor Third Officer Heighway stayed on the bridge since they were making navigational calculations in the chartroom.

Wrottesley infers that, since Illingworth's interference and his telling Wright not to worry about *Curacoa*, Wright seems to have forgotten the escort's existence. The trouble about Illingworth's statement, in Wrottesley's opinion, was that he was stating truths only for normal convoys in which the escorts are far more agile than the slow-moving merchantmen.

Wrottesley pointed out that Pilcher thought that *Queen Mary* was entitled to believe that *Curacoa* would get out of the way for four reasons:

(1) She had freedom of action.
(2) The overtaking rule did not apply.
(3) As a matter of seamanship *Queen Mary* was the stand-on vessel.
(4) *Queen Mary's* prime duty was to hold on to her zigzag.

Pilcher assumes that Boutwood should have agreed with these assumptions, whereas, of course, he did not agree with points (2) and (3).

Point (1) deserves some comment. *Curacoa* needed to keep close and maintain a straight and steady course or as straight and steady as yawing in the difficult following sea allowed. Boutwood was, in fact, constant to his signal of 1220 when he stated (a) his course – 108 degrees: and it is worth noting that when *Queen Mary* discovered her two-degree compass error and corrected the 108 to 106 degrees, she never told *Curacoa*. (b) His speed – 25 knots flat out, and (c) That he would fall in astern of *Queen Mary* on her mean course after having been passed. Because of these points, Wrottesley differed from the opinion of the learned judge and suggested that *Curacoa* did not have complete liberty of action.

As regards point (2), Wrottesley did not agree with the scrapping of the overtaking rule and reversal of roles, and therefore he found no reason to allow *Queen Mary* to become the stand-on ship. He considered neither the sanctity of Zigzag No. 8 nor any other zigzag sufficient reason to scrap the overtaking rule. And how was the captain of *Curacoa* possibly expected to know?

Lord Justice Wrottesley went on to point out that the deviation made to the zigzag between 1332 and 1340 in no way made a U-boat's task any easier, and nor would it if *Queen Mary* had kept out of the way of *Curacoa* at, say, 1408.

Another point he made: it would have been harder for *Curacoa* to gauge the movements of the zigzagging *Queen* than for the *Queen* to watch the straight-steaming cruiser. However, it is also arguable that since *Curacoa's* course was constant, bearings of the other ship should have been made with relative ease. Assuming *Queen Mary's* bearing between say 1407 and 1410 did not change, then it should have been imperative for *Curacoa* to go hard to starboard and damn the consequences.

Up in the ADP Holmes found himself mesmerised by the approaching disaster, yet even he thought it only inevitable during the last minute. He took a quick glance over his right shoulder to see what was happening on the bridge. Holmes comments:

> 'In my mind there is no doubt at all that *Queen Mary's* turn to starboard in obedience to the zigzag clock at 1404 should never have been made. Having been made it took three minutes for the liner to get onto the 131 degrees course, and if bearings of *Curacoa* had been taken then, and again at 1408, it must have been seen that unless the *Queen Mary* had gone hard-a-port at once – or even hard-a-starboard – there was going to be a collision. *Queen Mary's* course was altered without due thought, and Wright's handing over to Robinson without any mention of *Curacoa* was criminal. It seems to me that of all the four judges involved in the trial case and the Court of Enquiry, both Bucknill and Wrottesley came near to justice being done; and of the two, Wrottesley's views came nearest the truth.'

These two judges took the view that the blame for the accident should be apportioned as to two-thirds on the cruiser and one-third on the liner.

Accordingly, the appeal was allowed, and it was directed that costs were to be apportioned in accordance with the degree of blame.

HOUSE OF LORDS

'Each ship must take appropriate action when danger of a collision arises in her case, and is guilty of some negligence if she fails to do so.'

Lord Porter, House of Lords, 8 February, 1949.

More than six years after the collision the third and final act in the drama between *Queen Mary* and *Curacoa*, Cunard's appeal to the House of Lords, was played out on the eleven court days between 13 October and 1 November, 1948.

The case was held before Lord Porter,* Lord Merriman,† Lord du Parcq,‡ Lord Normand,§ and Lord MacDermott,¶ sitting with Vice Admiral Moore and Captain Chaplin RN as nautical assessors. Both Cunard and the Admiralty were represented by the familiar leading counsel as in the Court of Appeal.

At the end of the case judgement was reserved and was handed down on 8 February, 1949, nearly six and a half years since the tragedy. It had been a long haul.

It was a long hearing, repetitively tedious at times with leading counsel going over the same ground. Few could complain that any evidence or legal nuance, however small, had not been given an exhaustive and fair hearing.

---

* Baron Samuel Lowry Porter PC (1877–1956) Called to the Bar 1905; KC 1925. Judge of High Court of Justice 1934–38. Lord of Appeal in Ordinary 1938–54.
† Baron Frank Boyd Merriman (1880–1962). MP Rusholme Division of Manchester 1924–33 and became Solicitor General. Appointed President Probate Divorce and Admiralty Division of the High Court of Justice 1933.
‡ Baron Herbert du Parcq (1880–1949). KC 1926. Judge of the High Court of Justice 1932–38. Lord Justice of Appeal 1938–46.
§ Baron Wilfrid Guild Normand PC (1884–1962). KC 1925. Lord of Appeal 1947–53. MP and Solicitor General, and Lord Advocate for Scotland.
¶ Baron John Clarke MacDermott PC (1896–1979). Lord Chief Justice of Northern Ireland 1951–71. KC 1936. MP and Attorney General Northern Ireland. Lord of Appeal 1947–51.

The *Lloyd's List* Law Report on the House of Lords case headed 'The *Queen Mary*' spreads over forty pages of double columns; thirty-five of them were given over to the judgements. In the order in which the speeches were heard on 8 February, 1949, Lord Porter's judgement covered ten and a half pages; Lord Merriman's fourteen pages; Lord du Parcq's just a single column; Lord Normand's five pages and Lord MacDermott's also five pages.

Pat Holmes has calculated that the speeches took more than three hours to deliver; Lord Merriman's alone, probably lasted seventy-five minutes.

The hearing began with a recapitulation of the facts and arguments. Mr Hayward for the Cunard White Star Company reiterated his belief that *Queen Mary* was the stand-on vessel entitled to maintain her course until it became apparent that the cruiser could not by her own action alone avoid collision. On the question of interaction, he considered those aboard *Curacoa* should have taken avoiding action long before there could have been any suggestion of interaction: 'It was a matter of good seamanship,' he said.

He went on: 'It was the duty of the *Queen Mary* to keep her course and speed until the time when a prudent seaman would say collision could not be avoided by the *Curacoa's* own action.'

There were constant exchanges between the Lords and leading counsel; statement, question and answer, and typical of these was this. Mr Hayward said:

'It was clear from the evidence of Captain Boutwood that he conceived his duty to be not to embarrass the *Queen Mary*. What could that mean except keep out of the way? Lord Justice Bucknill in his judgement said: "I think good seamanship cast upon the cruiser the duty to keep out of the way of the *Queen Mary* as she performed her zigzag manoeuvres and to keep careful watch on her for that purpose." Lord Justice Wrottesley said: "The *Queen Mary's* alteration to starboard was one which the *Curacoa* might reasonably be thought to expect and provide for." Counsel submitted that "provide for" could not mean anything except take note of and act in accordance with. . . . He would point out that the unanimous findings of the Judges and the Court of Appeal were that if a good lookout had been kept on the *Curacoa* those on board her must have known that the *Queen Mary* at the material time was on her course of 131 degrees in pursuance of Zigzag No. 8. To refrain from causing embarrassment to the *Queen Mary* meant that she must be given reasonable seaway and that, in turn, meant that the *Curacoa* must not be on the *Queen Mary's* pattern at the moment she was on it. The position was quite different from two strange ships approaching each other.'*

Mr Carpmael presented the case for the Admiralty, submitting that *Queen Mary* should be held solely responsible for the collision. Argument centred on Collision Regulations. Carpmael submitted these points: he argued that both the captain of the cruiser and the master of the liner were bound to apply to collision regulations unless they were shown to be abrogated. They were not abrogated by the sailing instructions given to Illingworth. He was told to maintain his speed. That did not contravene the collision regulations (unless it was pursued in fog or in circumstances likely to lead to a collision). Illingworth was told to zigzag. That did not abrogate the regulations.

Mr Carpmael stressed the unprofessional-like manner in which the watch had been handed over: the two vessels were only two cables apart when Wright turned his back on the situation and handed over to his relief, Noel Robinson, simply with the words 'same course and speed'. No compass bearings of the cruiser were taken in the minutes before the collision. They must inevitably have given early indications that a risk of collision existed.

Captain Illingworth came in for criticism, as did his officers. When the master had been asked about the action of the officer on the bridge when *Curacoa* was four points on the bow and only two cables away he replied that the officer would know instinctively that he would have to call the master to the bridge. But in point of fact no one did call the master to the bridge. Furthermore, the officer on the bridge at this critical time did not know what the cruiser was doing. This, Mr Carpmael submitted, was a failure of the master to keep his officers informed on essential aspects of the operation.

The long ordeal by litigation over the *Curacoa* Incident came to a head on Tuesday 8 February, 1949, with the House of Lords judgement. Lord Porter's opinion, read by Lord du Parcq because of Lord Porter's indisposition, referred in detail to the facts of the evidence. Lord Porter:

'cited the relevant rules for the avoidance of collisions at sea, and said that he was of opinion that Rules 21 and 24 did not apply in reverse. As a matter of good seamanship it was the primary duty of the *Curacoa* to keep out of the way of the *Queen Mary*, but that did not mean that the *Queen Mary* was the stand-on ship. Each ship must take appropriate action when danger of collision arose in her case, and was guilty of some negligence if she failed to do so. He thought that Regulations 27 and 29 both applied.'†

* *Lloyd's List*, Law Report, October, 1948.
† *The Times*, 9 February, 1949.

Lord Porter's judgement went on to criticize the lookout aboard *Curacoa* which was 'obviously faulty'. It ought to have been detected immediately *Queen Mary* steadied on her course of 131 degrees that the two ships were converging and *Curacoa* ought to have altered course to starboard to get clear.

But the cruiser took no steps to do so until the liner was four cables away and possibly as close as two cables. And *Curacoa* evidently failed to realize the ships were converging until too late to take adequate remedial action. His Lordship recognized, however, that by the time this situation had been reached, *Queen Mary* herself should have acted when the distance apart was five cables, when she should have ordered hard-a-port, whereas she took no action until the ships were two cables apart and collision inevitable. When, at this stage she did take action it was to port the wheel only ten degrees, and the order to put the wheel hard over was only given when the ships were at most a cable apart when all hope of averting disaster had already gone.

Judge Porter's judgement as reported in *The Times* went on:

'But indeed, he doubted, so far as the *Curacoa* was concerned, if she could be held free from blame even though she were the stand-on ship. The *Queen Mary*, owing to her length, would be slow to turn, and owing to her speed it would be almost impossible to take any appreciable way off her until a considerable period of time had elapsed. The *Curacoa* was very much shorter and more handy to manoeuvre. Some time after it would be impossible for the *Queen Mary* by her unaided action to avoid a collision, the *Curacoa* alone could have done so. Therefore, even if she were the stand-on ship, she ought to have recognized long before she took action that the *Queen Mary's* unaided action could not have avoided a collision. The *Queen Mary* was under no duty to keep her course and speed, and even though, in his opinion, good seamanship and the circumstances of the case required the *Curacoa* to be under the primary duty to give way, he did not think that the *Queen Mary* could be excused from all blame. As the assessors had stated, she ought to have acted at not less than five cables instead of waiting until one minute of the collision.'

In his summary Lord Porter declared that in the circumstances *Curacoa* was plainly at fault in failing to recognize the change of bearing of *Queen Mary* as soon as it occurred, or immediately after; she also failed to take action in time to prevent collision and in taking insufficient action when she finally altered her course.

He also blamed *Queen Mary* for failing to recognize that an imminent risk of collision had arisen some minute and a half before she ported at all. He also blamed the liner:

'In failing to port sufficiently, and in the failure of the officer of the watch to call the captain at a time when he ought to have realized that to continue the zigzag in accordance with what he believed to be the captain's instructions was involving the ship in the immediate risk of collision.'

Lord Porter concluded by suggesting that he saw no reason to vary the majority decision of the Court of Appeal as to the ratio of liability that the *Queen Mary* was one-third and *Curacoa* two-thirds to blame. He recommended dismissing the appeal and cross-appeal and directing each party to pay their own costs.

Lord Merriman, in his seventy-five minute speech, explained:

'If I appear to deal at too great length with the issues involved, their gravity and the equal division of judicial opinion in the courts below upon what I regard as a very important question of maritime law, must be my excuse.'

Lord du Parcq opened with a short:

'My Lords, my agreement with the opinion of my noble and learned friend, Lord Porter, is so complete that I need do no more than express my own view in a summary form.'

He ended equally concisely with:

'For the reasons given by my noble and learned friend, Lord Porter, I agree that the decision of the majority of the Court of Appeal was right, and that the appeal and cross-appeal should be dismissed.'

The gist of his summary was this: that the two ships were engaged in a joint enterprise, each with a duty to perform. *Queen Mary* had to evade possible U-boat attack by zigzagging. *Curacoa* had to be ready to protect her from air attack. The troopship's movements, save in an emergency, were pre-determined. *Curacoa*, although with greater freedom of action might be compelled suddenly to take an unexpected course. Hence the need for particular rules for the avoidance of collision to have been laid down. Such rules would have superseded the Collision Regulations. No such rules existed and the two captains were not as one as to their rights and duties. This resulted in it being doubly important for a proper look out by each ship to be kept and in the end the question was: What, in the special circumstances, did good seamanship demand?'

Alone among the Lords, Lord MacDermott had an answer to this, namely obedience to Rules 24 and 21 of the Collision Regulations.

He said that there was no doubt that *Queen Mary* was an overtaking vessel within the meaning of Article 24 of the Regulations for Preventing Collisions at Sea, for it is clear that she was coming up with the cruiser from a direction more than two points abaft her beam. The Regulations have, according to the Merchant Shipping Act of 1894, statutory force so if they were not binding on *Queen Mary* one or other of the following propositions must be formally established:

(1)   That on the true constructions of the Regulations Article 24 was inapplicable.

(2)   That Article 24 was overridden and displaced by orders or directions of superior authority.

(3)   That compliance with Article 24 was excused by other provisions of the Regulations.

As to (1) Lord du Parcq judged (a) there is nothing about the regulations only applying to peacetime, nor (b) about the rules being different for warships and merchant ships for the rules contained in King's Regulations and Admiralty Instructions (KR and AIs) are identical with the Regulations for Preventing Collisions at Sea.

As to (2): Was Article 24 displaced or modified? It could be, under the Emergency Powers (Defence) Act of 1939. Under Regulation 43 of this, the Admiralty could issue navigation orders which, if contravened, were an offence. The written instructions handed to Captain Illingworth by the naval control at New York just before the voyage in question made no mention of *Curacoa* nor anything regarding action to be taken if involved in risk of collision with an escort.

Lord Normand felt that whereas *Curacoa* had a duty to give *Queen Mary* sea room as a general principle, when the troopship started to head straight on a collision course unexpectedly (that is as Captain Boutwood saw it) then it was *Queen Mary's* duty to alter that. However, had Boutwood realized in time that *Queen Mary* meant to carry on, he should have altered two points to starboard to run away as it were out of danger, and, in fact, as the liner was due to alter fifty degrees to port at 1412 all would have been well, but the captain of *Curacoa* did not know that, since *Queen Mary's* zigzag pattern was not clear to him.

Lord Normand also found communication between Robinson and Wright on relieving watch highly unsatisfactory. Wright was never told of *Curacoa's* signal about her course, speed and intentions of 1230 when he came up to enable Robinson to go to lunch. When relieved, in turn, at 1405 Wright never told Robinson of the conversation he had had with Captain Illingworth during the 1332 to 1340 period. That was casually left to Third Officer Heighway. The impression one gets is that neither of *Queen Mary's* First

Officers were really very interested in their escort and would have been happy not to have her around.

As to (3): Article 27 states: 'In obeying and construing these Rules, due regard should be had to all dangers of navigation and collision and to any special circumstances which may render a departure from the above Rules necessary in order to avoid immediate danger.' Here, the only departure from the Rules that needs to be considered is a departure from the plain injunction to keep out of the way. Would it have helped to avoid the 'immediate danger' of collision – and that on the evidence was the only immediate danger – if *Queen Mary* had been told not to keep clear? The appropriate manoeuvre for the *Queen Mary* to adopt in order to avoid the danger which confronted her at least three minutes before the collision was to go to port. And that would have meant obedience to, instead of departure from, the requirements of Article 24.

If Lord MacDermott is right that *Queen Mary*'s duty under the overtaking rule (No. 24) was to keep clear, and this duty was not discharged (for she ought to have gone to port earlier and was therefore at fault) then *Curacoa*, as the stand-on ship, also had the duty to turn away to starboard if *Queen Mary* showed no inclination to go to port and should have done so two minutes before the accident.

Both ships, therefore, were to blame. However, on the question of apportionment of liability Lord MacDermott was at first inclined that the basis of his conclusions would have made an equal division appropriate, but he found himself not disposed to dissent from the apportionment favoured by the rest of their Lordships and the majority of the Court of Appeal.

The verdict of the Court of Appeal and its confirmation by the House of Lords was to have repercussions for a long time to come. Relatives of the men who lost their lives in the cruiser sued the Cunard White Star Company for damages and loss of expectancy of life. Cunard agreed to two test cases – a bachelor and a married man – to agree settlements on which to base all the other claims. Despite Cunard having virtually won the case, it cost the company a considerable sum of money, in fact far more than it cost the Admiralty. The naval authorities were governed by conditions of service, limiting liability to the payment of naval pensions.

Doubts were raised at the time as to why expensive, protracted legal procedures were pursued in the *Curacoa* Incident. *Queen Mary*, after all, was under requisition to the Ministry of War Transport at the time of the accident, and it would be the Ministry which would be held responsible for all costs involved. Since the Admiralty was responsible for the cruiser, it would seem that this was a case of one government department suing another: transferring money from one pocket to another. But this was not so. The Liverpool *Journal of Commerce* commenting on the case, explained:

'Collision, so far as the terms of the liner's requisitioning was concerned, was excluded as a maritime peril, and because some of the blame has been apportioned to the *Queen Mary*, her owners, through their protection and indemnity association, are liable for a number of claims from next-of-kin of the 329 [338] members of the *Curacoa's* crew who lost their lives in the disaster.'

EPILOGUE

'The terrible responsibility was, of course, in the final count, that of the two captains. One went on to be knighted and become commodore of the Cunard Line, the other to win the DSO and to command minesweepers in the Mediterranean. Both men had a heavy burden of grief to bear for the rest of their lives.'

Patrick Holmes, 1991: surviving officer HMS Curacoa.

In 1945 Patrick Holmes joined the British Pacific Fleet as Fleet Recognition Officer. He travelled uncomfortably from England in an Avro York aircraft and landed in the sultry heat of Ceylon's capital city, Colombo, with its many beauties and oddities. His next form of transport was an oddity: HM Transport *Lancashire* was an ex-Bibby liner with three masts and one tall, lean funnel. It was a leisurely form of travel to Sydney, so leisurely that Holmes was too late to accompany the BPF on its sortie north in May. The war in Europe was over. In the east the formidable build-up for the grand assault from the sea upon Japan was proceeding rapidly. Holmes' missing the fleet's departure had its compensations. He missed the main waves of attack on the fleet by Japanese suicide bombers.

He was accommodated in the New Zealand-manned cruiser *Gambia* (Captain R.A.B. Edwards CBE) for a few weeks, then joined the destroyer *Troubridge* (Captain G.F. Burghard) from which he was transferred to the destroyer *Urania* (Lieutenant-Commander D.H.P. Gardiner DSC) by bosun's chair. Aboard each of these destroyers he trained guns' crews in aircraft recognition.

At this stage in the Pacific war this was not an onerous duty. Most Japanese aircraft had been shot from the skies. Those that remained were concentrating in Japanese waters to defend the homeland during the imminent assault on Japan itself. Holmes taught the gunners to recognize the Allied aircraft – Avengers, Hellcats and Corsairs.

Urania formed part of the majestic BPF, commanded by Admiral Sir Bruce Fraser. Among the assembled fleet was its second-in-command, Vice Admiral Sir Bernard Rawlings, and aboard the carrier *Implacable*, the commanding officer Captain C.C. Hughes Hallett, both of them past captains of *Curacoa*.

Urania helped screen the huge fleet of American and British ships bombarding targets in the south-east of the island of Honshu. Rawlings described the ships as 'forming a striking and unforgettable picture'.

Pat was watching the bombardments from the bridge of the destroyer when one of the officers asked him if he'd like to talk with a PO aboard who had picked up survivors from *Curacoa*.

'Up he came and we were chatting about it when out of the gloom on our port quarter there suddenly loomed another destroyer. Luckily we were both only doing about ten knots. She struck us near the stern, and bounced off back into the darkness. It must have been merely a graze but it damaged her stem and she had to return to Manus in the Admiralty Islands. The *Urania* was more or less okay. Radio silence was maintained in order to prevent the Americans hearing about it!

'My reactions were identical to those I had experienced nearly three years before. "Hang on!" I shouted and the black smoke that poured out of *Urania's* funnel reminded me of *Curacoa's* display.

'To be actually talking about the one and then witnessing a repeat performance was very eerie.'

A few days later Japan surrendered. An uneasy peace descended upon the world. Those of us who survived came home. Many thousands of sailors, like the 338 *Curacoans* of October, 1942, never made it. But we will remember them.

APPENDIX A
REAR ADMIRALS AND
CAPTAINS OF *CURACOA*
1918–1942

Rear Admirals:

July 1918 – May 1919	Sir Reginald Y. Tyrwhitt KCB, DSO, ADC
June 1919 – Sep 1919	Sir Walter H. Cowan KCB, MVO, DSO*
May 1921 – May 1923	Wilmot S. Nicholson CB
May 1923 – May 1925	Thomas D. Gilbert CB
May 1925 – May 1927	W.A.H. Kelly CB, CMG, MVO
May 1927 – Aug 1928	F. Larken CB, CMG
Dec 1928 – Dec 1930	A.J. Davies CB
Dec 1930 – Dec 1931	Barry E. Domvile CB, CMG
Jan 1932 – Oct 1932	F.L. Tottenham CBE

Captains:

January	1918	Barry E. Domvile CMG
April	1919	Charles N. Tindal-Carill-Worsley
January	1921	Harold E. Sullivan DSO
May	1921	Rafe G. Rowley-Conwy CMG
April	1922	Hugh C. Buckle
May	1923	Cecil N. Reyne
May	1925	C.B. Prickett
May	1927	F.T.B. Tower OBE
January	1929	H.E.C. Blagrove
March	1931	C.M. Graham
March	1932	H.B. Rawlings OBE
December	1932	The Hon. E.R. Drummond MVO
April	1933	R.L. Burnett OBE
December	1933	A.M. Peters DSC
April	1934	I.M. Palmer DSC
December	1934	C. Moody

January	1936	R.S.C. Nicholson DSC
January	1937	E.D.B. McCarthy
January	1938	R. Shelley
February	1939	G.D. Moore RAN
December	1939	E. Aylmer DSC
August	1940	C.C. Hughes Hallett
February	1942	S.M. Paton
June	1942	J.W. Boutwood

APPENDIX B
THE 'C' CLASS CRUISERS

Twenty-eight 'C' Class light cruisers were built in World War I from 1914 to 1918, although five were not completed until after the Armistice on 11 November, 1918.

The first six ships had three funnels and were very similar in appearance to the Arethusa Class of 1914.

HMS *Caroline*, whose name was given to the group, was still in existence throughout World War II as an RNVR gunnery training ship at Belfast. The five other 'C' Class three-funnelers were *Carysfort*, *Cleopatra*, *Comus*, *Conquest* and *Cordelia*. They were followed by two more ships, *Calliope* and *Champion*, which were identical with the *Caroline* group but for the absence of the narrow foremost funnel, due to their having geared turbines and fewer boilers.

Although the six later ships of the earlier 'Cs' had direct drive turbines, due to an unfounded lack of faith in the more economical and more powerful new geared turbines, the six larger boilers used in *Calliope* and *Champion* were used instead of the eight in the *Carolines*, and this allowed the foremost funnel to be dispensed with. This funnel arrangement was, in fact, the most characteristic feature of all the 'D' class and 'Cs' after the *Carolines*: namely, a broad funnel for'ard of a narrow one, both well raked with horizontal Admiralty-type tops.

These two further groups, named after *Cambrian* (four ships) and *Centaur* (two ships), brought to an end what is generally regarded as the earlier 'Cs'. The other *Cambrians* were named *Canterbury*, *Castor* and *Constance*.

All the *Carolines*, *Calliopes* and *Cambrians* had two 6-inch guns on the centreline and eight 4-inch guns, four on either side of the ship when built. Shortly after WW I they had four 6-inch guns and two 3-inch or 4-inch AA guns.

Centaur and *Concord* were the first of the 'C' Class to have five 6-inch guns and to position Number 2 gun abaft the foremast but for'ard of the funnels. In order to accommodate this arrangement both the foremast and bridge structure were moved forward.

All fourteen of the earlier 'Cs' had curved stems which added to their graceful appearance. All fourteen vessels of the later 'Cs' had straight raked stems. They formed three groups or sub-classes. There were originally four ships of the *Caledon* group, three of which were in the Reserve Fleet in 1939, and all ten ships of the *Ceres* (five ships) and *Carlisle* (five ships) groups also survived into WWII.

All the later 'Cs' had geared turbines, a form of propulsion tried experimentally in only two ships of the earlier groups, and all had five 6-inch guns on single centreline mountings.

The *Caledons* were geared turbine versions of *Centaur* and *Concord* but with a pair of revolving torpedo tubes on either side of the upper deck instead of submerged tubes. All four ships, *Caledon*, *Calypso*, *Caradoc* and *Cassandra*, were laid down in early 1916 and completed by mid-1917. *Cassandra*, sunk by a mine in the Baltic in December, 1918, was the only 'C' Class cruiser lost before 1940.

The five *Ceres* Class ships, laid down in mid-1916 and completed in 1917 or early 1918 were: *Ceres*, built by John Brown at Clydesbank; *Cardiff*, built by Fairfield on the Clyde; *Coventry*, built by Swan Hunter on the Tyne; *Curacoa*, built at Pembroke Dockyard, but engined by Harland and Wolff; and *Curlew*, built by Vickers at Barrow.

They differed from the *Caledons* in the arrangement of their main armament. Number 2 gun was raised and sited for'ard of the bridge. To enable this to be done the bridge and foremast were moved further aft as were the boiler rooms and funnels.

The last of the 'Cs' were the *Carlisle* Class, laid down in late 1917 and early 1918, but not completed until after the end of WWI. The group comprised *Cairo* and *Capetown*, both built by Cammell Laird at Birkenhead; *Calcutta* built by Vickers; and *Carlisle* and *Colombo* built by Fairfield. These ships were a repeat order of the *Ceres* group but for one important difference. All the previous 'Cs' and the Arethusa Class were notoriously 'wet' ships for'ard in anything of a sea, and it was decided to overcome this by giving the fo'c'sle more sheer.

The four *Caledons* all started with the letters Ca and had ancient mythical names. The five ships of the *Ceres* group originally had no cities among them, for *Cardiff* was laid down as *Caprice* and *Coventry* as *Corsair*.

In the case of the final group, *Carlisle* was originally named *Cawnpore* which would have given all five ships imperial city names, the others being *Cairo*, *Calcutta*, *Capetown* and *Colombo*, for in those days Egypt, India, South Africa and Ceylon (now Sri Lanka) were all part of the British empire.

Light cruisers in WWI were formed into squadrons to accompany the Grand Fleet to ward off torpedo attacks by German destroyers and torpedo boats, to act as scouts ahead of the fleet – like the frigates of old – and also in the Harwich Force to act as destroyer flotilla leaders.

Their maximum speed was 28 knots, increasing to 29 at their utmost power of 40,000 HP. They mostly had 2-inch side armour, increased in vital parts to 3-inch. They could tow balloons for observation purposes and some carried an aircraft above the fo'c'sle for reconnaissance. Some years before

WWII they had become obsolescent since their main armament of 6-inch guns was only designed for anti-ship or bombarding purposes. Belatedly, the Admiralty realized the great need for anti-aircraft ships.

In 1934, therefore, it was proposed to convert all the later 'Cs' to AA cruisers: the earlier ones, except for *Caroline*, which was an immobile training ship, had been scrapped or were designated to be so.

In the event, only eight of the thirteen were so converted. This was done by stripping them of their 6-inch guns and their torpedo tubes and by substituting, in most cases, four twin mountings of HA/LA (High Angle/Low Angle) dual purpose guns for convoy or fleet protection against enemy aircraft.

Two ships, *Coventry* and *Curlew*, were taken in hand in 1935–36 at Portsmouth and Chatham Dockyards respectively. *Cairo* and *Calcutta* were converted at Chatham in 1939 and were followed there by *Carlisle* and *Curacoa*, though the latter's conversion was not finished until early 1940. Owing to British shipyards being at full stretch throughout the war, only two further 'Cs' were converted, namely *Colombo* and *Caledon* in 1942–43.

So six ships, early in the war, and two more later in the war, became AA cruisers, while five more remained as somewhat antiquated remnants of a past era and were not used in the forefront of battle.

The first two conversions, *Coventry* and *Curlew*, originally had ten 4-inch guns mounted singly, but early wartime experience proved two of them unworkable, so they ended up with eight. This enabled eight separate targets to be engaged at once. HMS *Coventry*, incidentally, made history by destroying more enemy aircraft than any other British cruiser.

The next four ships had four twin mountings which could be more easily fired by the two directors. *Curacoa* differed in appearance from the other three by being the only flush-decked (i.e. *Ceres* group) vessel. She differed also from *Coventry* and *Curlew* by having four twin mountings instead of eight single ones. She was, in fact, unique.

The two last conversions looked quite different from all the others. *Colombo* with her marked sheer for'ard was identifiable from *Caledon* with her flush fo'c'sle, but both had six 4-inch guns in three twin mountings, two of which were for'ard of the bridge.

The 'Cs' were, all in all, a most successful and remarkable class of ship.

APPENDIX C
FATE OF 'C' CLASS CRUISERS

Caroline Class

Caroline	Drill Ship
Carysfort	Sold 1931
Cleopatra	Sold 1931
Comus	Sold 1934
Conquest	Sold 1930
Cordelia	Sold 1923

Calliope Class

Calliope	Sold 1931
Champion	Sold 1934

Cambrian Class

Cambrian	Sold 1934
Canterbury	Sold 1934
Castor	Sold 1936
Constance	Sold 1936

Centaur Class

Centaur	Sold 1934
Concord	Sold 1934

Caledon Class

Caledon	Scrapped 1948
Calypso	Lost 1942
Caradoc	Scrapped 1946
Cassandra	Lost 1918

Ceres Class

Cardiff	Scrapped 1946
Ceres	Scrapped 1946
Coventry	Lost 1942
Curacoa	Lost 1942
Curlew	Lost 1940

Capetown Class

Cairo	Lost 1942
Calcutta	Lost 1941
Capetown	Scrapped 1946
Carlisle	Scrapped 1949
Colombo	Scrapped 1948

APPENDIX D
CASUALTY LISTS
OFFICERS

Actg	= Acting	Pay.	= Paymaster
Capt.R.M.	= Captain Royal Marines	R.N.	= Royal Navy
Cdr.	= Commander	R.N.R.	= Royal Naval Reserve
(E)	= Engineer	R.N.V.R.	= Royal Naval Volunteer Reserve
(G)	= Gunnery	Surg.	= Surgeon
Lieut.	= Lieutenant	Temp.	= Temporary
(N)	= Navigation	Wt.	= Warrant Officer

BODGER	Douglas H.J.	Lieut. (G) R.N.V.R.
BRITTAIN	Norman A.	Lieut. R.N.V.R.
BROCKLESBY	Philip W.	Temp. Sub-Lieut. R.N.V.R.
CALDWELL	Stanley B.	Temp. Sub-Lieut. R.N.V.R.
CAY	Maurice	Surg.Lieut.-Cdr. R.N.
COLE	John S.	Capt. R.M. (Actg.)
DAWES	Alfred E.	Temp. Pay Lieut. R.N.V.R.
FROST	James E.	Gunner (Actg.) R.N.
GARDNER	Daniel H.W.	Temp. Lieut. R.N.V.R.
GRANT	James L.	Warrant Engineer R.N.
HARMAN	John T.	Temp. Lieut. R.N.V.R.
HIDDLESTON	James	Temp. Lieut. (E) R.N.
HOWLAND	Arthur R.	Temp. Pay Sub-Lieut. R.N.V.R.
JOHNSON	Anthony P.C.	Lieut. (N) R.N.
MACHIN	Edward H.	Temp. Wt.Electrician (Actg.) R.N.
MAXWELL	John	Lieut. R.N.
NAUGHTON	Douglas J.	Temp.Surg.Lieut. R.N.V.R.
OSBORNE	Stanley R.	Temp.Sub-Lieut. R.N.V.R.

ROBERTSON	Douglas M.	Cdr.(E)(Actg.) R.N.R.
SPEARMAN	Alexander Y.	Lieut.-Cdr. R.N.
SUTTON	Geoffrey C.	Pay. Lieut.-Cdr. R.N.V.R.
THOMPSON	Matthew P.	Lieut. (E) R.N.R.
TILLEY	Albert J.	Schoolmaster R.N.
VAUGHAN	Eric H.	Lieut. R.N.
WOODCOCK	Sydney	Gunner (Actg.) R.N.

SHIP'S COMPANY
ABBREVIATIONS

AB	=	Able Seaman
Act.	=	Acting
C. or Ch.	=	Chatham
C.P.O.	=	Chief Petty Officer
E.A.	=	Electrical Artificer
E.R.A.	=	Engine Room Artificer
Ldg.	=	Leading
M.A.A.	=	Master-at-Arms
(O)	=	Officers'
O.A.	=	Ordnance Artificer
OD	=	Ordinary Seaman
P.	=	Portsmouth
(Pens.)	=	Pensioner
P.O.	=	Petty Officer
R.D.F.	=	Radio Direction Finding (Radar)
R.F.R.	=	Royal Fleet Reserve
R.N.S.R.	=	Royal Naval Special Reserve
R.N.V.R.	=	Royal Naval Volunteer Reserve
S.A.	=	Supply Assistant
S.B.A.	=	Sick Berth Assistant
Sto.	=	Stoker
Tel.	=	Telegraphist
Temp.	=	Temporary
1	=	1st Class
2	=	2nd Class

SHIP'S COMPANY

ABBOT	Robert S.	AB	C/JX235175
ABBOTT	Ronald B.	Act.Ldg.Stoker (Temp)	C/KX115226
ADAMS	Walter E.	AB	C/JX173051
ADAMSON	Alexander F.	Stoker 1.	C/KX105391
ADLEN	George B.	Officers' Cook 1 (Temp.)	C/LX 21021
ALDRED	James	O.D.	C/JX351443
ALEXANDER	Maurice J.	Stoker 1.	C/KX114720
ALLCROFT	David F.	O.D.	C/JX299044
ALLEN	James E.	O.D.(R.D.F.)	P/JX321862
ANGER	Harold	C.P.O.Tel.(Pens.)	C/JX 40064
APPLEBY	Denis	O.D.	C/JX351445
ARMITAGE	Thomas D.	O.D.	C/JX351446
ASH	Kenneth R.	Ldg.Cook (O)	C/MX 65016
ASHTON	George W.	O.D.	C/JX316156
ATKINSON	Geoffrey C.	O.D.	C/JX351675
ATKINSON	James J.B.	Marine	Ch. 23783
ATTOE	Percy J.	A.B.	C/JX151752
AULTON	John	A.B. R.N.S.R.	C/SR 59075
BAILEY	Stanley A.	A.B.	C/JX203323
BAIRSTO	John A.	A.B.	C/JX207285
BAKER	George A.	Stoker 2	C/KX147052
BAKER	Gordon J.E.	Stoker 1	C/KX134039
BAKER	Ronald J.	O.D.	C/JX351184
BARBER	Sidney F.	Marine	Ch/X100195
BARDEN	Dennis	O.D.	C/JX318882
BARNET	John T.	O.D.	C/JX318875
BARRETT	Herbert W.	Stoker 1.	C/KX134467
BARRETT	Kenneth R.	O.D.	C/JX351451
BARRETT	Robert A.	A.B. R.N.V.R.	C/HDX 40
BARROW	John H.D.	Marine	Ch/X 1827
BATES	Stanley	O.D.	C/JX351450
BATEY	Thomas W.B.	Ldg.Cook (Temp)	C/MX63356
BEALE	Albert R.	Ldg.Seaman R.F.R.	C/J 92989
BEARD	Rowland D.	E.R.A.3	C/MX 56948
BEATON	Peter	E.R.A.4	C/MX 76194
BEATTIE	James	O.D.	C/JX251017

BEEBY	Harold F.	O.D.	C/JX317626
BENTON	George	Stoker 1	C/late JX211125
BERMAN	William H.	Marine (Pens.)	Ch 23494
BINGHAM	Thomas E.	O.D.	C/JX351452
BISHOP	Philip K.	C.E.R.A.	C/M 35328
BIXBY	George F.	Stoker (1)	C/KX120562
BLOTT	Arthur W.	Stoker (2)	C/KX147054
BLUNT	Lewis F.	Act.Ldg.Sto.(Temp)R.F.R.	C/K 51758
BOWLE	Frank D.	Act.Ldg.Sto.(Temp)	C/KX106929
BRAYSHAW	Alfred	O.D.	C/JX351459
BREAKNELL	Edward	O.D.	C/JX351460
BREWER	Alec A.	O.D. R.D.F.	P/JX349726
BROAD	William E.R.	Stoker (1)	C/KX109258
BRODIE	Oswald	Stoker (1)	C/KX117162
BROWN	Kenneth E.	Marine	Ch/X 3528
BROWN	Russell H.	Act.P.O.(temp)	C/J 114792
BROWN	William R.	O.D. R.D.F.	P/JX350016
BROWNSETT	Frank	O.D.	C/JX316182
BRUCKSHAW	Leslie	O.D.	C/JX351464
BRYAN	Gordon E.	O.D.	C/JX316021
BULL	Harry P.	A.B.	C/JX189323
BULMAN	John R.	E.R.A. (4)	C/MX59009
BUNDAY	John G.	A.B.	C/JX189365
BURTON	Geoffrey D.	Ldg. S.A. (Temp)	C/MX66777
BURY	John F.	O.A.(5)	C/MX56091
BUTLAND	Edgar J.	C.E.R.A.	C/M 305089
BUTLER	Albert	Chief Stoker	C/K 55519
BUTLER	James H.	A.B.	C/JX202896
CAIN	Reginald N.	A.B.	C/J 78777
CALDWELL	Robert	A.B. R.D.F.	P/JX207935
CALEY	Kenneth	A.B. R.N.V.R.	C/HDX 112
CANEY	Robert A.	A.B.	C/J 107852
CARD	Francis A.W.	S.B.A.	C/MX
CECIL	Thomas	P.O.(Temp)(Pens.)	C/J 43783
CHALLIS	Edward R.	Act.Ldg.Sto.(Temp)	C/K 55765
CHAPPLE	Robert L.	A.B.	C/JX238762
CLARK	Patrick F.	A.B.	C/JX150309
COLDRON	Walter R.	Stoker P.O. R.F.R.	C/K 65893
CONEY	Cyril	Supply C.P.O.	C/M 37885
CONLAN	Peter	Stoker (1)	C/KX135129
COPELAND	Cyril	O.D.	C/JX346813
CORDON	Frederick J.	A.B.	C/JX205102

CORNELIUS	Robert E.	Marine	ChX 3461
CORNELL	Percy W.	Yeoman of Signals	C/JX132321
COTTAM	Hubert	A.B.	C/JX237605
COULSON	Samuel	A.B.	C/JX240712
COX	Alfred H.S.	O.D. R.D.F.	P/JX358298
COX	George H.C.	Chief O.A.(Temp)	C/M 36713
CRAWFORTH	Stanley	Act.P.O.(Temp(R.N.V.R.)	C/HDX 48
CREHAN	William L.	Corporal	Ch/X 1695
CRICK	Frank D.	Marine	Ch/X101769
CROUCH	James W.	Act.Ldg.Sto.(Temp)	C/K 66493
CUNLIFFE	George P.W.	Shipwright (1)	C/MX 47481
CUTHIL	David A.	S.A.	C/MX 81040
DAVIS	Ernest F.	Marine	Ch/X105087
DEAL	Leonard G.	S.A.	C/MX83008
DEAN	Harry	O.D. R.D.F.	P/JX304317
DEAN	Robert F.	Stoker (2)	C/KX147065
DEARSON	Charles G.J.	A.B.	C/JX206996
DELAMAINE	Robert A.	Stoker (2)	C/KX147068
DOCHERTY	James	Marine	Ch/X100118
DONOVAN	Jerimiah	Ldg.Sto.(Temp)	C/KX 85041
DOUGLAS	Robert G.	Signalman	C/JX224194
DOWNER	Joseph A.	M.A.A.	C/M 39869
DREW	Frederick	P.O.Steward (Temp)	C/L 14802
DRIVER	Stanley F.	Ldg.Stoker	C/KX 90453
DUNNING	Royston	O.D. R.D.F.	P/JX349472
DYASON	Robert G.	Stoker (2)	C/KX137482
EATON	Donald E.	Act.Ldg.Signalman	C/JX144843
EGAN	Harold	A.B. R.N.V.R.	C/HDX 4
EDDY	William	Act.Ldg.Sto.(Temp)	C/KX 84571
EDMUNDS	Bernard A.J.	P.O.Writer (Temp)	C/MX 60866
ELLIS	Charles	O.D.	C/JX346793
ELLIS	Victor H.	Marine (Pens.)	Ch.23440
FERGUSON	Alexander	E.R.A.(4)	C/MX73700
FORREST	William A.M.	P.O.	C/J 105800
FRASER	Francis R.	Marine	Ch/23185
GARGET	Sydney	Blacksmith (1)	C/MX45530
GARNER	Frederick C.	O.A. (3)	C/MX 58512
GARWOOD	William F.	Ldg.Seaman (Temp)	C/JX125247
GAZE	Francis E.	O.A. (5)	C/MX55239
GILLINGS	John N.	O.A. (1)	C/MX 46416
GLACKEN	Patrick O.	Act.P.O.(Temp)	C/SSX21956
GLANFIELD	William L.	Ldg. Cook	C/M 37713
GLAZIER	Lewis W.	Ldg.Stoker	C/KX76281
GLOVER	Frederick	A.B.	C/JX214721

GOODBURN	Frederick C.	Act.Shipwright (4)	C/MX 53806
GOWER	Leonard F.	C.P.O.Cook	C/MX 46136
GOZZETT	Alfred H.	Coder	C/JX272440
GRANT	Edgar J.	E.A.(5)	C/MX92737
GREEN	Albert	R.P.O.	C/MX 58435
GREEN	Harold	A.B.	C/J 41819
GROVES	Albert B.	P.O.(Temp)	C/SSX17166
HALL	Arthur K.	Ord.Tel.	C/JX216117
HALL	Charles W.	Ord.Tel.	C/JX233636
HARDING	George	O.D.	C/JX346927
HARLING	Peter G.	Stoker (2)	C/KX117869
HART	Ronald J.	A.B.	C/JX236917
HAWKINS	Henry M.	Sick Berth P.O.	C/M 37726
HAWTHORNE	James	Act.Ldg.Seaman(Temp)	C/JX151563
HENDERSON	Robert	Canteen Assistant	(NAAFI)
HEPBURN	George	Joiner (4)	C/MX66747
HEWITT	Sidney H.	P.O.	C/J 98633
HEWSON	Arthur	Chief Yeoman	C/J 72276
HIGGIN	John A.	A.B.	C/JX169136
HILL	Albert E.S.	Ldg.Tel. R.F.R.	C/J 49972
HOLDER	Leslie	Stoker P.O.	C/KX 77841
HOLMAN	Harry A.G.	A.B.	C/JX193227
HOLTBY	Phillip L.	A.B.R.N.V.R.	C/HDX 7
HOOPER	James T.	A.B. R.F.R.	C/SS11049
HORNER	Kenneth	Signalman	C/SSX30455
HOUSTON	W.J.	Cook (S)	C/MX 92438
HOWARD	Henry	a.B.	C/JX125052
HOWARD	Roy	O.D.	C/JX346873
HOWE	Freddy	a.B.	C/JX172658
HOWLETT	Edward H.J.	Stoker (1)	C/KX122494
HULME	Harry	Steward R.N.S.R.	C/SR 8756
HUNT	William H.	Stoker P.O.(Temp)R.F.R.	C/K 53830
HUNTER	Harold G.	Stoker (1)	C/KX130132
HUTCHINSON	George	Cook (0)	C/MX 81820
HYLTON	Reginald W.	Marine	ChX 1635
INGALL	William M.	Ldg.Seaman	C/J 81390
IVESON	Basil T.	A.B. R.D.F.	P/JX197565
JAMES	Edwin G.H.	E.R.A. (4)	C/SMX 59
JAMFREY	James	Act.Sto.P.O.(Temp) (Pens)	C/K17091
JANAWAY	James H.	Act. A.B.	C/JX257413
JEEVES	Ernest E.	O.D.	C/JX345798
JEFFREY	Frederick J.W.	Chief Stoker	C/K 62836
JEFFREY	Sidney T.	Marine	Ch/X 976

JENNINGS	Edward A.	A.B. R.N.V.R.	C/HDX 13
JOHNSON	Stanley	Officers' Cook (1)	C/LX20344
JONES	George	O.D.	C/JX346696
JONES	John W.	O.D.	C/JX346693
JOYCE	Ralph P.	Act.Ldg.Tel(Temp)	C/JX178006
KELDAY	Jerry W.	Seaman R.N.R.	C/X 19238
KEEVILL	Raymond C.T.	O.D. R.D.F.	P/JX349432
KIRKLAND	Douglas	A.B.	C/JX197528
KNIGHT	Robert J.	Mechanician(2)	C/KX 78320
KNOWLES	Albert T.	Chief Painter	C/M 37986
LAKER	William	Stoker (1)	C/KX130176
LANE	Stanley C.	O.D. R.D.F.	P/JX321114
LAZARUS	Leonard	Ldg.Radio Mechanic	P.MX 89463
LEASK	Frederick J.	O.D. R.D.F.	P.JX342866
LLOYD	William J.	A.B.	C/JX 19851
LOCKYER	James A.	P.O.	C/JX178322
LOVE	Eric A.	Marine	Ch/X 2744
LOVEJOY	James A.	Marine	Ch/X106091
LOW	Walter J.H.	Stoker P.O.	C/K 64776
LUGAR	Christopher E.	Canteen Assistant	(NAAFI)
LYALL	Donald F.	O.D.	C/JX346839
McDONALD	Charles	Stoker P.O.	C/K 65691
McHARDY	Roderick P.	Telegraphist	C/JX232064
MacIVER	Donald	A.B.	C/JX259465
MacLAREN	Thomas A.	C.P.O.	C/J 94539
McLEAN	Thomas	E.R.A.(4)	C/MX 76384
MADDISON	George	Ldg.Stoker R.F.R.	C/KX 99575
MALTBY	Francis A.	Cook	C/MX 92451
MANN	Fred S.	Marine	Ch/X1559
MANN	Frederick H.	Stoker (2)	C/KX136787
MARTIN	John P.	A.B.	C/SSX25559
MASON	Frederick F.	Cook R.N.S.R.	C/SR 61338
MASON	John	Coder	C/JX229685
MATTHEWS	Sydney	A.B.	C/JX195691
MEIKLE	John	O.D.	C/JX317857
MOIR	William	Stoker P.O.	C/KX77485
MONK	Reginald J.	S.B.A.	C/MX 65419
MOODY	John J.	O.D.	C/JX316927
MORGAN	Francis J.	O.A.(4)	C/MX 65549
MORRIS	James L.	A.B. R.N.V.R.	C/HDX 17
MOSES	John	Stoker (1)	C/KX129583
MUMFORD	James F.C.	Stoker (2)	C/KX135643
MURLEY	Harold G.	OD	C/JX317477
MURRAY	William C.	Act.Ldg.Seaman (Temp)	C/J 111921

MYERS	Richard S.	P.O. R.F.R.(Pens)(Temp)	C/J 58522
NEATHAM	Jack M.	Assistant Cook	C/MX 94515
NICHOLL	George A.	AB R.D.F.	P.JX258837
NICHOLLS	Ronald G.	Stoker (2)	C/KX136492
O'CONNOR	Terence	Marine	Ch/X103748
OSELTON	Ronald	OD R.D.F.	P/JX315572
PARISH	John	Ldg. Seaman	C/SSX17875
PHILBURN	Donald	Stoker (1)	C/KX127001
PIMLEY-POPE	Cyril A.	OD	C/JX299478
PINKERTON	Joseph E.	Stoker (2)	C/KX110207
PITT	William	Stoker (2)	C/KX136391
PORTER	Arthur H.	Stoker (1)	C/KX127003
POWLEY	Thomas J.	Cook (5)	C/MX65032
QUEST	Alfred C.	Supply P.O.(Temp)	C/MX57077
RAPALLE	Brian T.	E.R.a.(4)	C/MX60444
RAWDON	Eric	Ldg.Radio Mechanic	P/JX269108
REASON	William R.	Act.Ldg.Seaman(Temp)	C/JX130616
REDMAN	George W.	Stoker (2)	C/KX137508
RHYMES	Albert F.	Ord.Signalman	C/JX273485
RICHARDSON	John R.	Ord.Signalman	C/JX269717
RICKETTS	John E.	Marine	Ch/X100230
ROACH	William C.	Act.P.O. (Temp)	C/JX137434
ROBINSON	Eric	Ord. Telegraphist	C/SSX35111
ROBINSON	William H.	OD R.D.F.	F/JX322082
ROWE	Walter D.	Canteen Manager	(NAAFI)
SADLER	Charles W.	Stoker (1)	C/SKX1534
SALISBURY	Harold	OA (4)	C/MX69273
SAUNDERS	Alfred K.	S.A.	C/MX71662
SAUNDERS	Geoffrey	Marine	Ch/X101595
SAYWELL	George H.	Act.P.O. R.N.V.R.(Temp)	C/HDX 73
SCOTT	Thomas A.	O.A.(5)	C/MX56132
SEARBY	Arthur W.	Act.Ldg.Stoker (Temp)	C/KX115263
SERVICE	Adam B.	AB R.D.F.	P/JX195467
SETTERFIELD	Charles H.	AB R.F.R.	C/SS10302
SHARP	Ronald D.	Stoker (2)	C/KX136498
SHARP	Thomas W.	AB R.N.V.R.	C/HDX 28
SHAW	Alfred W.J.	AB	C/JX199978
SHORTEN	George D.J.	P.O.Steward	C/L 14780
SHROPSHIRE	Stanley	AB	C/JX262395
SKIDMORE	Stanley	AB	C/SSX29628
SLADE	Frank H.	AB	C/JX198695
SMALLSHAW	Jack K.	Ord.Signalman	C/JX252592
SMITH	Arthur L.	OD	C/JX350750
SMITH	Joe	AB	C/JX196735

SMITH	James A.E.	Ldg. S.A.(Temp)	C/DX 110
SMITH	Reginald C.	AB	C/SSX27488
SMITH	Tom G.	Stoker (1)	C/KX114968
SPOONER	Richard C.	C.P.O. (Pens.)	C/J 27956
STANDING	Thomas G.	E.A. (1)	C/MX36036
SUGDEN	Hubert	AB R.N.V.R.	C.HDX 30
TADMAN	Charles T.	Ldg.Steward	C/LX23176
TAYLOR	Cyril A.	OD	C/JX301391
TAYLOR	John	Marine	Ch/X 1951
TAYLOR	Louis R.	OD	C/JX351857
THOMAS	Cyril V.	Coder	C/JX229690
THOMAS	Stanley M.	AB R.N.V.R.	C/TDX 2048
THOMPSON	Ernest H.L.	Stoker (1)	C/KX117524
THORBURN	Leslie H.	Act.E.R.A.(4)	C/MX 56546
THORPE	John	AB R.N.V.R.	C/HDX 32
TODD	James	Marine	Ch/X 2161
TRUNDLE	Eric G.	Act.AB	C/SSX32498
TURRELL	Frederick	AB	C/SSX20725
TUTTY	Wilson F.	Marine	Ch/X 3444
TWOMEY	Jeremiah	Chief Stoker (Pens)	C/K 20027
VERRALL	Reginald R.	Stoker (2)	C/KX117870
VOYCE	George H.	Marine	Ch/X 100069
WALKER	Harry	Marine	Ply/2298
WALL	Albert E.	Chief Stoker (Pens)	C/K 32083
WANT	Robert W.	Stoker P.O.	C/K 60581
WARD	Frank E.	Writer	C/MX95265
WARE	James W.	AB R.N.S.R.	C/SR 147
WATKINS	Arthur J.	P.O. Telegraphist	C/JX133378
WATSON	John	Ldg.Seaman (Temp)	C.JX128078
WATSON	Thomas W.	AB	C/JX221743
WEATHER-STONE	John H.	Plumber (1)R.N.V.R.	C/TDX 263
WELLS	Edward J.	Mechanician (1)	C/KX 82754
WELLS	Frederick J	AB	C/JX215290
WELSH	Sydney E.	OD	C/JX260086
WEST	Albert O.	Act.Ldg.Seaman (Temp)	C/JX145528
WESTRAY	George W.	Stoker (2)	C/KX146846
WHEELER	James	Stoker (1)	C/SKX 1536
WHEELER	Vernon J.	Stoker (1)	C/KX115685
WHITAKER	Edward	Stoker (1)	C/KX106505
WHITE	Edward R.G.	Sergeant	Ch/X 1094
WHITELAW	George A.N.	OD R.D.F.	P/JX248303
WHITTING-STALL	Wilfred	AB R.D.F.	P/JX263313

WILKINSON	Roy	Stoker (1)	C/KX127018
WILLIAMS	Alun	Stoker (1)	C/KX116553
WILLIAMS	Eric	Signalman	C/SSX31475
WILLMOTT	Wilfred J.	Act.O.A.(4)	C/MX96183
WILSON	Frederick W.	AB	C/SSX33576
WINDSOR	William T.	AB R.F.R.	C/J 87205
WISE	George L.	Marine	Ch/X 3485
WOOD	Alec	OD	C/JX318817
WOOD	Dennis	AB R.N.V.R.	C/HDX 81
WOOD	Geoffrey W.	OD	C/JX352168
WOOD	Samuel	Stoker P.O. R.F.R.	C/KX77407
WOODFINE	Frederick W.	AB R.F.R.	C/J 84725
WOODS	Denis S.	Act.Ldg.Stoker (Temp)	C/KX91462
WOODS	William	OD R.N.V.R.	C/HDX 80
WOODWARD	Ralph	Coder	C/JX251538
WRIGHT	Claude N.	Sailmaker	C/JX134508
WRIGHT	Jack	Act.Ldg.Stoker (Temp)	C/KX105626
YOUNG	Joseph	AB	C/JX148378

APPENDIX E
DIRECTION, DISTANCE
AND SPEEDS

(A) DIRECTION

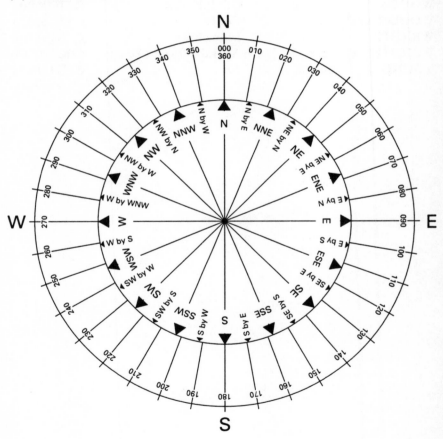

The inner circle 'boxes' the compass, the angle between each point being
11¼ degrees. There are therefore 32 points – 8 in each quadrant.

174

The outer circle shows the three-figure numbers used for steering the ship. Points, however, are useful for describing positions of other vessels relative to one's own, as shown below.

Angles in degrees after Red (for port) and Green (for starboard) are also used.

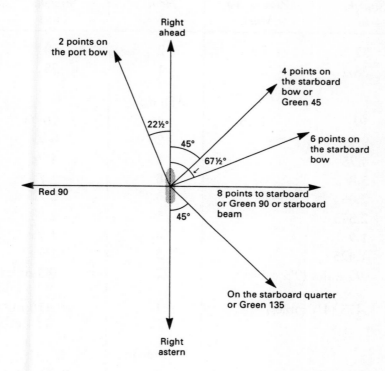

(B) DISTANCE AND SPEED

All distances in this book are in the Imperial and not the Metric system. The miles referred to are nautical miles of 6080 feet. A cable is 608 feet or one tenth of a mile. This is roughly 200 yards or 600 feet, which equals 100 fathoms.

For easy conversion, 8 kilometres correspond to 5 land or statute miles and 9 kilometres is about the same as 5 sea or nautical miles.

A knot is a nautical mile per hour.

60 nautical miles (about 69 land miles) equal one degree of latitude.

DISTANCES TRAVELLED

By *Queen Mary* at 28½ knots		By *Curacoa* at 25 knots	
Straight Miles	*Zigzagging Miles*	*Hours*	*Straight Miles*
57	53	2	50
28½		1	25
		Minutes	
19	17.6	40	16 ²/₃
9½		20	8 ¹/₃
4.75		10	4 ¹/₆
3.8		8	3 ¹/₃
2.85		6	2 ½
2.375		5	2 ¹/₁₂
1.9		4	1 ²/₃
1.425		3	1¼
.95 miles (9½ cables)		2	.83 miles or 8 ¹/₃ cables
.475 (4¾ cables)		1	.416 miles or 4 ¹/₆ cables
		Seconds	
About 2.4 cables		30	About 2.1 cables
" 1.6 "		20	" 1.4 "
" .8 "		10	" .7 "
" .4 " (80 yds)		5	" .35 "(70 yds)

28½ knots corresponds with 48 feet per second.
25 knots corresponds with 42 feet per second.
Queen Mary's length of 1018 feet is covered in 21 seconds at 28½ knots.
Curacoa's length of 450 feet is covered in just under 11 seconds at 25 knots.

Appendix F
Regulations for
Preventing
Collisions at Sea

Article

21   Where by any of these Rules one of the two vessels is to keep out of
      the way, the other shall keep her course and speed.
      Note: When in consequence of thick weather or other causes such
      vessel finds herself so close that collision cannot be avoided by the
      action of the giving-way vessel alone, she also shall take such action
      as will best aid to avert collision. (See Articles 27 and 29.)

24   Notwithstanding anything contained in these Rules, every vessel
      overtaking any other, shall keep out of the way of the overtaken
      vessel. Every vessel coming up with another vessel from any direc-
      tion more than two points abaft the beam (i.e. in such a position,
      with reference to the vessel which she is overtaking, that at night she
      would be unable to see either of that vessel's side lights,) shall be
      deemed to be an overtaking vessel; and no subsequent alteration of
      the bearing between the two vessels shall make the overtaking vessel
      a crossing vessel within the meaning of these Rules, or relieve her of
      the duty of keeping clear of the overtaken vessel until she is finally
      past and clear.
      As by day the overtaking vessel cannot always know with certainty
      whether she is forward or abaft this direction from the other vessel,
      she should, if in doubt, assume that she is an overtaking vessel and
      keep out of the way.

27   In obeying and construing these Rules, due regard shall be had to
      all dangers of navigation and collision, and to any special circum-
      stances which may render a departure from the above Rules
      necessary in order to avoid immediate danger.

29   Nothing in these Rules shall exonerate any vessel, or the owner, or master, or crew thereof, from the consequences of any neglect to carry lights or signals or of any neglect to keep a proper look-out, or of the neglect of any precaution which may be required by the ordinary practice of seamen, or by the special circumstances of the case.

APPENDIX G
CORRESPONDENCE WITH
CAPTAIN HEIGHWAY

Pat Holmes, now residing in Western Australia, managed to contact Captain William Heighway in New South Wales through the magazine *Sea Breezes*. Their edited letters provide an interesting postscript to the story. Sadly, William Heighway died during the production of this book.

9 June 1989

Dear Captain Heighway,

. . . I wonder if, over the years, you have had further insights into what went wrong. My own views, for what they are worth, are that the verdict should have been a 50:50 one since the apposite regulations for avoiding collision at sea – Nos. 24 and 21 – were the main cause of blame.

The remark about sheep being blameworthy if it allows the sheepdog to bite it wears a bit thin if the sheep is twenty times bigger and also faster than the poor ruddy dog.

To you, who probably couldn't see us at all during those final seconds, it may have seemed we were committing suicide by crossing your bows. On reflection, how I wish *QM* had altered to starboard and *Curacoa* to port so that *QM* missed our stern. However, of course, this is merely being wise after the event and probably neither ship was going to answer the helm quickly enough.

I found Captain Boutwood alive in August, 1989, nearly ninety-one, and although he had had a stroke six weeks previously I found he still had a twinkle in his eye. He didn't seem to be a very positive witness, however and I wonder if this fact influenced the decision of the courts?

Yours sincerely

PAT HOLMES

Dear Mr Holmes,

I was most interested to receive your letter and learn that you may write a book on the *Queen Mary – Curacoa* collision. I certainly wish you well in such a project and will be pleased to help . . .

As regards blame: my belief is that the Admiralty Court Judgement was the correct one – zero Cunard, 100% Navy. We – and I am speaking for the other officers also – considered that the escort had to keep clear of the vessel being escorted – but don't let the B get too close! Had the *Curacoa* been a merchant ship then *Queen Mary* would have been 100% to blame. In those moments just prior to the collision my thoughts were: 'Why doesn't *C* alter course to starboard?' (You had no chance of avoiding *Queen Mary* by going to port.) Maybe my own action in giving an order to go to port was delayed because I thought *C* was only closing to take photographs. In any event the order to alter course to port had already been given by Mr Robinson and *Queen Mary* must have been swinging to port when I spoke.

You will note in the judgement that 'Shiner' Wright (Junior First Officer and my watchmate on the 8 to 12) did not appear very bright and from his performance in court, the judge was entitled to that opinion. However, it is my sincere belief that there would not have been a collision had he been on the bridge (about five minutes or so before the collision the captain had called him into the chartroom and he passed and spoke briefly to Mr Robinson on his way there.) But you cannot change history. Captain Boutwood gave false evidence but whether this was deliberate or not I cannot say. He stated that after we passed under your stern about 1.40 we ceased to zigzag and steered the main course. Then, later, for no apparent reason, we altered course to starboard and hit *Curacoa*. At no time did we cease zigzag although there was an interruption to it just before passing under the stern of *Curacoa*.

If Cunard were held ever 1% to blame, then, for legal reasons unknown to me, Cunard would be held 100% to blame for compensation sought by next of kin.*

Best wishes,   Yours sincerely
                           BILL HEIGHWAY

Friday 23 June '89

Dear Captain Heighway,

Very many thanks for your interesting letter of 19th June and the invaluable enclosures . . .

I have often wondered if the unlucky coincidence of four officers and two helmsmen being involved in relieving or being relieved during the vital time

---

* It has not been possible to confirm or deny this.

around 2 pm had anything to do with the collision and so I find your remark about had Mr Wright been on the bridge the accident would not have occurred, particularly pertinent. Was, as it were, the chain of command fatally broken?

As for *Curacoa's* course, it seemed to me, apart from some yawing to be dead straight throughout. We certainly did not close to obtain photographs. Though I remember seeing one or two officers below me taking them but this was several minutes before the collision. When I first became worried about the *Queen Mary* apparently bearing down on us, I looked down to our bridge and saw that Captain Boutwood was looking at *Queen Mary* and then speaking down the voicepipe to the helmsman, another look – and then another order – what, of course, I do not know; but on our way from the shore to HMS *Argus* in the Clyde for the court of enquiry, he asked me if I had noticed our altering to starboard and I told him 'No, nor to port.' But that doesn't mean of course I was necessarily right – too much else was happening!

First, in the ADP, we were looking at *Queen Mary's* starboard bow and she was heading directly at us and – luckily for us, but not others – we saw her port bow as she hit. I saw the stern disappear apparently 'miles' away before we left the ADP. Although I shouted 'Hold on!' one, if not two, look-outs disappeared overboard. Ensuring that all had blown up (or were blowing up) their 'Mae Wests' I followed them down to the break of the fo'c'sle when the 80 degree list to starboard had come back to nearly upright and we were slipping back into the sea stern first (backwards a more appropriate word, perhaps – the stern having been severed some minutes before.)

I remember seeing 'the pilot' – navigating officer Lieutenant Johnson – on the bridge putting code books into the weighted bags and then I entered the water on the starboard side with the Officer of the Watch Lieutenant John Maxwell and never saw him again – I believe he may have climbed back on board – and I was dreadfully saddened by the loss of all my other friends, too. As you know, among the officers only Captain Boutwood and I were picked up.

What has always worried me *vis a vis* your zigzag is this: why didn't we know exactly when you were doing your course alterations? Surely if we had known them your final alteration of twenty-five degrees to starboard should have been foreseen. I suppose, because of that alteration putting us in danger, Captain Boutwood thought you'd never make it, but continue straight until you were on our port bow at least: i.e. because we were in the way you'd realize that being the overtaking vessel you'd keep clear! Does this make sense to you?

Please address me as Pat, Mr Holmes sounds much too formal.

Yours very sincerely,
PAT HOLMES

24.7.89

Dear Pat,

I have now read Ralph Barker's article on the collision and consider he has done an excellent job of marshalling the salient points of the evidence. Referring to page 7 I would not agree that Wright gave the order 'Hard-a-starboard' to commence the next part of the zigzag. Rather just to avoid the cruiser.

Bill Heighway then went on to explain how, if Captain Boutwood had been right in assuming that *Queen Mary* had stopped zigzagging but continued on a straight course until, for no apparent reason, she made the turn to starboard into *Curacoa*, then in the interval between 1336 when, he suggests, *Queen Mary* passed under the cruiser's stern and 1412 at 28½ knots, she would have steamed 17.1 miles, and *Curacoa* at 26 knots only 15.6 in 36 minutes. Since *Queen Mary* was about ½ mile astern at 1336 she would have been about a mile ahead at 1412. Taking lengths of ships into account the actual clearance would be about ¾ mile.

Pat Holmes agrees with these figures, and adds:

> 'Although I think the time of *Queen Mary*'s crossing our wake was more likely 1339 but that our speed was probably only 25 knots. Thus we get *Queen Mary* at 28½ knots doing 15.675 miles in 33 minutes, and *Curacoa* in that time doing only 13.75 miles – an even greater difference. There is no doubt Captain Boutwood was mistaken.'

Bill Heighway continued with his letter of 24 July:

As regards your query about four officers (five counting the captain) and two helmsmen being on the bridge: firstly, forget the helmsmen as they could not contribute anything towards the accident. It is customary for two helmsmen to be on watch, one does the first two hours, the other the final two. Under the wartime conditions they could not see outside the wheelhouse anyway.

I don't think that 'four officers' stuffed things up. Looking for a single incident I will blame Captain Illingworth. Wright and I were on the starboard wing. Captain called Wright into his chartroom, leaving me alone – for perhaps a minute before Hewitt appeared. About a minute later Robinson appeared. All this occurred over three minutes, say 1406 to 1409. I said previously that if Wright had been on the bridge the whole time the collision would not have occurred. This now appears that I have cast doubts on Robinson's competence and I do not mean that at all. What I meant was that Wright's competence impressed me and I knew him much better than I did Robinson. So why blame Illingworth?

182

Well, perhaps he had no right to remove a senior officer from the bridge without ensuring that it was safe to do so. By the same token, could you throw the blame back on Wright and say that he should have sent me instead with an explanation as to why he remained on watch? If there were special orders to be followed by senior officers on watch in wartime, all I can say is that I never saw them.

I must say that I was impressed with the Cunard officials with whom I spoke before giving evidence. Not one suggested that I should colour my evidence to help their case. The Marine Superintendent emphasized that it was my job to tell the truth as best as I remembered even if it seemed to advance the RN case. In the legal department I asked for a copy of the previous proceedings but was refused. They told me, however, that no one could prevent me from reading newspapers and the best coverage was given in *Lloyd's List* – which I obtained. I did not see Cunard's counsel (Mr Hayward) until I got into the witness box.

   Yours sincerely
   BILL

In a further letter dated 29 November, 1989, Bill Heighway elaborated on the situation on *Queen Mary's* bridge just before the collision:
I don't think I wrote 'that had Wright not handed over to Robinson' the collision might not have occurred, although that was the germ of the matter. In my view Wright *did not* hand over to Robinson. The captain called him into his chartroom and according to the evidence Robinson and Wright spoke very briefly at the doorway of the chartroom. Normally it takes about five minutes to hand over the watch: navigational data, course, speed, leg of the zigzag, RPM, any specific captain's orders, the beautiful stern of the Wren cypher officer, and so on. This would take at the very least five minutes. At nighttime time is necessary for the eyes to become adjusted to the light – but still the five minutes would cover that; and in this case there would be no way that the relieving officer (Wright) would go below while the cruiser was so close on the bow. The situation would be full of interest – it would be unthinkable to leave the bridge (even if the watch had been handed over) until finally past the cruiser.

So, if we rewrite history both Wright and Robinson would have been together on the bridge until say 2.15 pm. And I believe that Wright would have altered course to port before Robinson and thus no collision. They would certainly have been continually discussing the situation and two heads are better than one. As I said earlier in another letter, maybe Illingworth can be blamed for calling Wright into his chartroom and thus leaving the bridge in charge of a junior officer. Or else Wright is to blame for leaving the bridge and not sending a junior officer (me) to explain to Illingworth why he could not come at that moment.

There is another matter which I did not mention to the Cunard solicitors and therefore was not questioned about in court. I was not trying to hide anything – it just never entered my head at an appropriate time. I am not sure of the time, but it was noticed for at least two minutes – let us say approximately 2.06 to 2.08. During this time the bearings of *Curacoa* remained constant and it would have been about 50 to 60 degrees on the bow. During this time I could see right through a large doorway approximately square in the after part of the cruiser. And, of course, the Collision Rules state that if the bearing does not appreciably change, risk of collision exists. However, the bearing did change, but whether it broadened or narrowed I cannot say. My guess is that it broadened.

*   *   *

If Bill Heighway's recollection is correct then *Queen Mary* in relation to *Curacoa* was gaining. Had it been narrowing *Queen Mary* might just have missed the cruiser's stern. The alteration to port merely made matters worse.

SELECT BIBLIOGRAPHY

BARKER, Ralph, *Against The Sea*, Chatto & Windus, 1972. An excellent account of the collision and summary of the court cases.

BEHRENS, C.B.A., *Merchant Shipping and the Demands of War*, HMSO, 1955. See Chapter XI for voyages of the Queens.

BENSTEAD, C.R., *Atlantic Ferry*, Methuen, 1936.

BISSET, Commodore Sir James, *Commodore*, Angus & Robertson, 1961. An inaccurate, secondhand account of the *Curacoa* Incident, but useful primary source document.

BONSOR, Noel, *North Atlantic Seaway*, Vol I, David & Charles, 1975.

BRAYNARD, Frank O., *Lives of the Liners*, Cornell Maritime Press, 1947.

BUCKLEY, Christopher, *Norway, The Commandos, Dieppe*, 'The Second World War 1939–1945,' A Short Military History, HMSO, 1952.

BROOKS, Clive, *Atlantic Queens*, Haynes, nd.

COLEMAN, Terry, *The Liners: A History of the North Atlantic Crossings*, Penguin Books, 1976. A poor account of the incident.

CONNELL, G.G., *Valiant Quartet*, William Kimber, 1979. Extremely readable account of four 'C' Class cruisers.

DOMVILE, Admiral Sir Barry E., *By And Large*, Hutchinson, 1956.

GRAVES, Charles, *Atlantic Queens at War – War History*. Cunard wanted a readable and interesting account of the company's war service written. Several well-known authors were considered for the project. Charles Graves, a popular travel writer and author of many books, was selected and a contract was signed on 5 March, 1946. The book was completed by the beginning of July and publication was set for 11 September. This was postponed for over a year until 1 October, 1947. On 26 August the Chairman, Sir Percy Bates, cancelled the publication despite 20,000 copies of the book having been printed. All copies, including recovered review copies, were pulped. Graves received 25 guineas per thousand words, about £1500, for the book. The MS is in the Cunard Archives. Graves dismissed the *Curacoa* incident in a couple of paragraphs.

GRATTIDGE, Captain Harry, *Captain of the Queens*, Oldbourne Press, 1956. Chapter 13 covers the account of the collision when Grattidge was staff captain of *Queen Mary*. Some obvious inaccuracies but a useful account.

HARDING, Stephen, *Grey Ghost: The RMS Queen Mary at War*, Pictorial Histories Publishing Co, 1982. Good source for facts and figures.

HOLMAN, Gordon, *The King's Cruisers*, Hodder & Stoughton, 1947. A good eye-witness report.

HUGHES, Tom, *The Blue Riband of the Atlantic*, Patrick Stephens, 1973.

HUTCHINGS, David F., *RMS Queen Mary*, Kingfisher Railway Publications, 1986. Contains Harley Crossley's painting of the collision.
————————— See also under MILLER, Williams H.

HYDE, Francis E., *Cunard and the North Atlantic 1840–1973*, Macmillan Press, 1975.

LACEY, Robert, *The Queens of the North Atlantic*, Sidgwick & Jackson, 1973. Short but mainly accurate account of the incident.

McCART, Neil, *Passenger Ships of the Cunard Line*, Patrick Stephens, 1989. Especially interesting for Allin Martin's brief account of his escape and survival.

MacLEAN, Commodore Donald, *Queen's Company*, Hutchinson, 1965.

MADDOCKS, Melvin, *The Great Liners*, The Seafarers Series, Time-Life, 1978.

MAGUGLIN, Robert O., *The Official Pictorial History of the Queen Mary*, Wrather P.P. Ltd, California, 1985. Text by Maguglin; historical comment by Bill M. Winberg. Good photographs but poor on coverage of the collision.

MARR, Commodore Geoffrey, *The Queens and I*, Adlard Coles, 1973.

MARRIOTT, John, *Disasters at Sea*, Ian Allan, 1987. Good account of the lead up to the collision and the court hearings.

MILLER, William H. and HUTCHINGS, David F., *Transatlantic Liners at War: The Story of the Queens*, David & Charles, 1985. Contains eye witness accounts and Norman Blundell's statement.

MILLS, Sir John, *Up In the Clouds, Gentlemen, Please*, Weidenfeld & Nicolson, 1980.

PADFIELD, Peter, *An Agony of Collisions*, Hodder & Stoughton, 1966. An excellent account of the incident and the subsequent court cases as to be expected from such an author, though *Curacoa* is wrongly spelled throughout.

PATTERSON, A. Temple, *Tyrwhitt of the Harwich Force*, Macdonald & Janes, 1973.

POTTER, Neil and FROST, Jack, *The Mary*, Harrap, 1961. Two chapters are devoted to the dramas at sea and in court. Graphically told but judgement is debatable.

READE, Leslie, *Ocean Liners of the Past No. 6*, (The Cunard-White Star Quadruple Screwed Liner *Queen Mary*), Patrick Stephens, 1972. One of a series of reprints from 'The Shipbuilder and Marine Engine-Builder'. Accurate but short account of the drama.

ROSKILL, Captain S.W., *The War at Sea*, History of the Second World War, Vols I and II, HMSO, 1954 and 1956.

TAFFRAIL, [Captain Taprell Dorling.] A history of the Cunard Company was written but not published. The MS lies in the Cunard Archives.

THOMAS, David A., *The Atlantic Star 1939–45*, W.H. Allen, 1990. Useful for background information.

TUTE, Warren, *Atlantic Conquest*, Cassell, 1962.

WATTON, Ross, *The Cunarder Queen Mary*, Conway, nd.

WINTER, C.W.R., *Queen Mary: Her Early Years Recalled*, Patrick Stephens, 1986.

BOOKLETS, MAGAZINES, CATALOGUES ETC

A Catalogue of the Archives of the Cunard Steam-Ship Company, Vols I and II, held at the University of Liverpool, Harold Cohen Library, 1980.

Cunard: Christmas 1931. Special number, 'Construction of the New Giant Liner,' Cunard Steam Ship Co Ltd, 1931.

The Etruscan, staff magazine of the Bank of New South Wales, Vol 18 No. 3, December, 1969, 'Collision at Sea,' by Oswald L. Brett. A sound account.

The History of Ships, Vol 4, New English Library, nd. 'Disaster 12: *Curacoa*.' Parts publication pp. 1473–7.

Illustrated London News, RMS *Queen Mary* Number, Vol 188 No. 5066, 23 May, 1936.

Launch of the Queen Mary, Cunard Steam Ship Co, nd circa 1934. Useful for facts and figures about the liner.

The Naval Review, Magazine of the Association of Royal Navy Officers, Vol 36 No 2, May, 1948, 'Experiences with the Rosyth-North-about Convoys 1940–42,' by Valor (Charles Hughes Hallett.)

Sea Breezes, issues of August, 1977 and May, 1990.

Ships Monthly, issues of December, 1979 and January, 1980, 'Keeping the Peace,' by Jack Philip-Nichols. Vivid account of his early days in *Curacoa*.

The Stateliest Ship: Queen Mary, published by the Steamship Historical Society of America, Staten Island, New York, nd. circa 1982.

Time Magazine, Vol 1 No. 6 Article about the *Queen Mary* and Captain Illingworth, August, 1947.

Transactions of the Royal Institute of Naval Architects, Vol 8, No. 91, 1949: article 'Interaction Between Ships,' by Dr A.M. Robb.

INDEX

148, 152. Family background, 43–4; disciplinarian, 44–5; 'abrupt, rude, deaf', 46; married, 48; act of courage, 48; known as 'yellow peril,' 49; character assessment, 49; interview aged 91, 49
Career, 47, 49–50; Leys School, 44; midshipman, 47; Cambridge University, 47; Lieut-Cdr gunnery expert, 45; HMS *Berwick*, China, 45, 48; Commander, 48; commands *Whitley*, 48; *Curacoa* in command, 43, 66; Commands 12th minesweeping flotilla, 44; DSO, 50; *Report 12 August*, 71, 73; taped report rejecting shame, 50; *Report of Proceedings*, 58, 71, 72, 73, 75, 76; meets Illingworth, 80; early lunch, 82; tactics, 85–6; stirring of doubts, 87; ETA, 89; Abandon Ship, 94, 103; rescued, 100, 108; Court of Appeal, 112; account of collision and rescue with Holmes, 113–4, 116; gives evidence, 119–25, 131, 132; judgement against, 133–5; judge reviews evidence, 136–7; Appeal court, 139–44; lack of memory, 148
Bower, Royal Marine Eric, 106–7
Bramham, HMS, 79, 96, 100, 102–3, 105, 107–8, 109, 111, 112, 113, 114

Brazil, troopship, 75
Brisbane, Captain Charles, 1
Bristol Channel, 75
Britain, Battle of, 32
Brittain, Lieut. Norman, RNVR, Principal Control Officer, 144
Britten, Commodore Sir Edgar, 60
Brocklesby, Sub-Lieut. Philip, RNVR, 42, 56, 100
Broke, HMS, 47, 52, 69, 70
Brown, John, shipbuilders, 58–60; ship designer, 130
Brown on Resolution, film, 12
Browning, H.E.G., 139
Brownsett, Ordinary Seaman, Frank, ADP lookout, 55, 110
Bruckshaw, Ordinary Seaman, ADP lookout, 55
Bucknill, Sir Alfred Townsend, Lord Justice, 139, 141–8
Bulgaria, 9, 10; Boris, King of, 10
Bulldog, HMS, 79, 96, 102
Burnett, Admiral Sir Robert, 11
Burial sites, 115
Bushell, Able Seaman, ADP lookout, 55–6

Cairo, HMS, 15, 29, 31, 33, 52, 78
Calcutta, HMS, 15, 31, 33
Caledon, HMS, 8, 78
Caledonian Hotel, Edinburgh, 42
Calliope, HMS, 8
Calypso, HMS, 8
Camberley, 12
Cambrian, HMS, 8, 47
Campbell, HMS, 47

Canadian Pacific Line, 50, 52
Cape Bon, 31, 78
Cape of Good Hope, 64
Cape Town, 61, 62, 78
Caradoc, HMS, 8
Cardiff, HMS, 8, 10, 13
Carlisle, HMS, 13, 33, 78
Carol, King of Romania, 10
Carpmael, Kenneth S., KC, 118–21; 126–31, 135, 139, 149
Carter, Telegraphist Geoffrey, 94, 108, 109
Castleton, HMS, 75, 76, 77
Cartwright, Ken, 102, 105
Cay, Surgeon Lieut.-Cdr. M, 54
Champion, HMS, 11
Channel Dash, 64
Chaplin, Captain, naval assessor, 147
Charlton, Mr, gunner, 22–3
Chatham, 5, 14, 15, 28, 32, 35, 47, 50, 51
China Station, 48
Christiania, (Oslo), 4
Churchill, Winston S., Prime Minister, 32, 62–3
Clark, General Mark, US Army, 93
Clarke, Supply Assistant, Len, 107
Clarkson, Ken, 102
Clay, Peter, Ordinary signalman (later Lieut. RNVR) 31–2
Clock Point Gate, 76
Clover, Sub-Lieut. Robin K. (later Lieut. RNVR) 15, 32
Clyde (bank), 19, 27, 58, 59, 65, 68, 69, 72, 74, 76, 77, 78, 82, 89, 95, 97, 114
Clyde Light Vessel, 70, 77